EACH BOOK
A DRUM

EACH BOOK A DRUM

Celebrating Ten Years of Halifax Humanities

THE HALIFAX HUMANITIES SOCIETY

HALIFAX 2015

Cover images:
"What's Behind her Skull?" © 2011 by Brenda DeLorenzo.
Photograph courtesy of Lamont Dobbin.

"North is Freedom" © 2007 by Doug Bamford and Stephen Braithwaite.
Photograph courtesy of Victoria Goddard.

Interior lay-out and book design © 2015 Victoria Goddard.
Cover design © 2015 Jesse Hiltz and Victoria Goddard.

Library and Archives Canada Cataloguing in Publication

    Each Book a Drum : Celebrating Ten Years of Halifax
Humanities / The Halifax Humanities Society.

Includes bibliographical references.
ISBN 978-0-9947336-0-3 (paperback)

    1. Humanities--Nova Scotia--Halifax. 2. Education--Nova
Scotia--Halifax. I. Halifax Humanities Society, issuing body

AZ103.E23 2015   001.3   C2015-902842-6

CONTENTS

VIGILS

HOME AND AWAY

SELF AND OTHER

SURPRISES

EACH BOOK
A DRUM

$\mathscr{P}$ REFACE

(to a poem)

GEORGE ELLIOTT CLARKE

O.C, O.N.S., Ph.D.

I'M HONOURED THAT Halifax Humanities Society should seek a preface from me for this volume celebrating, righteously—but not self-righteously—a decade of charitably radical labour in educating the less-lettered and the less-connected in time-tested classics, so that they may feel inspired or compelled to transform their individual circumstances and/or social policies and morals. I appreciate this honour because I am an Africadian (African-Nova Scotian), born into the struggling classes, and brought to political literacy by my autodidact intellectual and social-worker father (Bill) and by my Kindergarten-founding and Early Childhood Education-expert mother (Gerry) and by various teachers, beginning with Ms. Alexa McDonough, my own Kindergarten teacher, and eventually a leader of Nova Scotian and Canadian democratic socialists. Raised in the working-class, struggling-class North End of Halifax, I remember very well how we black kids and poor kids were "streamed" into classrooms from which we would exit as under-educated, under-employable, low-skill, low-wage, fresh candidates for the dole, the drunk tank and the doldrums.

I received my Social Insurance number at age 13, in Grade 7, at Bloomfield Junior High School, because an agent of Canada Manpower (as

Employment Canada was then titled), interrupted my math class to encourage us blue-collar- and pink-collar-parented kids to acquire our SINs so we could quit school (as soon as possible) and start earning our own wages. Of course, there's nothing wrong with earning any kind of legal income; any job is a good job. But there was—and is—something unjust about a society that conspires to under-educate some citizens so that they may be more easily exploited as cheap, disposable labour or even as unsuspecting cannon fodder in the Armed Services.

In my own case, encouraged to pursue a love of letters and to become a writer, I benefitted, not only from dedicated teachers (Fred Holtz, Carol Gibbons, etc.) in Halifax, North End schools, but also from the attentiveness of librarians at the North End Memorial Library—like Dee Amyoony, Terry Symonds, and Janet Doyle. I also enjoyed the excellent tutelage of socio-political activists and artists like Burnley "Rocky" Jones, Joan Jones, Jackie Barkley, Walter Borden, Sylvia Hamilton, and Bev Greenlaw, all of whom opened up their libraries and music collections to my avid interest and who encouraged my poetry and challenged my thought, I mean, my critical evaluations of Occidental, North American, Canadian, Nova Scotian, and Haligonian histories, societies, governments, cultures, and practices.

To my mind, Halifax Humanities exemplifies this same true principle of pedagogy: To teach us to discover for ourselves the philosophies (and theologies) and principles of the (mal)functions of our governments, economies, and cultures—so that we are enlightened *persons*—that is to say, *empowered* citizens. I end with a poem. Perhaps it demonstrates my understanding about the nature of things, as a poet, well, for better or worse.

Early Spring in the Annapolis Royal Historic Gardens

This grey, frigid, wintry March Sunday—
the "Innovative Garden" says "not yet," not "yes":
It fields closed buds and brown-black leaves
and winter cabbage that looks dowdy,
gone pale-green or dead-purple.
Shrivelled weeds and grisly fragments—
studs—
of pallid green crop up here and there—
like gangrene bone shards after a plane crash—
such ultra-light dreck,
such darkly remarkable wreckage.

Snow shrouds, or strives to shroud, all:
Its cold sweat glistens,
but is too frail to touch.

Even graveyards splay snow-scoured;
frost glazes the dust
and the obstreperous grass,
each brown blade its own soft, anonymous headstone.

A path pays out slick green, brown spruce needles:
Slipping—
or irreverent, accidental, backbone-breaking "skating"—
is a winter expedient.

Over a field of see-through snow,
dog paws chase
three-pronged bird-tracks.
Crows caw a raucous, kiss-my-arse chorus.
A brisk wind prods me into the vacant rose garden,
just as fresh snow flares, snares,
annoying,
like hail:

There's been too much already!
(Banished cold, that's summer!)

Winter lingers so long,
Our weariness becomes *Worry*.

December defoliates all,
and January is as injurious as *Time*,
February is as boisterous
and as violent as untrue *Valentines*.
March ushers in the bitter whiteness
of squall and squelching slush,
so winter seems to plaster all
as irrevocably as gravity.

So much Beauty is withered—
like political promises.

I tromp on white snow that's crusty,
beneath the superficial softness,
and view rime-racked roses—
only thorns now, bushels of thorns,
the blooms all deadheaded.
The plants look spindly cacti—
and yet *Beauty* will burst from these stems—
intoxicating, erotic, tea-scent tantalizing—
once March ebbs into May-month charm.

Now, my pen must push through snow pellets—
striking and sticking to the conquered page.

I close my book; the snow stops.
I open it again, and my fingers freeze.

Near me, there's a puddle—
impossibly solvent water!
It should be ice—
at least a silken lockup!

The pond looks a sepulchral mirror.

(Ice paints even rain white.)

Maps preserve nothing.

I glance over at the railway bridge—
its iron's rusted,
the colour of dry blood—
the sordid ink of geopolitics.

The sky hulks grey-white, white-grey,
and blustery over the gold-brown marsh;
clouds seem thin, vacant pearls—
as plain as unwritten poems.

My fingers feel freshly numb—
my pages turn cold as snow—
black ink flits, drops, crow-like.

I'm a clerk,
skulking among snow,
voicing vain verses to the wind,

that bullish, bullhorn roar:

The Fundy tide is a-comin in!

The Annapolis River flings forth petals
of drops,
so many icy tears,
arriving as all-pervasive swells.

Currents collapse, muddled, upon mudbanks.

This cold spring, late March, feels unbearable—
just damp, dark, and disgusting;
the cold wet showering down
is just sleazy hygiene.

I open a gate unto the marsh,
and winds hit as hard as a freight train.

I stand now where tracks once lay:
They're as disappeared now
as notions of *Justice*
for Indigenous peoples—
so Canadian….

Drizzling snow hazes the Gardens
with blurs of cream.

Bleak is the marsh and the hills beyond—
just snow and spruce and fir and pine and snow—
but the snow now blooms
as if to cancel buds.

My fingers, freezing, I gotta leave off ink.

I yield to the white chill,

the lily-bleaching snow—
the falling whiteness—
this torrent of cobwebs!

There's no pristine sunlight here.
Instead, tree branches share slices of light,
facets of shadow,
while chill still abounds.

(Is *Goodness* graspable
when cold clasps the hand?)

In pure, Canadian exhaustion,
as dusk turns snow to dust-like stars,
I back off from writing up these gardens,
hardening again with dark and ice,
until April—
metaphysical April—
renews a fiscal legacy
of burnt grass and churned earth
and blossom and dandelion and milkweed
and tax returns and geese returning.

I've seen—tried to see—enough.

I exit, hoping for warmth.

Look it!
A crow whickers upward in the glorious finale of light.

The poet is a voyageur:

For nothing is as voyeuristic as light.

—George Elliott Clarke

$\mathcal{E}$DITORS' $\mathcal{J}$NTRODUCTION[1]

THE EDITORS

People on low fixed incomes are so consumed with surviving day to day that there is virtually no room in their lives where they are able to concentrate on anything other than getting by. Living this way, for whatever reason, robs you of your strength and energy. More importantly, it wipes out your capacity to dream and plan.

It threatens defeat again and again.

This course, Halifax Humanities 101, was a gift that opened our eyes to what we are able to accomplish, given the opportunity. It was a window that was finally opened on a room that had been forced shut for some time ... a room that had been starving for fresh air.

The scope of knowledge we were exposed to did not come from books and lectures alone. As a class, we learned to bond and value one another's thoughts and philosophies.

Deep lasting friendships were formed and, for a while, money or the lack of it was not what was most significant in our lives.

—Jymy Tanner and Helen Langille, Halifax Humanities 101 valedictorians, 2006

---

1   The Introduction and order of the anthology were prepared by Susan Dodd in consultation with the Halifax Humanities Editorial Committee (Susan Dodd, Shari Clarke, Lamont Dobbin, and Mary Lu Redden) and the Chair of the Board, Colin Starnes.

WE HOPE THAT this book of poems, reflections, and essays will be here for you when you crave good company.

Enjoy it, like a cup of tea with an old friend … your most intense old friend; the one who spikes her teapot with challenges to your complacency, your ingratitude, your defeatism.

We talked for years about collecting writings from the Halifax Humanities community, and we were moved to action by the untimely death of our friend, Jymy Tanner, and the then-approaching 10-year anniversary of Halifax Humanities.

Jymy was among our first students, she was a constant presence in the Seminar, and for years a Director on our Board. We tried to create a book that Jymy would enjoy: a meeting place, on the page.

All of us know troubles, but we do not all know material want and social exclusion. It is hard to define the challenge at the heart of any serious study of the humanities, and it is impossible to describe the friendship that such study generates. Studying the humanities together is, as Laura Penny says, "serious fun."

Halifax Humanities counters the prevailing view of education as the transmission of marketable skills to potential labourers. In all that we do, we aspire to affirm that people are so much more than "useful." And, as Alexander MacLeod puts it, this makes us a lively contender in a "scrap that shouldn't be ignored."

This book is about the simple, amazing fact that studying the humanities can bring us together in our diversity without collapsing us into indifference.

Halifax Humanities: What we do

HALIFAX HUMANITIES CONSISTS of three interrelated programmes, and numerous offshoot activities.[2] The original course is *Halifax Humanities 101.*

---

2   The Halifax Humanities Society began as the Saint George's Friends of Clemente Society in 2004. We changed our name in 2013 in part because we are not, formally, a "Clemente" programme. "Clemente" means, literally, *mild* and *merciful*; it

HH101 is an introduction to selected classics in Western thought, taught as an historical narrative. We offer HH101 "barrier-free" to people who live on assistance, disability, pension, or with other financial constraints. The course attracts those who seek a community beyond the isolation that can be imposed by economical, physical, and social barriers. As Jymy and Helen put it in our first valedictory speech: "for a while, money or the lack of it was not what was most significant in our lives." These first valedictorians went on to stress that the friendships of a lifetime emerge from these common studies. Halifax Humanities 101 runs for eight months, twice weekly, out of the North Branch Memorial Library on Gottingen Street.

The Seminar—as we call the weekly gathering of HH101 graduates, volunteer professors, and coordinators Scott MacDougall and Paul Bowlby —considers great works from past and contemporary ages following an agreed upon theme.[3]

Halifax Thinks offers lectures and tutorials to adult students who want to read the humanities in good company and for whom time is the greatest barrier to study. The modest fee paid by Halifax Thinks participants goes to support Halifax Humanities 101 and The Seminar.

Professors from the University of King's College, Dalhousie, Saint Mary's, the Nova Scotia College of Art and Design, Mount Saint Vincent and Acadia volunteer in Halifax Humanities classrooms. Guest speakers have included Earl Shorris, George Elliott Clarke, Alex Colville, John Hartman, Rose Adams, Anne Emery, and Howard Epstein. Students from King's and the Halifax Humanities Seminar volunteer to support our Director Mary Lu Redden. The North Branch Memorial Library, the Alderney Gate Library in Dartmouth and the University of King's College all donate class-

is also the last name of a baseball player—Roberto Clemente—and his namesake community centre in Lower East Side Manhattan where the inspiration for our programme, Earl Shorris, began his barrier-free liberal arts classes for those living in poverty. Angus Johnston, Gary Thorne, Colin Starnes, Brian Flemming, Mary Lu Redden, Colin Dodds, William Barker, Tracey Moniz, Ben Franken, Mike Murphy and Scott MacDougall all reflect on the history of Halifax Humanities in their contributions.

3   Angus Johnston started the Seminar and coordinated it for its first eight years; see Scott MacDougall's essay, "The Smallest Kindnesses—'The Seminar' Redefined."

room space. Saint George's Anglican Church donates Mary Lu's office space just around the corner from the North Branch Library.

Halifax Humanities provides books, bus tickets, tea, coffee, snacks, and childcare subsidies to our HH101 and Seminar students. Always breaking even—if only just—we do everything we can to open the cultural life of our city to our participants. Neptune Theatre, Symphony Nova Scotia, Opera Nova Scotia, and the Art Gallery of Nova Scotia are among those that have opened their doors in welcome by donating tickets to events.

We offer writing support, too. Law students and Masters students volunteer as writing tutors. Each week, HH101 grads workshop their writings as they munch cheese, crackers and grapes in William Barker's writing seminar. Many contributions that we include in this collection were conceived and polished by Bill's "writing groupies," as Gillian Webster calls them. Tracey Moniz offers a writing group at Mount Saint Vincent University, which she describes as the empowerment of making a "masterpiece" of our own writings.

Our extra-programme offerings change, but they include joint outings to opera, music and plays. Angus Johnston's sole aim may be to inculcate a love of opera in participants so that he always has good company at Opera Nova Scotia, Dalhousie Theatre and Opera events, and screenings from the Met.

The Dalhousie-Schulich Law School presents a Literary Moot Court every year, with proceeds going to Halifax Humanities. Odysseus, Alice (from Wonderland), Victor Frankenstein … all have faced judgment. Students from King's hosted a poetry and music evening with performances from many, including Ben Caplan, in the lovely acoustics of the King's chapel. Twice now, teams from across the city performed *Odyssey Live!*—a book-an-hour reading of the 24 books of Homer's epic.

We fundraise continually, and by purchasing this book, you are contributing to the ongoing work of the Halifax Humanities Society, and we are grateful.

Books, Poems, Lives …

THE AUTHORS OF our volume are participants in Halifax Humanities as students, teachers, and supporters.

Our anthology's title, *Each Book a Drum*, comes from a George Elliott Clarke poem inscribed on the sculpture that greets visitors to the North Branch Memorial Library on Gottingen Street. George Elliott Clarke is our honorary patron and we are delighted that he wrote not only our preface, but also the poem "Early Spring in the Annapolis Royal Historic Gardens."

Corrine Gritten completes our introduction with her consideration of the North Branch Library's poetical sculpture in "Education Matters."

On the back cover of our book, you will see Brenda DeLorenzo's remarkable self-portrait, "What's Behind Her Skull?" conveying the intensity and psychological complexity common to us all.

The real heartbeat of Halifax Humanities is our common reading, talking, and listening. We are not primarily a writing class, and we do not have a full set of our valedictory addresses from over the years for this very reason. David Ferguson, for instance, spoke without a prepared text, capturing in a few words the core paradox of humanities studies: reading great texts makes us at once humble … and newly confident.

When we gathered the writings that authors offered us, we found six themes that we used to organize this anthology: *attention, adventure, vigils, home and away, self and other,* and *surprises.* Each section begins with a transcript of a valedictory address, includes divers writings by students, professors and founders of Halifax Humanities, and concludes with a reflection on the power and purpose of humanities studies.

Attention

WHAT DOES IT mean to attend to one another—to really pay attention?

Halifax Humanities answers this question by posing it. It's one of those performative moves where the question is the answer and the answer is the question.

Shari Clarke's Valedictory Address from 2013 recalls returning to "life's big questions" in the company of new friends and thinkers from across the ages. In "Childhood Joy," Bonita Shepherd reminds us to attend to the play of childhood. Anne Beek shows how joining Halifax Humanities was a great act of courage. In "My Teachers," Kathleen Higney thanks her books for years of challenge and support. Lamont Dobbin describes the work of caring in "A Day at the Food Bank." Jesse Blackwood's character in "J.D. Salinger" cannot attend even to himself, fretting distractedly about everything, including his great teacher's underwear. Through Augustine's *Confessions* Ron Haflidson argues that to be ready to learn is to be intellectually open to a kind of faith that releases us from prejudice. John Baxter marvels at spirits attuned to beauty in a transcribed talk on Shakespeare's *Merchant of Venice*. In "The Education of Attention: Simone Weil on the Right Use of School Studies," Warren Heiti argues that the greatest imperative is to learn to be fully present. Gary Thorne, who along with Angus Johnston was inspired to found a barrier-free humanities programme in Halifax, recounts his discovery of the writings of the New York visionary, Earl Shorris. Father Thorne explains how he shared this vision with the parish of Saint George's Anglican church in the North End, then with faculty in the Foundation Year Programme at the University of King's College, and, finally, how we realized this vision at the North Branch Memorial Library on Gottingen Street.

Adventure

HALIFAX HUMANITIES IS an adventure. Ask anyone who has been involved in any way. It is an adventure, and that is that.

In the Valedictory Address from 2012, Lisa Comeau recalls some of the most important texts in her year, especially Alice Munro: "Billy Pope and Flo were not protected. Things could get at them." This awareness of vulnerability turned, in Halifax Humanities, to a new kind of audacity. Gillian Webster recalls her first leaps into the unknown in "My First Parachute Jump." Barbara Whitby takes us on a "Hitch-hiking" journey from just-bombed London into the mystical legacy of England's first Christians. Jannette Vusich invites us to visit a Gothic church in "'Bright is the Noble Work': Abbot Suger and the Church of Saint-Denis, Paris." Christopher Rice takes us on a whale of an adventure, from the classic American master piece back to the foundational structure of so much tragedy in "*Moby-Dick* and Aristotelian Tragedy." In "Doing Descartes Backwards," Steven Burns leads us on an adventure into Descartes' study, into his radical method, and into the workings of our own minds. Finally, Colin Starnes, the current Chair of the Halifax Humanities Board, argues that the study of the humanities outside of universities is the adventure of a lifetime, in "Free Humanities: Truffles for the Mind are the New Soul Food."

Vigils

HALIFAX HUMANITIES IS a watch we keep over suffering, loss, and remembrance. There is not a text that we read or a day that passes where we aren't invited to explore troubles in and through the works before us. Recalling our intellectual inheritances can liberate us into new perspectives on today's predicaments. Reading—now alone, now together—we share our burdens but without being forced to expose our inner scars.

In his Valedictory Address from 2011, Lamont Dobbin reflects on gifts and exchanges across difference. Bonita Shepherd gives pain a personality in "It Comes In." John Cox looks to the ancient poem *The Epic of Gilgamesh* and marvels at our reluctance to face death, despite the pains and anxieties of life. Rose Adams depicts emotional distance and severed communication in "The Length of the Court." In "The Procedure," Brenda DeLorenzo shows brutal efficiency at work. Dawn Hale guides us from the blankness of abuse to the brightness of learning in "Empty Eyes." Gillian Webster explains how books are a refuge and an inspiration in "Horses, Dogs and Other Heroes." In "Patricia's Song," Kathleen Higney remembers the quiet faith of her friend. "What is a Vigil?" asks Susan Dodd, as she puzzles over the relationship between the politics of vigilance and vigils of remembrance. In "Memory Work in Three Parts," Sylvia Hamilton recalls us to Nova Scotia's shame as a slave-holding culture, and inspires us to seek justice without being destroyed by vengeance. In "Earl Shorris: *Sophos* and *Agape* in Halifax Humanities," Angus Johnston—one of the founding visionaries of our programme—remembers his friend and considers Shorris' concerns that Halifax's distinctive version of barrier-free humanities privileges the enjoyment of community over the inculcation of autonomy in our students.

Home and Away

A PARADOX LIES at the heart of Halifax Humanities: to know our homes we must travel—through time, across distance, and away from our presuppositions. The works collected here consider the familiar and the strange, voyage and homecoming, as well as exile and diaspora.

In her 2010 Valedictory Address, Grace Morris says, "I have gone through many changes in the time since I read the advertisement for Halifax Humanities, as I am sure my classmates have. It was like a window opening, a breath of fresh air. And now the door is open and we are ready to go through." Bonita Shepherd invites us to the holiday feast table at her childhood home in "Christmas Grotto." We're lucky in our natural home, as Laura Legere recalls in "Weather Patterns." Barbara Whitby takes us into the World War Two bombing of London in "Feeling Alone." In "One Star," Rose Adams wonders about our capacity to navigate. For Madeline Reid Comeau, homecoming is wistful in "Torn." Corrine Gritten shows us her neighbourhood in its starkest character in "Darkside: The Ghetto." Into Wonderland we go, with Alice and long-time Halifax-Chebucto MLA, Howard Epstein, in "Alice and Wonderland." Vernon Provencal guides us through the foundational tale of exile and homecoming in "The Song of Odysseus: life lessons learned." Roni Gechtman offers a timely plea for alternatives to territory-based nationalisms by recalling the optimism and death—at Nazi hands—of a turn-of-the-century thinker in "Simon Dubnow: Jewish Historian, Diaspora Nationalist and Social Hegelian." Scott MacDougall describes the intellectual hospitality of *The Seminar* in "The Smallest Kindnesses: 'The Seminar' Redefined."

Self and Other

OUR COMMON STUDY can transform us from isolated selves into a community of readers, thinkers, talkers, and listeners. In this, Halifax Humanities can be intensely empowering, especially, it seems, for women who were marginalized by single parenthood, poverty and/or violent relationships, and for people emerging from the isolation of addiction.

In her Valedictory Address from 2009, Jennifer Conroy says to her fellow Halifax Humanities 101 graduates: "I hope that when our paths cross one day in the future, I will hear your song, as Walt Whitman says—I want to hear it loud and clear." In "Naptime with Elizabeth," Madeline Reid Comeau invites us into the intimacy of curling up with a sleeping baby. Brenda DeLorenzo gives us a rather less intimate view of dealing with a young adult in "Lady Godiva." In "Interview with an Inuksuk," Laura Legere plays with a curious appropriation of cultural symbols. David MacEachern poetically considers variations in "Self-Respect." In "Freedom of Expression and the Crusade for Human Rights: Joseph Howe and Carrie Best: Two Nova Scotia Pioneers," Kim Kierans recounts the origins of the free press in Canada, and its development in the civil rights activism of an African Nova Scotian woman journalist. In "Roland in Paradise: teaching the *Song of Roland* in Halifax Humanities," Neil Robertson makes the startling claim that today's secular freedom is rooted in the ethical ground of a medieval warrior's zeal. Roberta Barker takes up Shakespeare's challenges around race and gender in "'I Loved Her That She Did Pity Them,' or, How I Learned to Love *Othello*." Warren Heiti tries on the mind-body distinction in the poem "Descartes." In "Public Space, Democracy and *Silas Marner*," Stephen Cloutier argues that the high modern period, the time of George Eliot, is the opening of a new kind of free space of recognition between equals. Finally, in "Clementia: On the Uselessness of Reading Together," Mary Lu Redden, long-time Director of Halifax Humanities, considers the distinctiveness of our version of Shorris-inspired "Clemente" courses and concludes that our class is, in a sense, Halifax's cultural Central Park.

Surprises

HALIFAX HUMANITIES SURPRISES. Participants are surprised by the direct and personal challenges that the texts pose to them. Professors are surprised by the direct and personal challenges that the participants pose with their remarkable questions and interpretations.

As Kathleen Higney brings out in her Valedictory Address from 2008, Halifax Humanities is about action words—verbs, but friendly ones. Madeline Reid Comeau remembers the surprise dealt out by "The Gift." Kathleen Higney considers the challenges of boredom in "Needing Entertainment." In "Sorry, Mr. Connors!" Catherine Joudrey apologizes to the teacher she surprised—and mortified—with her reading material. David MacEachern perplexes with his intriguing "Justified Conclusion." Steven Burns' character redefines a "platitude" in "Could You Please Define That Word?" Nicholas Hatt presents Augustine's final conversion—and the brilliant thinker's ultimate surprise about the answer to the riddle that has tormented him until then. Jesse Blackwood's "Boxmaker" makes something out of nothing, building room for joy and friendship beyond measure, and so beyond utilitarian grasp. Ben Franken and Mike Murphy describe the how the annual Dalhousie Law School's Moot Court does "terrible things to great literature." Colin Dodds reflects on his consistent support for Halifax Humanities, and finds its roots in his career-long commitment to public education. William Barker poetically confesses: "I Want To Be a Crow," and describes "What I Learned" from his years of writing workshops with Halifax Humanities participants. Tracey Moniz explains her writing workshop, which inspires participants to write their lives as "Our Own Masterpieces." Brian Flemming insists: "If ever there was an argument for improving access to higher education at low, or no, cost, Halifax Humanities provides that argument."

Conclusion

WE BEGIN OUR conclusion with two tributes to the feisty side of Halifax Humanities. Laura Penny shows how the decade-long realization of Gary Thorne's and Angus Johnston's vision of a barrier-free humanities class in Halifax enriches the lives of students and professors alike. Penny argues that the "Serious Fun" of studying the humanities together flies in the face of prevailing views of "poor people" as necessarily, and properly, excluded from "fun"—and that it makes a mockery of prevailing views of "fun" in the process.

In "A Scrap We Can't Avoid: The Essay I Didn't Write About Halifax Humanities (and the One I Did)," Alexander MacLeod contrasts the kind of self-satisifed 10th Anniversary celebration that we *might* have had with a call to recognize that the humanities are under attack from utilitarians on all sides.

Each book a drum, indeed.

We conclude our celebration of the books we share, the friends we enjoy, and the community we build by going back to the foundation, with Jon David Welland's reflection on the interplay between spirit and matter in his poem "Elements."

***

ON BEHALF OF the Halifax Humanities community, we hope you enjoy the company of this book, and that you take up its quiet challenge:

Sit with us, and read ...

ℰDUCATION ℳATTERS

CORRINE GRITTEN

North is freedom–
Uptown, down-home:
Each book a drum;
Each life a poem.

—George Elliott Clarke

IN FRONT OF the Halifax North Public Library on Gottingen Street sits a poignant metal sculpture that evokes a connection to this seaside community. Etched into the soaring, rusty façade are the voices of the people of Halifax telling their history: historical Africville, the Halifax Explosion, a favourite recipe for a hearty, home-cooked meal. On top sits the crowning glory: a strong figure, secure and safe, extends a helping hand, reaching down to another who is striving to make it up.

This sculpture could not grace a more apt location. Inside this library, something wondrous occurs twice weekly from September until May. In a donated conference room, for two hours, sit twenty or so enthusiastic students and a rotation of volunteer professors from any of Halifax's fine universities, gathered there to study philosophy.

Welcome to Halifax's "alternative" university. This is the gateway for adults of all ages to engage with higher learning in a pressure-free, tuition-free environment. This is *Halifax Humanities 101*. It is where students facing financial hardships can reconnect with post-secondary education or experience it for the very first time.

Inclusiveness through education seems key to bringing people a means of participation in life and community rather than the sense of being on the outside looking in. To engage with Halifax Humanities' proffered consciousness-expanding curriculum is to encourage a greater sense of self and a grander concept of the complexities of this modern world.

"Treasure," "gift," "fortunate," "life-changing," and "blessing" echoed across the lips of students throughout the term. By the end of this time together many have discovered something unexpected in their lives, the joy of accomplishment, the ability to have a "voice" and engage in the community as a relevant part of it, sometimes for the first time, and the desire to pursue further academic advancements.

Outside on the grounds of this alternative campus sits a poignant metal sculpture that evokes a connection to this seaside community. Students are the climber reaching for the top. Education is reaching down to give a hand up. It is only from the top that we are able to extend our reach to those who struggle upward behind us.

$\mathcal{A}$TTENTION

VALEDICTORY ADDRESS
2013

SHARI CLARKE

WE ARE NOW officially the graduating class of 2013. It doesn't get much better than this! I am thrilled and humbled to have the honour of giving the valedictory address on behalf of such a wonderful group of fellow graduates.

For the past eight months, we have met for two hours twice a week, united in our shared passion for books and the knowledge and ideas contained within them. We probably all shared some measure of trepidation and anxiety in the beginning. Some of us had been away from formal education for decades, some had not pursued education past high school, while still others of us have had negative experiences within an educational system.

What we knew for sure was that we were being offered the opportunity to meet with people we didn't know to read and discuss authors we might not have heard of, with professors who weren't being paid, and who were neither going to grade nor evaluate us. We were being offered free books, snacks, transportation, and childcare. Throughout the eight months, we were also offered tickets to concerts, operas, and plays. To quote from a Kelly Clarkson song, "Some people wait a lifetime for a moment like this."

This seems like an opportune moment to thank a number of people. First, I would like to thank Father Thorne and Professor Angus Johnston who first dreamed of the idea of offering a course such as this in Halifax. Without your vision, optimism, planning and dedication, none of us, the graduates of years one through eight would be here today.

Thank you to all the sponsors and financial supporters, both individual and corporate. Needless to say, without your recognition of the intrinsic value of this program, and your follow-through of financial gifts and resources, this program would have remained a dream.

To our esteemed professors and instructors: thank you for your incredible generosity. With you as our guides and supporters, we have traveled to wonderful places and met an impressive cast of characters. How far have some of our travels been? Well, next year going to Dartmouth for the seminar class will seem like nothing!

We have listened in awe with Odysseus to the wondrous song of the sirens, and wrestled many monsters along side of him in a twelve-year journey home. Along the way we have cheered every new self-discovery which he made.

We have suffered along with Job and marvelled at his strength, tenacity, and resilience through adversity.

We have stood on the battlefield with Roland surrounded by his dying army. Would we have made the same fateful decision in his place?

If we came to this program hoping for answers to life's big questions, we would be disappointed. Instead, we were offered the opportunity, through the reading of great authors, to ponder and reflect on some of life's great questions, and perhaps to re-define some questions in the light of our own experiences.

Many of the world's great visionaries and thinkers have grappled with profound questions: What is the nature of the universe? What does it mean to be human? What does it mean to believe or not believe in God? It is astonishing how closely some of these questions relate to: How will I pay my bills? How will I feed my children? What can I do to become whole?

The seekers of knowledge, and the askers of questions: these people have become role models for us. In many cases, the fact that they dared to question, to take risks, and ultimately have the courage of their convictions has changed the world, and how people think: Descartes, St. Theresa of Avila, Martin Luther, George Eliot, George Elliott Clarke, Hannah Arendt ... and the list goes on.

So what exactly has happened to us over the course of the last eight months?

First, there are a few more people to thank: Mary Lu Redden. You are Halifax Humanities. You are our First Contact, the Captain of our Starship, The Upholder of the Prime Directive. (For anyone who knows *Star Trek*, that is saying a whole lot!!) You work tirelessly on our behalf, fundraise, take care of a myriad of practical details, and mother hen us, in the nicest sense. Thank you for everything you do.

To our family and friends: thank you for all the ways you have encouraged and supported us. It has meant everything. While I still have the platform for a few minutes more, I would like to give a personal and very special thank you to someone in my life who has been a rock and support to me for more than a dozen years. Anne Houstoun. You have been an advocate for me during difficult times, and a cheerleader through the good. I trust your counsel, and value your opinion when there are no easy answers. I am glad for this opportunity to give you a public thank you.

So, back to the past eight months: like Silas Marner, many of us have had our share of life's adversities. Like Silas, we have been ridiculed, robbed and betrayed. And like Silas, we have received something in our life that has profoundly changed us. We will, from now on and always, be the graduating class of 2013. We have become new members of a family (and I use that word quite intentionally). So again, I thank everyone who has made this possible.

And so I will end as I began: on behalf of the graduating class, "Oh I can't believe it's happening to me. Some people wait a lifetime for a moment like this."

Thank you.

CHILDHOOD JOY

BONITA SHEPHERD

MARY LAWSON WAS the elementary school that I and my four older siblings went to many years ago. We grew up in Westphal, a suburb of Dartmouth N.S. I remember how I cried when I was first left there alone, I was very scared and so I stayed very close to the teacher. I remember sitting in the front row and how a few of the other kids kept calling me to talk; when I did, I would always get in trouble for turning around to listen to them.

I remember there was a piece of equipment that we could play on in the school yard; it was called the rocket; it was long and cylindrical in shape. It started out blue in color but the paint gradually faded, rusted, and chipped off of it. On the end of it there was a ball shaped part to this equipment originally painted red. I used to love to scrunch up like the other kids inside of it. In fact, some of them, including my brother and sisters, didn't believe that I could, so I would have to keep showing them that even the chubby kid could fit inside of it.

In fact I used to go up there by myself all of the time to check and see if I could still fit into the smaller part. I think that I was also very scared of it in some ways. In one way it was quite a challenge and a feat for me but I was also concerned even at that young age about maybe getting stuck in it, and then what would I do? Thankfully that never happened.

There was a big hill beside the school that we used to ride our toboggans down—those were the days, and I could never do that again! Pity really, I remember it being so much fun as our toboggans would hit all of the bumps, and fly up into the air; being covered in snow, and racing all the other kids, screaming and laughing all the way down the hill—what fun.

$\mathcal{F}$INDING $\mathcal{M}$Y $\mathcal{W}$AY

ANNE BEEK

I JOINED HUMANITIES IOI in September of 2012. I was looking for something to join now that my boys were older. I had heard about the Seminar Class from Bonita and Gail. At that time I wasn't sure if something like that was for me. After being at a food bank and getting more information and seeing the books we were going to read and about how it is for people on low income from Corrine, I decided to send in the application to see if I would be accepted as the programme sounded like it was really nice, though I was still unsure but willing to try. Mary Lu called to go for an interview. This was a good start. I met with her and talked about my life and what to expect if I was accepted. I was very excited about being accepted and started in September. I found some of the reading I did harder to understand than others. The professors were very knowledgeable and the information very interesting. This always kept me looking forward to the next class. What I found nice was being able to get tickets to the Neptune Theatre, never having been there before; this was a treat to get out with friends from class. To my surprise and to the surprise of my family I was able to stick it out and graduate and then move up to the Seminar Class, which is just once a week, not twice like Humanities IOI. I find I still look forward to my Wednesday class as I find it very stimulating.

I am very glad that I took the first step and joined Humanities IOI. Going on to the Seminar Class was one of the biggest and best decisions for me. I hope others are able to enjoy the class as I have as it has enriched my mind about so many different things. I'm very grateful to Mary Lu and all of the professors for volunteering their time as without them we would not have this opportunity to learn what we do.

My Teachers

KATHLEEN HIGNEY

I hear the call
Come and dine
Come—the food is prepared
Your attendance is desired

Sit in the presence of men and women
World-shakers and culture-shapers
Often not appreciated in their day
And have to walk alone

Experts of past and present thought
And predictors of the future
Are engaging my mind
Teaching me to think for myself

I am invited to join the conversation
With the few who dare
To examine, question, form opinions
And then argue them—with friends

As I participate—something is happening
I am becoming more like them
Awake, unafraid—modeling a good society
I am gaining strength through the example
    of my teachers

A Day at the Food Bank[1]

LAMONT DOBBIN

WHEN YOU FIRST come into the food bank, Frances gives you a number and invites you to relax at the tables and chairs sprinkled with *Heralds*, *Metros*, and other local reading material. Joanne and the two Bettys have coffee and donuts at the back of the room. Off to the right are clothing and footwear donations and beyond that a large collection of books both hard-cover and paperback free for the taking. After a few announcements and a short prayer service, Carl and Gordon will call the numbers and, one by one, they'll get the family information they need to make up a food packet. This goes to Biggy, Helen, and Marg in the pantry. They make up a custom package of soup, milk, KD, cookies, beans, pasta, cereal, crackers, jam, rice, and canned fruit, veggies, and meat, depending on family size and the children's ages. They'll also include a personal package of toiletries if you've requested it. While you're waiting, you can talk to Tom about jobs, education, or other programs. Heather, Glenn, and Martin will then call your number again and combine the package from the pantry with bread, veggies, and whatever else is available that week. When you have your food, Jim and Ralph are ready to give you a lift home. If you're the very first person in the line-up, you could be on your way in less than half an hour, but for most it takes a bit longer. This is what it looks like every Wednesday morning at Stairs United Church on Hester Avenue in Dartmouth.

The food bank here got its start quite informally many years ago with

---

1   An earlier version appeared in *The Dominion*, June 18, 2012.

parishioners bringing food to the church and the minister handing it out from his study to those who came in need. The church then set aside a small cupboard under the stairs and opened up the food bank regularly to the neighbourhood. As the need increased, Stairs built the much larger, present-day pantry, used the cupboard for storage, and hired several coordinators to run a full-fledged food bank. The coordinators are long gone, an official charitable society has been established, several outreach services have been added, and two part-timers, Frances and Tom, now lead a troupe of dedicated volunteers in operating one of the largest and busiest food banks in the area. Farrell Hall Bingo and Investors Group are mentioned as generous supporters but, along with Feed Nova Scotia, the vast majority of donations come from anonymous, caring individuals.

Frances Hunter was introduced to me as "she who must be obeyed." Her official title is Food Bank Manager. I wouldn't dare ask how old she is but I do know her son took early retirement a few years ago when he turned sixty, so you do the math. Frances has been working here since the beginning, traveling around to various grocery stores collecting day-old bread, and emptying the food bank bins. She's never thought about quitting: "It's just something I was called to do." She's very animated when discussing the clients. "Each one is different. They need to feel they are respected. Each one has a story and they want to be listened to. They want to be hugged and see a friendly face and that's what I do—give them a hug and a big smile. That's my reward too, the hugs and smiles I get."

The palpable sense of family and friendship that permeates the food bank was noticed by Lillian Kai on her first visit. Lillian is neither a volunteer nor a client. She came by to drop off a donation over a year ago and has been here almost every week since to have a coffee and keep in touch with the friends she's made. "If I miss a week, I owe Tom double the hugs." This week is special. She got engaged Easter Sunday and she's showing off her engagement ring. (It's really nice.) "I enjoy dropping in to chat and encourage people but I get encouraged too." Jessie is another example of the food bank family attitude. She's a volunteer on Tuesday, a client on Wednesday, and a parishioner on Sunday. A woman of few words, her only comment is a big smile and thumbs up.

Martin Walker from Grace United Church is the current president of the Society for the North Dartmouth Outreach Resource Centre, the people who now officially run the Stairs food bank. Martin took early retirement a few years ago and wanted to do work with a sense of purpose. "I wanted to do something practical rather than just chair meetings. I'm really impressed by the hands-on attitude of the volunteers here, the get-it-done attitude. They know that people need this and they just do it." Martin was also struck by the positive environment and sense of family among the workers and clients. "There's almost no turnover here among our volunteers. Once people come here to help out, even if they didn't plan a long-term commitment, they really tend to stay."

Before Martin took over in January, Gordon McKeen was the president of NDORC for the past ten years and he's the man responsible for their motto "Gentle, Humble, Frugal." He explains the slogan this way:

> Our clients can be very fragile because of the problems they have and also because of the way that society treats them and, for many people, it's not easy to come to a food bank. One woman told me she walked past half-a-dozen times before she came in. For this reason we want to be very gentle in our dealings. We also want to be humble. But for grace there go I. Any of us can fall victim to circumstance. Finally, we need to be frugal both with our assets and our energy so that we can make sure every client gets help and shares the resources we have to offer.

Tom Clarke joined the food bank for what he thought was a one-year stint. Fifteen years later he's still the outreach coordinator. Tom's been very impressed with the assistance the food bank has received from other organizations in the community. Every week he delivers a car packed full of food from the relatively small congregation at St. Andrew's Anglican Church, while the Port Wallace United Church has agreed to pay for lost health cards and emergency bus tickets for clients in need. Tim Horton's on Wyse Road donates donuts and muffins, the *Chronicle Herald* drops off ten free newspapers each Wednesday, and we're all amazed at the huge donation dropped off each month by a couple who quit smoking and now spend that money on food for the poor. Donna Perrin and Tom O'Neil come by on the last Tuesday of each month to unload an enormous pile of food purchased with the proceeds of their new, healthier lifestyle.

Tom provides the latest postings from the job bank each week and pamphlets or notices from Tenants Rights, Circle of Care Society, and as many other groups as might be useful. He says that from the very beginning they wanted to offer more than just food. "Our clients have a lot of challenges, not just financial but physical, mental, emotional and otherwise." That's why other helping hands are invited to visit each week. Today someone is here from Dartmouth Family Center, Dartmouth Community Health Team, and, of course, Reverend Sarah Reaburn will spend the morning talking to folks while they wait for their food.

I asked the Reverend what kinds of things people want to talk about. "People frequently want to discuss their grief, often old grief that hasn't been dealt with. There are also relationship problems and these often involve addiction issues. Lots of people just want to pray." There's a quiet room just off the kitchen and almost every week Sarah will spend time with someone in private prayer and discussion. "Of course, some people just want to chat! Since I've been doing this for over five years, I know these folks and they know me so there's always lots of catching up." The food bank has actually expanded Sarah's ministry quite considerably since many of these clients now have a spiritual connection to the church without actually being parishioners or attending regular services. Their only regular contact is the Wednesday morning food bank.

Kevin Little from the Public Good Society isn't here today but he's been a regular most Wednesdays since 2008. Kevin has connections all over the community and he can point clients in the right direction and help them make contact with the right people and organizations for their particular needs. Whether it's employment training or opportunities, education needs, a health-wellness navigator, housing connections or other requests, Kevin serves as a conduit, linking clients with people and services they might otherwise never find. Recognizing the special needs of the people he serves, Kevin often takes it one step further and provides transportation or even accompanies folks to their first appointment to make sure the connection is made.

Finally, when people have collected all their food parcels and spoken to the people they need to see, Ralph MacKenzie and Councillor Jim Smith offer to drive them home. Jim's been offering rides to clients for many years now and it was his suggestion that got Ralph started about a year ago. He drove his own vehicle for the first eight months but now uses the recently purchased community-based van shared by the Public Good Service and several other charitable organizations. Jim was a key player in getting funds for the van, Esso donated $1,500 worth of gas cards, and the various community groups share the other operating expenses. Ralph doesn't feel that a ride home is in any way an extravagance. "Some people wouldn't come to the food bank at all without a ride home. They can't afford cab-fare and physically can't carry the groceries home." Like the other volunteers, Ralph doesn't feel he's doing anything exceptional. "People talk about what a great thing you're doing but I feel really rewarded. I'm building relationships with these people. I know their names, where they live, and what's going on in their families. I'm making friends. I love it."

At 11:00 the doors are closed, the last few clients are served, and the volunteers and Ron, the church janitor, will clean up and put away everything. Throughout the week, in churches, businesses, and homes around the city, people will set aside food and other donations for those in need. Tuesday morning, Feed Nova Scotia will drop off another allotment of groceries to be sorted and packaged. And next Wednesday at 8:30 AM we'll do it all again and, as long as there's a need, every Wednesday after that.

J·D· SALINGER

JESSE BLACKWOOD

I WASN'T SURE what to do when I woke up. I was anxious as hell to get some good writing done. I was anxious because I didn't think it was going to happen. I'd been reading that goddamn J.D. Salinger and I couldn't get his way of talking out of my head. And it isn't that he's not a good writer too. It isn't anything like that. It's just like wearing someone else's clothes. You might be able to put them on all right but you're not going to feel like you're wearing your own clothes. That's fine and all too. When I'm drunk or I'm feeling like horsing around or something, then I don't mind pretending I'm someone else. But I just wasn't feeling like pretending when I woke up. For one thing I was only wearing my underwear and I sure as hell didn't feel like wearing J.D. Salinger's underwear. Some people might be into *that* but I'm not. And for another thing, I had just woke up, and usually when I just wake up I don't feel much like horsing around. So instead I just stood there getting colder and colder because I was still just wearing my underwear until I finally had the good sense to put on some of my own clothes. Even if no one was around and I couldn't get the voice of that goddamn J.D. Salinger out of my head, at least I was wearing my *own* clothes.

What's even weirder than walking around in someone else's underwear is just feeling like you're someone else. I mean, I was wearing my own underwear and all but I sure as hell didn't feel much like myself. I thought maybe it was because I hadn't had any coffee yet. I usually don't start feeling like myself each day until I've had at least a couple of coffees and maybe more than that. Some days I can drink coffee all day and never get to feeling like myself. Take yesterday for example, I had about six coffees before it was even one o'clock and I still felt hungover as hell.

So this morning what I did, I did the only thing I could do. I started boiling some water to make coffee. Only I don't have a kettle or anything. I have just the one pan. It's nice looking too, non-stick Teflon so it's easy to clean or something. Anyway, I still wasn't feeling much like myself and I was shivering cause I'd only just got my clothes on and I didn't know what to do. So I just stood there watching the water in the pan. It was sort of peaceful just watching the little bubbles form on the bottom of the pan. I know water isn't supposed to boil when you watch it, or it's supposed to take longer or something but I didn't care. I even kinda hoped it wouldn't. I saw the little round pockets of air just forming around the edges of the pan and I sorta hoped they'd just stay like that forever. Before the water really gets going it seems like they just might too. It seems like they're holding onto the bottom of the pan just as long as they can, like they know they're going to disappear as soon as they let go.

Anyway, for a moment I thought I might get my old self back, like I was when I was a kid, cause I was enjoying watching those little pockets of air hold on as long as they could. But then the center really started to go and I felt like that goddamn J.D. Salinger again. I'd like to believe in old wives' tales because I don't care much for science but it just isn't true that the watched pot never boils. That pot just doesn't give a goddamn how hard those little pockets of air are trying to hold on and neither does science.

It depressed me to think that Salinger was probably right about all the beautiful moments breaking apart or dying. I didn't see any way out of it either. So I just shut off the water and poured it over my coffee. Usually I love drinking coffee but it was depressing as hell just then. The coffee I had was this fair trade coffee from Nepal that cost about twice as much as a regular package of coffee and it isn't better or anything but they say some of the money is supposed to go to the farmers who grew the coffee in the first place. That's why I bought it. But it was depressing as hell thinking about those poor farmers in Nepal squashed between China and India, trying to eke out a living on coffee that costs twice as much and that no one was ever going to buy except out of pity. It was really depressing thinking about raggedy-dressed farmers growing coffee beans in Nepal and surviving on my pity. Pity is a terrible thing to live on. But I figured I'd drink the coffee anyway. What was I supposed to do, just throw it out and quit drinking coffee altogether?

Well I've thought about it. I even came to Asia in the first place because I'd hoped to disappear. Boy was I wrong about that. Most of the time I'm the only white guy around. Plus I'm about a foot taller than everyone else and I have curly hair. Disappear. Ha. Like the pot that never boils. Goddamn science.

There was a moment, before I even got on the plane to come over here, that it seemed like it might be true, that I might just be able to come to Asia to disappear. I was in the garden at my parents' house. I wasn't doing anything really, just walking and thinking. It seemed then, those ten thousand miles ago, like it might just be a good idea. Boy, that idea boiled over pretty quick once I got here. I felt even more like myself. I mean, like I couldn't pretend to be anyone else and I was walking around naked or something, the way everybody noticed me. Anyway, I sure as hell didn't get to disappear and re-invent who I would be. I was still just drinking fair trade coffee from a farmer that depressed the hell out of me.

And because I didn't have a fridge or anything, because I'd just moved into the apartment, I had to drink the coffee black. Normally I like to have my coffees about half sugar, half milk, and half coffee. Cream is even better than milk when it's there. I can be quite a prima donna about my coffee. I've drunk coffee all over the world. I mean, I used to drink world famous coffee every day back when I was living in Rome. Then I didn't care where the coffee came from.

Boy it depressed me to think about how good coffee can be. All I had was a flimsy little French press with yesterday's coffee stains along the rim. The coffee really wasn't going to make the day any easier. At least French press sounded sexy. It was better than Bodum or some other brand name. I hate brand names. God do I hate them. Don't even ask me why. Ask the goddamn psychologist if you have to know. He has all the answers.

Anyway I was feeling pretty lonely being on the other side of the world in an apartment that still had the last tenants' dust and plates and books and shit all over the place. And thinking about the French press didn't make me less lonesome. It just reminded me of this guy Eric something. I don't remember his last name but we worked together at the same school teaching English. I mean the kids there are really great, really so goddamn wonderful it just makes me want to cry sometimes. Kids can do that to you. Especially when they're six or seven and they haven't grown up or anything.

But that wasn't why I started thinking about Eric. It was his birthday the night before last and that was the reason I'd had so many coffees yesterday morning and was feeling so hung over. But the reason the French press made me think of him, was after he'd had a couple of drinks he kept talking about the kinds of girls he liked to shag. Now I can be pretty social when I have to be and because it was his birthday I didn't let on how much of a selfish asshole I thought he was. But then he started talking about this one girl in particular who was a ballerina. She was from Russia or something and trying to make her career as a dancer. He said that he'd shagged all her friends but she was the only one he really wanted. She was the only really hot one. I thought that was really something. I could see her all done up for a show and pirouetting right on the tips of her toes, maybe even to something really beautiful Tchaikovsky had written. And all Eric could think of was what a terrific body she had and what a terrific shag he might get. And what made it worse was that I still felt like that J.D. Salinger and that Eric only ever felt like Eric. I could tell by the way he talked about himself. He loved being in Asia. He felt like a celebrity. I couldn't blame him for that either. I really couldn't.

It was all a very depressing way to drink my coffee and I was still anxious as hell to figure out what J.D. Salinger meant. If he thought you just kept falling and falling and putting on other people's clothes. Or if he thought there was a way not to disappear, a way to get older without letting go of everything.

AUGUSTINE, FAITH, AND LEARNING

RON HAFLIDSON

BY THE TIME Augustine sat down to write his *Confessions*,[1] he was an undisputed intellectual superstar who, as a Bishop, was regularly called upon to articulate and defend his faith. The first nine books of *Confessions*, which can (somewhat accurately) be described as autobiographical, tell the story of his life from his birth to the death of his mother. While Augustine does tell us a lot about himself, at times with shocking detail, *Confessions* is not the 5th century equivalent of a 21st century celebrity tell-all best-seller. He is up to something else. Even the most casual readers will quickly discover that, if you're not a Christian, Augustine's out to convert you; if you already are a Christian, he's out to encourage you in your faith. In so doing, Augustine offers those interested in Western intellectual history insight into how one of the great defenders of the Christian faith sought to establish Christianity's superiority over all the other many religions and philosophies on offer in that formative age.

We might suspect, given this description, that such a book would not endear itself to we contemporary Canadians who, for the most part, pride ourselves on affirming a beautiful diversity of religions, cultures, etc. And yet my experience of teaching *Confessions*, in *Halifax Humanities* and elsewhere, is that a delightfully motley crew of people, from the Dawkins-quoting atheist to the enlightened Buddhist, can't help but adore Augustine.

---

1   Augustine, *The Confessions* (New York: New City Press, 1997). Maria Boulding, translator.

Certainly much of this adoration has to do with just how naughty Augustine was and how much (and how beautifully) he tells us about his naughtiness. More significantly, though, I think is that Augustine was equally adept at analyzing ideas as he was at analyzing people. So, even if you find all of the Jesus-y bits boring or downright offensive, there's still insight into human beings that, in many ways, still seems fresh.

One way of approaching *Confessions* is as a story about how human beings learn. It's often been noted that the major changes in Augustine's life come about when he reads a good book; while certainly that's true, books are only one feature of how he learns. Thus I thought it appropriate, given that *Halifax Humanities* specializes in learning, to reflect on what *Confessions* has to tell us about learning. The whole of *Confessions* could be read in this way but I'll confine myself to Book III, which describes two of Augustine's conversions, first to philosophy and then to Manicheanism. In these conversions we see several essential features of Augustine's understanding of learning.

As a young man, Augustine learned primarily as a means of self-advancement. He followed his parents' wishes and studied rhetoric, the study of how to use words to persuade others; yet Augustine was not hoping to persuade others of what was just and true, rather he was after a prestigious and powerful career. When describing his time as a student of rhetoric, Augustine also describes his love of the theatre. He could not get enough of plays; and the more they made him cry or laugh, the better. He writes: "I rejoiced with lovers on the stage who took sinful pleasure in one another, even though their adventures were only imaginary and part of a dramatic presentation, and when they lost each other I grieved with them, ostensibly out of compassion; yet in both instances I found pleasure in my emotions … A person who sorrows for someone who is miserable earns approval for the love he shows but if he is genuinely compassionate he would far rather there were nothing to sorrow about" (III.2.3, p. 44). Based on this passage, Augustine is often taken to be against theatre, but I think there is something more complex going on here. Augustine is not criticizing theatre as such, rather he is criticizing his relation to it. The key phrase is "I found pleasure in my emotions." Augustine cared little whether the plays made him happy or sad, he just damn well wanted to *feel*, and feel *intensely*. The problem he identifies with this, when looking back, is that he was treating emotions as an end in themselves. Emotions, the mature Augustine would conclude, are meant to attune us to reality; if I'm saddened by TV footage of refugees forced to leave their homes, that emotion connects me, in some dim way, to the experience of other people. It may be that as a result of that emotion I'll be moved to act in some way. Yet Augustine's emotions in response to the theatre aren't about connecting, not only because the actors aren't real people but, more importantly, because he was enjoying how his emotions stimulated him. This is a dangerous habit to get into. If I enjoy being compassionate, then, in a certain way, I affirm others' suffering that provides the opportunity for me to be compassionate, whereas compassion, as Augustine notes, ought to be based on wanting suffering to *end*. His love of theatre gives us insight into the kind of student he was: above all, he sought knowledge as a means of getting what he wanted; like the thrill of laughing and crying in the theatre, Augustine's studies placed himself at the centre, and all else was subordinate to him.

All that changes when Augustine reads a good book. Lost to us now, the first century Roman statesman and philosopher Cicero's *Hortensius*, was a key text in the rhetorical curriculum. Augustine notes that they were to focus on Cicero's words, not the substance of what he was saying. But Augustine, through no credit of his own, took in the substance with the words. He writes, "The book changed my way of feeling and the character of my prayers to you, O Lord, for under its influence my petitions and desires altered. All my hollow hopes suddenly seemed worthless, and with unbelievable intensity my heart burned with longing for the immortality that wisdom seemed to promise." The contrast with the theatre is very revealing. Whereas in the theatre Augustine just wanted to feel anything, as long as he felt it intensely, after reading Cicero Augustine tells us his feelings are re-oriented towards genuine knowledge. And not just knowledge as a means to a prestigious and powerful career, but knowledge that he describes as "the immortality of wisdom" (III.4.7, p. 46). For Augustine, knowledge is no longer about providing tools to manipulate others so he can get his way; I take "immortality" to refer to a desire for a kind of knowledge that is beyond manipulation; it cannot be put at his disposal. Augustine has opened himself up—or rather, he has been opened up—to a knowledge that is an end in itself. Further, it is not mere "knowledge," but "wisdom." I take it that wisdom is not knowledge of one branch of knowledge among others; rather wisdom is a knowledge of the whole, to see reality in its beautiful coherence and so to know one's place in relation to that coherence. Augustine describes his desire for knowledge in starkly erotic terms, "... by [wisdom's] call I was aroused and kindled and set on fire to love and seek and capture and hold fast and strongly cling not to this or that school, but to wisdom itself, what it might be" (p. 47). Augustine has, it would not be inaccurate to say, fallen in love with wisdom, or, quite literally, he has become a philosopher, a lover of wisdom.

As a result of growing up in a Christian family, Augustine associates wisdom with Jesus. So after he has become a philosopher thanks to Cicero, Augustine's love of wisdom leads him to read the Bible. While he finds much about Christ there, he is, he tells us, repulsed by it: "My swollen pride recoiled from its style and my intelligence failed to penetrate to its inner meaning, scripture is a reality that grows along with little children, but I disdained to be a little child and in my high and mighty arrogance regarded myself as grown up" (p. 47). Looking back, Augustine sees the inspired nature of the Bible at work on him; he believed that the Bible was written in such a way that there was something for everyone, from the barely-literate simpleton to the philosophically-educated genius, and yet, the price of admission for all is humility. Yet Augustine's point, I think, need not apply only to the Bible. Notice how he says he turned from the Bible because he was not yet ready "to be a little child." Learning, he is saying, takes time; and it takes the willingness to become a beginner again (and again ... and again ...). Or, as the Zen Buddhists call it, we must cultivate "Beginner's Mind." Augustine decidedly did not have a "Beginner's Mind." The beauty of Cicero's prose got through to him because its rhetorical brilliance flattered his pride; he was willing to learn from a text that conformed to his identity of himself as an advanced student of rhetoric. Whereas if he were to glean any meaning from the Bible, he would have to admit his ignorance about what wisdom lay there and take the time to learn. He doesn't tell us what of the Bible he read, but we may speculate that in his search for Christ he opened it to the New Testament; and so he could, say, have read one of Jesus' parables about farming or one of Paul's commentaries on how to act in church. What does all of this, Augustine no doubt asked himself, have to do with the immortality of wisdom?

One way we might interpret Augustine's repulsion at the Bible is as a battle between two of his loves. He had decidedly fallen in love with know-ledge, which is essential to learning, and yet his love was not willing to take the time to learn; and so, it seems, his love of knowledge is in conflict with a certain love of himself. In our often very moralistic age, the term "selfish-ness" gets thrown about left and right. Augustine preferred to distinguish between an ordered self-love and a disordered self-love. That is, there are ways of loving ourselves that are in harmony with, often in the service of, our love of others and of God; taking regular rest, for example, is not just good for us, it makes us more ready to care for whoever is in our lives. On the other hand, there are ways of loving ourselves that are in opposition to loving others and God. The young Augustine who is repulsed by the Bible is an Augustine whose self-love resists any need for change. He is in love with knowledge, but he's also in love with himself in a way that prevents him from taking the time and undergoing the change that knowledge demands.

Augustine, then, converts to Manicheanism. What led Augustine to Manicheanism at this point in his journey? The details of Manicheanism sound utterly bizarre to us these days, though, I think, the fundamentals of it still underlie many very popular contemporary forms of religion, philo-sophy, politics, and science. Augustine emphasizes that Manicheanism was materialistic and dualistic. Materialistic refers to how Manicheans believed that all things, including their two gods, were material. And dualism refers to how the grand Manichean story that explains the current state of things involves a conflict between two (dual) gods: a good god of light and an evil god of darkness. Augustine says, in retrospect, that materialism and dualism appealed to him because of his disordered self-love. To be a materialist, to Augustine's mind, is only to ascribe reality to what is most immediately observable by you; and, similarly, to be a dualist is to divide up the world into who's in and who's out, and, to locate yourself as someone who's in. Manicheans claimed to give him answers right away so he didn't need to take any time to learn, and, further, they didn't demand he make any changes in his life. The knowledge Manicheanism offers, then, flatters the self as it is, rather than demanding that change is essential if we're ever to truly know anything. Thus Augustine's descriptions of the Manicheans are among his most harsh: "I fell among a set of proud madmen, exceedingly carnal and talkative people in whose mouths were diabolical snares" (III.6.10, p. 48).

Later in *Confessions*, Augustine will identify one of the key "diabolical snares" of the Manicheans as promising its followers that all their teachings are rationally defensible. In contrast, as a student, Augustine found the claim of the Catholic church, that one had to have faith in the teachings of the Church, to be equivalent to intellectual suicide. Yet after his honeymoon with the Manicheans had ended and he was on his way out of the sect, Augustine reflects: "... how innumerable were the things I believed and held to be true though I had neither seen them nor been present when they happened. How many truths there were of this kind, such as events of world history, or facts about places and cities I had never seen; how many were the statements I believed on the testimony of friends, or physicians, or various other people; and, indeed, unless we did believe them we should be unable to do anything in this life" (VI.5.7, p. 100). In other words, Augustine began to discover that it was not the Catholic church alone that demanded faith as an essential step towards knowledge; faith is demanded in every area of our lives almost at every moment. To begin to learn is to reach out in trust—to have faith—that there is more to know and it is worth knowing. That involves, inherently, taking a risk. Thus Augustine comes to conclude that the Manicheans' whole approach to learning is false: no religion (or philosophy or science or person ...) can claim to immediately give you the truth based on reason alone because you must begin at the beginning and such a beginning involves stepping out in faith. The Catholic church, the mature Augustine would conclude, is far more honest about how learning happens: you must start out in faith as a necessary first step on the way to knowledge. That's not to say that you might not eventually discover that your faith was wrong, but the mistake was not to have faith, the mistake was to have faith in the wrong object. The love of knowledge, for Augustine, always reaches out in faith; it is certainly a risk, and it demands the searcher change and take time; and, of course, it leaves one open to failure, but no true form of learning can immunize you against such risk. The love of knowledge leads us to reach out in trust—to books, friends, teachers—and to discover, Augustine would assure us (and so too, I hope, would participants in *Halifax Humanities*), that it is only by such seeking that we will ever find.

"Your Spirits are Attentive"
Convocation Address, Halifax Humanities 101 Graduation, June 14, 2008

JOHN BAXTER

I AM DEEPLY honored to have been asked to speak to you on this occasion and to be able to participate more generally in the wind-up festivities of the Halifax Humanities Programme for this year. It's a wonderful programme and I consider myself lucky to have had some small involvement in it over the past couple of years. I've given my brief address to you this afternoon a title: "Your spirits are attentive." It's a quotation, so you have to hear it with the quotation marks around it: "Your spirits are attentive." Now, you may have supposed that this convocation would simply be an occasion for you to relax, sit back, and look pretty (or handsome), collect a certificate or two, and receive the accolades you so richly deserve. Well, I have to admit that you *are* a pretty handsome bunch and I'm more than happy to congratulate you all on a job well done. You've come through—in style—and it's an impressive achievement. Congratulations! And congratulations, too, to your friends and families and supporters!

But I wonder if Mary Lu, attentive as she is to every detail of the programme, has alerted you to the possibility that there could still be a test this afternoon? Humanities seminars are never over till they're over and this one isn't over. I will be expecting you to identify the quotation that is my title. Where does it come from? Who says it? What does it mean? Any guesses?

"Your spirits are attentive."

You may remember that when we talked about *The Merchant of Venice* last winter, we spent most of our time on figures such as Shylock (why *does* he want a pound of flesh? does he get more than justice in the end?) or Portia (why *should* she obey the terms of her father's lottery, and why does she make such a big fuss about the ring her husband lost?) or Bassanio (who does he think he is to deserve a huge loan just to impress his girlfriend, and does *he* get more than he deserves in the end?). But we didn't spend any time on two other figures, Lorenzo and Jessica (Shylock's daughter), and now is the time to make up for that omission—and to make ourselves ready for the final test. Lorenzo and Jessica have eloped; they have already escaped from Venice and are just hanging out in Belmont, waiting for their friends to return. It's a night scene and they are looking at the sky. Lorenzo speaks first:

> How sweet the moonlight sleeps upon this bank!
> Here will we sit and let the sounds of music
> Creep in our ears. Soft stillness and the night
> Become the touches of sweet harmony.
> Sit, Jessica. Look how the floor of heaven
> Is thick inlaid with patens of bright gold.
> There's not the smallest orb which thou behold'st
> But in his motion like an angel sings,
> Still quiring to the young-eyed cherubins.
> Such harmony is in immortal souls,
> But whilst this muddy vesture of decay
> Doth grossly close it in, we cannot hear it. (5.1.54-65)

At this point, a group of musicians enters the scene and Lorenzo turns from Jessica to address the musicians: "Come, ho! and wake Diana with a hymn." He says "Diana" but he also means "Jessica"; he equates her with Diana in this context most probably because he identifies her with the moon and Diana is the goddess of the moon in Roman myth. "With sweetest touches," he continues, "pierce your mistress' ear/And draw her home with music" (5.1.66-9). Diana/Jessica, however, is not so sure she wants to go home—having left her father, she may be a little uncertain about just where her home now is—and she responds in a very reflective way: "I am never merry when I hear sweet music." To this meditative response, Lorenzo replies with a quick and kindly reassurance. He has an explanation for her mood at this moment for her very personal way of reacting to the stillness of the night and its "touches of sweet harmony." "The reason is," he says, "your spirits are attentive" (5.1.70-71).

Here, then, in the last act of *The Merchant*, we have our quotation and we are already half-way prepared for the test. But what does our quotation mean? The singing of the stars, or planets, in their fixed spheres was a commonplace, originating in ancient thought. It can be found, for example, in Plato's *Republic*. "While the human soul is immured in the corporeal body ('this muddy vesture of decay') it is unable to hear or respond to celestial music," at least not in the way that the angels can. The French philosopher and essayist Michel de Montaigne says, "what philosophers deem of the celestial music, which is that the body of its circles, being solid smooth, and in their rolling motion touching and rubbing against one another, must of necessity produce a wonderful harmony." This line of thinking, incidentally, is why Lorenzo speaks of the "*touches* of sweet harmony." Montaigne continues, "but that universally the hearing senses of these low world's creatures, dizzied and lulled asleep ... by the continuation of that sound, how loud and great soever it be cannot sensibly perceive or distinguish the same" (Oxford ed., 215n). Jessica and Lorenzo, however, even though they too are among the creatures of the low world—that is, our world, our human world—are still able on this heightened occasion to catch a hint of the celestial harmony. They have a harmony in their own immortal souls that is in touch with something much larger. The reason why Jessica is never merry when she hears such music is because she is possessed by an emotion much more profound than merriment. She is possessed by a sense of wonder or awe at the magnificence and beauty of the universe. Her spirits are "attentive."

And what Lorenzo says to his new bride in *The Merchant of Venice* is what I want to say to you as the newest graduates of Humanities 101: "*Your* spirits are attentive." *The Merchant of Venice*, like our world, is full of "muddy" things: revenge, jealousy, anger, betrayal, profligacy, prejudice, and selfishness. Shakespeare gives full scope to each of these things—he depicts the real world as it really is—but he also knows, as most of his characters know, that there are better things and that, ultimately, there are best things. The love of Jessica and Lorenzo is one of the good things in the play but it is certainly not without its flaws. It is not perfect. But in the last act of the play they are particularly attractive and engaging characters precisely because of the way they sense a world that is yet more perfect, more fully harmonious than their own. They look to the sky, spangled with stars, or in Lorenzo's better words, "thick inlaid with patens of bright gold," and they become aware that what seems like the roof of our world is merely "the floor of heaven." Their attentiveness to each other is magnified and improved by their attentiveness to what is beyond them.

I have often asked myself, after the occasions when we discussed Shakespeare together, what makes this group so engagingly candid and outspoken, so unpredictable and refreshing. Actually, what I said to myself after one session was "why do they ask so many hard and unanswerable questions?" I know that some of you like to play the "let's try to stump the professor" game; let's ask as many off-the-wall questions as possible; let's see what he *doesn't* know. It's a great game, though I like it better when you play it with Angus or Neil than with me. All the same, the game works because of the kind of life experience that you bring to your studies. Some of my younger undergraduates seem not greatly to care whether their experience in the class connects up with their lives outside of class. In fact, they sometimes seem to expect that there isn't or needn't be a connection. But you bring a quite different set of attitudes to the whole operation. You seem on the whole to be admirably committed to finding the connections or, if necessary, to making them if they already seem not to exist. You come prepared to travel from Halifax to Venice to Belmont and back again. And this attitude, this sense of a journey, this experience of the continuity of the journey that is your own life with the journey through the realms of imagination and ideas, is why "your spirits are attentive."

A convocation, of course, is a bitter-sweet experience. On the one hand,

there is a justifiable sense of pride and accomplishment. You've brought the
project to completion and fulfillment. You've made some new and important friendships, with colleagues and instructors and with the authors you've
studied. Be sure to re-visit them all. These friendships will last. On the other
hand, the end always also brings a bit of sadness. The project is over, at least
this stage of it, and that fragile and evanescent community that is a seminar
will never be quite the same again. Its very essence is that it is distinct—and
temporary. There are lots of attempts in the modern university to evaluate
the experience of education so we devise questionnaires measuring the
effectiveness of the instruction or the quality of the discussion or the difficulty of the material or the clarity and coherence of the syllabus. And on the
whole these are good things to do. But we all know that a really good class
is never quite caught by these statistical means or even by the assembling
of a dozen different opinions and perspectives. A really good class offers
something more intangible, more ineffable. It offers you a home. Lorenzo,
remember, wants to draw his mistress "home with music." It offers a kind
of community distinct from the community of the street or the family or
the office or the mall. A good seminar is a place where your spirits can be
attentive in Shakespeare's sense.

And in the end neither the sadness nor the happiness matters as much
as just being there. In another play that Shakespeare wrote very near the
end of his career, perhaps a dozen or more years after *The Merchant*, he provided his own farewell to the stage, that is, to the project that had occupied
him for more than two decades. The play is *The Tempest* and, if you don't
already know it, you should add it to your list. Humanities 101 wouldn't be
doing its job if you didn't come away with a list much longer than the list of
books you actually read or dipped into. The central figure in *The Tempest* is
Prospero and near the climax of the action he is obliged to relinquish his art
and his magical powers and return to the time-bound world of our ordinary
humanity and to this "low world's creatures," in Montaigne's phrase. Here
is Prospero's farewell to his own version of Humanities 101. He begins by
addressing his prospective son-in-law Ferdinand.

You do look, my son, in a moved sort,
As if you were dismayed. Be cheerful, sir;
Our revels now are ended. These our actors,
As I foretold you, were all spirits, and
Are melted into air, into thin air,
And like the baseless fabric of this vision,
The cloud-capped towers, the gorgeous palaces,
The solemn temples, the great globe itself,
Yea, all which it inherit, shall dissolve,
And like this insubstantial faded,
Leave not a rack behind. We are such stuff
As dreams are made on, and our little life
Is rounded with a sleep. Sir, I am vexed.
Bear with my weakness, my old brain is troubled. (4.1.146-59)

Your revels, too, are now ended. The term is over. But the sort of vision that Shakespeare conjures up, while he also laments that it is dissolving, is always there to be re-activated and re-animated by returning to this scene—and others like it—and by reading and studying with spirits that are attentive. I hope you will do so. Shakespeare needs you.

Bibliography

Montaigne, Michel de. *Essays and Selected Writings: A Bilingual Edition.* Ed. and trans. Donald M. Frame. New York: St. Martin's Press, 1963.

Shakespeare, William. *The Merchant of Venice.* Ed. Jay L. Halio. Oxford: Oxford University Press, 1993.

Shakespeare, William. *The Tempest.* Ed. Stephen Orgel. Oxford: Oxford University Press, 1987.

THE EDUCATION OF THE ATTENTION:
Simone Weil on the Right Use of School Studies

WARREN HEITI

The French philosopher Simone Weil is responsible for having introduced, to philosophical ethics, the concept of attention. This concept seems neither complicated nor unfamiliar but here I agree with Weil: "Not to understand new things, but by strength of patience, effort and method to come to understand those truths which are evident with one's whole being."[1] Weil's thinking about attention is closely connected with her philosophy of education. Her "Reflections on the Right Use of School Studies" belong to a posthumous collection of writings that Weil bestowed upon J.M. Perrin (the priest who tried, unsuccessfully and not entirely sympathetically, to persuade her to become baptized in the Catholic church). Let me anticipate the aim of her essay; Weil writes, "Although people seem to be unaware of it today, the development of the faculty of attention forms the real object and almost the sole interest of studies."[2] Elsewhere, in a set of complementary aphorisms, edited by her friend Gustave Thibon and titled "Attention and Will,"[3] she repeats this thought: "Teaching should have no aim but to prepare, by training the attention, for the certain application of full attention to an object.//All the other advantages of instruction are

---

1   Weil, *Notebooks*, Vol. 1, p. 144; cf. Pétrement, *Simone Weil: A Life*, 30-31.
2   Weil, "Reflections," *Waiting for God*, 57.
3   Weil, "Attention and Will," *Gravity and Grace*, 116-122.

without interest."[4]

I want to pause and notice how astonishing this claim is. Some of us might think, not without justification, that we go to school to train for a *job*—that school is a kind of accreditation programme for the workforce. Or perhaps we think that school is where we go to learn stuff—and that learning is the accumulation of information or data: when I graduate, I will *know more* than when I started. Weil is insisting that these ideas of, and approaches to, education are *without interest*. What then is the point of education? Why go to school? Isn't it important that I know that *modus ponens* is a valid argument-form; that Odysseus blinded the cyclops, and that Oedipus blinded himself with his wife's (his mother's) brooches; that the "Indian Residential School" system is a great injustice; that climate change is actually happening; et cetera? Am I not a better human being for having learned these facts?

Weil is saying no: "There must be method in it. A certain way of doing a Latin prose, a certain way of tackling a problem in geometry (and not just any way) make up a system of gymnastics of the attention ... "[5] By analogy with the gym, where one's physical body is exercised, school is a place where one limbers up one's attention, makes it stronger, more flexible.[6] Consider this claim: "So it comes about that, paradoxical as it may seem, a Latin prose or a geometry problem, even if they are done wrong, may be of great service one day ... Should the occasion arise, they can one day make us better able to give someone in affliction exactly the help required to save him, at the supreme moment of his need."[7]

Again I want to pause. First Weil claimed that learning facts (becoming a human encyclopedia) was not the point of school. Now she is claiming that doing your geometry homework can save lives—even if you get the answers wrong. When I was learning how to conjugate the verb "to be"

---

4   Weil, "Attention and Will," 120.

5   Weil, "Attention and Will," 120.

6   Weil is drawing on Plato here. He says: the soul is like the body. Just as there is a health of the body, there is a health of the soul. The health of the soul is called "justice" and, as your body becomes stronger through exercise in the gymnasium, so your soul becomes stronger by practising music and mathematics.

7   Weil, "Reflections," 65; translation altered.

in ancient Greek, tediously writing the conjugations out on recipe cards, I was learning how to be ethical? That claim is incredible. But here is the question which, according to Weil, school studies train us to ask: "'What are you going through?' It is a recognition that the sufferer exists. For this reason it is enough but it is indispensable to know how to look at him in a certain way."[8]

The question expresses perfectly the quality of attention which she is elucidating in her essay. We ask this question almost every day: "How are you?"—but we rarely mean it. We tend to ask in a perfunctory way and heaven forefend that someone should really tell us how she is. Weil imagines us asking this question differently, leaving space for the other person to respond. She does not pretend that such openness is easy—on the contrary, she says that it is "a very rare and difficult thing."[9] Learning how to do it well is a life's work. For Weil, the attention expressed by this question is at the very root of ethical responsibility.

Let me say a few words about Weil's *method*. The attention she is after is not merely a feeling of pity or charity—such a feeling could be entirely inefficacious. What is needed, she repeatedly insists, is method: "a certain way" of looking. "In every school exercise," she writes, "there is a special way of waiting upon truth ... There is a way of giving our attention to the data of a problem in geometry without trying to find the solution or to the words of a Latin or Greek text without trying to arrive at the meaning ... // Our first duty toward school children and students is to make known this method to them, not only in a general way, but in the particular form that bears on each exercise."[10] Frustratingly, after having emphasized the indispensability of these *specific* methodological forms—for example, attending to a geometry problem is *different*, she insists, from conjugating a Greek verb—she never discloses their contents.

However, she does offer some helpful remarks about a *general* method. These remarks draw the distinction between attention and will. "Most of-

8   Weil, "Reflections," 64.
9   Weil, "Reflections," 65.
10 Weil, "Reflections," 63.

ten attention is confused with a kind of muscular effort"—but such effort, namely, exerting the will, gritting our teeth, contracting our brows—"has practically no place in study."[11] Those of us who have stayed awake until four o'clock in the morning, reading the heaps of text needed for the next day's lesson, might disagree. It required a tremendous force of will, we might protest, to keep ourselves from losing consciousness. But Weil would say that is irrelevant. Perhaps will-power is needed to pass your eyes across the text. But *learning* is something different.

"The intelligence can only be led by desire," Weil writes. "The joy of learning is as indispensable in study as breathing is in running."[12] She is not promoting the shallow idea that teaching can be "entertaining." Joy, she suggests, is like oxygen. It is not frivolous; it is, quite literally, *necessary* to the life of the mind.

Will is what keeps our eyes open when we are tired. But it is joy that lets us learn. Joy (and here is a Spinozistic thought) is the experience of becoming more clear in the presence of something beautiful. This clarification occurs by itself while the student maintains a stance of patient receptivity. "All wrong translations, all absurdities in geometry problems ... are due to the fact that thought has seized upon some idea too hastily and being thus prematurely blocked, is not open to the truth. The cause is always that we have wanted to be too active ..."[13] Here, Weil is offering a theory of error which she has derived from Descartes. According to Weil and Descartes, error is the result of mis-coordinating the functions of attention and will.

Recall Meditation Four ("Concerning the True and the False"). There, Descartes draws a distinction between the faculty of the intellect and that of the will (roughly analogous to Weil's distinction between attention and will). These two faculties have different functions. The intellect perceives and, when it perceives well, it perceives clearly. The will, on the other hand, does something else: in the practical and theoretical realms, it says *yes* or *no*. For example, I perceive some water and am thirsty. My will says, "Yes, drink"

11   Weil, "Reflections," 60-61.
12   Weil, "Reflections," 61; cf. Weil, "Attention and Will," 118.
13   Weil, "Reflections," 62.

or "no, don't." Or: I perceive "2+3=5." My will says, "Yes, that's true" or "no, that's false." Error is when the will pre-empts (or outstrips) the intellect. Before the intellect has perceived clearly, the will issues its verdict. [If we accept Plato's definition of justice—performing one's proper function—then the will's impetuosity is a kind of epistemic injustice.] For example, I glimpse some liquid and my will yanks on its leash and barks, "Yes, drink"—but the liquid is gasoline. Or: I see "252+373=255," and my will impulsively blurts out, "Yes, that's true"—but really it's false (the correct answer is 625). It is for this reason that patiently waiting is crucial for both Descartes and Weil. One keeps one's will on a leash—or better yet, one trains one's will so that a leash is unnecessary.

Something remarkable emerges from this way of thinking: action *is* attention. It is a radical reconceptualization of freedom, agency, and action. What Descartes claims will likely sound paradoxical: "In order to be free I need not be capable of being moved in each direction; on the contrary, the more I am inclined toward one direction ... because I clearly understand that there is in it an aspect of the good and the true ... the more freely do I choose that direction."[14] He is claiming that *freedom* consists in having one's thinking *determined* by the truth (or in having one's action determined by what is good). Consider: "2+3=5." Descartes is saying that if you let your intellect focus this proposition clearly, if you really understand it, then your will cannot help but say "Yes! True!"

This is the experience of necessary truth, and it is this idea which Weil develops in greater detail in the set of aphorisms titled "Necessity and Obedience."[15] Most of us take it for granted that we are actors. We cause our actions, which effect changes in the world. Weil's conception of agency is different. When I understand, I see that I am not an actor but a *medium*: I should be like an arrow, "impelled," "driven": "To be only an intermediary between the uncultivated ground and the ploughed field, between the data of the problem and the solution, between the blank page and the

---

14   Descartes, *Meditations*, AT VII.57-58.
15   Weil, "Necessity and Obedience," *Gravity and Grace*, 43-50.

poem, between the starving beggar and the beggar who has been fed."[16]
My primary ethical responsibility, odd as it may sound, is *not* to rush around
manipulating the world and making it better; my primary responsibility is
witnessing—perceiving the world as clearly as I can.

Compare Steven Burns' discussion of Weil's example of a child attending to a mathematical problem: "In Weil's eyes, the real accomplishment of
the child is a negative one; he has lost sight of his own ability and of the
challenges and rewards of arithmetic, and has concentrated his attention
purely on the numbers. If the sum is correctly done, then the sum itself is
the reason for this."[17] Weil's thought involves much trust. The trust is that
clear perception is enough for action. Just as clearly understanding the formula "2+3=5" compels us to say "yes, true," so clearly perceiving someone's
real need should compel us to *respond* to that need. The conception is ultimately Platonic. The trust is that *desire is for what is true* or *what is good*. If we
really perceive what is good, we cannot help reaching out. In other words,
virtue is knowledge.

---

16   Weil, "Necessity and Obedience," 46.
17   Burns, "Justice and Impersonality," §1 (479).

Bibliography

Burns, Steven. "Justice and Impersonality: Simone Weil on Rights and Obligations." *Laval théologique et philosophique* 49.3 (October 1993): 477-486.

Descartes, René. *Meditations.* Third Edition. Trans. D.A. Cress. Indianapolis: Hackett Publishing Company, 1993.

Pétrement, Simone. *Simone Weil: A Life.* Trans. Raymond Rosenthal. New York: Schocken Books, 1976.

Weil, Simone. *Attente de Dieu.* Paris: Éditions Fayard, 1966.

Weil, Simone. *Gravity and Grace.* Trans. Emma Craufurd and Mario von der Ruhr. London: Routledge Classics, 2002.

Weil, Simone. *Notebooks.* Volume One. Trans. Arthur Wills. London: Routledge & Kegan Paul, 1976.

Weil, Simone. *Waiting for God.* Trans. Emma Craufurd. New York: Perennial Classics, 2001.

THE *B*EGINNINGS OF *H*ALIFAX *H*UMANITIES 101

In the beginning the rich were rich
and the poor were poor
—or so it seemed

GARY THORNE

What if people gathered together to read great works of philosophy and literature, and to contemplate both ancient and modern art in all its forms, in order to learn how to know the world, to love the world, and to live passionately and compassionately in it?

As our culture made the turn into the 21st century, even the most traditional 'liberal arts' universities had come under the spell of the global corporate agenda such that the university seemed to be almost the last place where this learning could happen.

Then in 2001 I was reminded of an initiative in the United States that made the substantial resources of the university available to seekers after a 'new life' outside the strictures of the corporate mandate of the contemporary university. A few years previous I had read a 1997 article in *Harper's Magazine* that described a group of people who were gathering precisely in order to learn how to know the world, to love the world, and how best to live in the world passionately and compassionately. In 2001 Earl Shorris expanded his description of the beginnings of the Clemente Course in the Humanities in his book *Riches for the Poor*. This programme seemed ideally tailored for those in Halifax's North End inner city for whom every day was a struggle for physical and psychological betterment. The Clemente Course promised something solidly practical for those desperate on the streets, viz. poetry, art, music, reflection with others on Beauty and Truth, informed exchange of ideas, conversation about the Good, and the possibility of thoughtful and passionate civic engagement.

Over a three-year period, Earl had interviewed hundreds of people living on the margins as part of a study he was conducting on poverty in America. The direction of his thinking changed when he met a woman prisoner in a maximum security prison outside New York City. Earl asked a group of inmates: "Why do you think people are poor?" It was only a discussion starter—Earl thought he already knew why people lived in poverty and why poverty had such a strong grip on so many: "numerous forces—hunger, isolation, illness, landlords, police, abuse, neighbors, drugs, criminals, and racism, among many others—exert themselves on the poor at all times and enclose them, making up a 'surround of force' from which, it seems, they cannot escape."[1]

But on that particular afternoon a female inmate showed Earl that he was missing something. The "moral life of downtown" was the key, she explained. The way out of poverty to a life of reflection, freedom, and active civic engagement was through the plays, the concerts, and the lectures of "downtown": i.e., the humanities. Earl set aside his research on poverty and established the first free humanities course in the Roberto Clemente Family Guidance Centre in Lower Manhattan.

At first Earl found it difficult to recruit students. Then, he told those living in poverty that they had been cheated:

> Rich people learn the humanities; you didn't. The humanities are a foundation for getting along in the world, for thinking, for learning to reflect on the world instead of just reacting to whatever force is turned against you. ... If you come to the Clemente Course, you must do it because you want a certain type of life, a richness of mind and spirit. That's all I can offer you: philosophy,

---

1 Earl Shorris, 1997 *Harper's Magazine* Foundation, Magazine Collection: 90J0851, Electronic Collection: A19745126

poetry, art, history, logic, rhetoric, and American history.[2]

In 2001 I was Rector of Saint George's Round Church, situated in the Halifax North End. I was keen to create as many opportunities as possible for friendships to develop between the well-educated middle class parishioners, many of whom did not live in the neighbourhood, and the extremely marginalized people who lived near the church or spent much of their time there accessing support centres, advocacy organizations, and various community services. The Clemente Course seemed to be a perfect match for the neighbourhood, and an opportunity for the 'liberal arts' to be engaged with an integrity now lost to the middle-class university experience. But to establish such a project required more resources than I had at my disposal.

Then, I received an unlikely offer from a complete stranger: Susan Barthos was coming to live in Halifax for six months, and she offered her skills, commitment and passion for a "significant worthwhile project." A full-time commitment for six months from such a capable consultant could well bring a Clemente Course in the Humanities to Halifax. I leapt at the offer and Susan threw herself into the project.

First, we asked key members of the Saint George's congregation if they believed that such a programme would be suited to Halifax and if Saint George's was the right community to take this on. One person responded that the parish would not only provide the needed stability but was also a community that "encompasses and embraces the poetry of the poets and the lives of the poor." The director of the parish YouthNet neighbourhood youth programme wrote: "YouthNet parents have often remarked that they wish they had opportunities like their kids get here." One response made it clear that others were thinking along the same lines as myself:

> This programme will be a means of transformation for people. Students will be given the chance to think their own lives in terms of the great books of our culture. I suspect that they will think their lives in terms of these books in a way that is very difficult for middle-class kids. For us (the middle-class), we as-

2   Ibid.

sume a freedom in relation to urgent questions that is deceptive and often precludes the transformative power of reading Plato, for example. I can't but think that the engaged student from the inner-city will feel powerfully the themes of oppression, exile, tyranny etc. that permeate the texts of the canon.

Support grew in the parish for a Halifax Clemente Humanities Course. The next step was to put together a substantial discussion paper outlining our vision and business plan for the Halifax Clemente Course.[3]

The Discussion Paper that we drafted promoted Halifax Humanities 101 as "An Educational Journey from Poverty to Empowerment." We would offer this course to:

> … the poorest of the poor who have no access to traditional post-secondary education. The university-level course material teaches reflection and critical thinking, enabling the disadvantaged and disenfranchised to navigate their way through poverty and actively to participate and contribute to their communities and in the political processes that will effect change.

We anticipated a class size between 20-30: students would be between the ages of 17-45,[4] live below the poverty line, be able to read a tabloid newspaper, be available to attend two two-hour sessions a week, and be willing to read 5-10 hours per week outside of class. Potential students would complete a simple application form and submit a one-page statement describing their interest. Selected applicants would attend a 45-minute interview during which the programme would be outlined in detail, and a short reading introduced and discussed to determine comprehension skills. Books, transportation, childcare and class snacks would be of no charge to the students. Instructors were to be drawn from local universities. The Discussion Paper anticipated that students would receive a half-credit at a local university.[5]

---

3   The University of British Columbia had begun a Clemente Course in 1998 that it called *Humanities 101*. We did not take on the name *Halifax Humanities 101* until 2005, but for convenience I will use that designation for the remainder of this history.

4   We would remove the upper age limit before recruiting for our first class.

5   This did not materialize and, in retrospect, the equation of the course with a

With Discussion Paper in hand, from January through to June 2004, Susan, with considerable assistance from Henry Roper, patiently but efficiently guided a very small team of us through hundreds of hours of meetings with all levels of government, the six universities in Halifax, community agencies, potential corporate sponsors, and community leaders. By the summer of 2004, we knew where our support would be found, and we were confident that it was sufficient to pilot one year of Halifax Humanities 101. In addition, Susan researched and submitted funding applications that would bear the fruit we required. We also knew that it would take another year of planning. The corporate sponsors agreed to defer their grants until our first class of 2005/6.

There were interesting moments. No level of government would support us because Halifax Humanities 101 was not about skills development or a guarantee of immediate employment. At one meeting with the Provincial Minister of Community Services, the Minister became enthusiastic and he himself began to speak eloquently of the potential of Halifax Humanities 101 to break the cycle of poverty. I could see the eyes of the senior bureaucrats begin to roll. When the Minister left the meeting, the bureaucrats wasted little time in telling us that our proposal did not "fit the mandate" of the Department. Another significant meeting was with Social Work students who had been involved with the earlier attempt to establish a Clemente Course in Halifax. They were appalled that our proposed curriculum would be nothing more than an indoctrination into patriarchal, white, western culture. Where were the women's studies, African history, Asian studies, etc.? One director of a continuing education department of one of Halifax's largest universities asked if I had ever met anyone who lived on the margins. Why, she asked indignantly, would we offer classical humanities to the poor, instead of something more "realistic."

Early in 2004, before the energetic team of King's faculty took the lead on the project to make Halifax Humanities 101 happen, one day I attended a lecture in the Foundation Year taught by one of the professors I hoped would provide this leadership (which he did). At the mid-lecture break we

university credit could be problematic.

chatted, and he asked me quietly what would be more sad than to hear "the song of a poet who died in the gutter"?[6] After a pause I suggested that it would be more sad for one to die in the gutter without a poem and without having been given a voice to sing that poem. Halifax Humanities 101 would help those who died in the gutter to be singing the poetry of their life for us all to hear. Thus even the "gutter" becomes a place where freedom and redemption can be found.

In the end, we discovered many in Halifax who understood our vision and committed themselves to Halifax Humanities 101. Dr Colin Dodds, President of Saint Mary's University, became an early and resolute champion of the initiative. Dr Bill Barker of the University of King's College clearly understood that Halifax Humanities 101 would be as much value to the university as it would be for the students: it would remind universities of the real purpose of humanities education. The other four Halifax universities gave their support as well. Tracey Jones, Manager for Literacy/ESL/Diversity Services for the Halifax Public Libraries offered constant advice and encouragement, and gave us space in the North End Library where Halifax Humanities 101 still meets twice a week. Senator Terry Mercer caught the vision early on and was a dependable and effective spokesperson from the conception to the birth of Halifax Humanities 101.

In the six months leading up to the formal launch of Halifax Humanities 101 on 17 October 2005,[7] the Board of the Saint George's Friends of Clemente Society worked hard to solidify the curriculum, hire a Director, finalize the funding, offer opportunity to teach in Halifax Humanities 101 to the finest teaching professors in Halifax, and recruit the twenty-five students for the first class. For the record, the first student to sign up was Bonita Shepherd who first heard me speak of the initiative at a Board meeting of the Metro Non-Profit Housing Association. Bonita, who lived in supportive housing, could not contain her excitement at the

---

6   Bob Dylan, *A Hard Rain's a'Gonna Fall.*

7   17 October is the Unite Nations International Day for the Eradication of Poverty. Many of the inaugural students came along to the launch with their first assigned reading in hand, *The Epic of Gilgamesh.*

thought that she might be able to participate in a humanities-based education. She would not let me leave the meeting without a promise that she would have this dream opportunity of a lifetime.

My part of the story ends here, as the first Halifax Humanities 101 class is about to begin.

Earl Shorris' *The Art of Freedom: Teaching the Humanities to the Poor* was published in 2013, the year after his death. In that book, Earl notes the unique vision of the Halifax Humanities 101. Many Clemente Courses developed out of Earl's original vision, and he visited as many as he could. In all the other Clemente Courses that Earl had visited, the organizing theme was that of *sophia* (wisdom). Here in Halifax, Earl concluded, something was different: the driving force behind Halifax Humanities 101 was not *sophia* but *agape* (love). I think Earl was almost correct. Love was the driving force behind the establishment of Halifax Humanities 101, but it was a combination of loves.

First and foremost it was a love of *sophia*. The Halifax Humanities 101 founders wanted to share their love of *sophia* with those who had been prevented from knowing *sophia* in the particular way that had transformed their own lives (through great works of philosophy, poetry and literature). But the second love that Earl saw so clearly during his visit to Halifax was not *agape*, but rather a friendship love (*philia*) that developed from the way that Halifax Humanities 101 was taught. Friendship, Aristotle teaches, exists only between equals. Friendship becomes possible in the Halifax Humanities 101 classroom when the instructors recognize their own poverty. Riches for the poor, yes. The teachers give to the students who are poor, and the students offer riches to the teachers who recognize that they too are equally poor, though in different ways.

The consistent and defining image for the Clemente Course in the Humanities since the day that Earl spoke to the woman prisoner in the maximum security prison in New York State is that of Plato's Allegory of the Cave. Earl learned that because poverty was an absence of contemplation and beauty, not simply an absence of money, it was comparable to the experience of people chained to the wall of the cave. Those living in material poverty can identify with the metaphorical chains that allow them only to see the shadows on the walls, and assume that is all there is in life. But the Allegory of the Cave equally applies to the university professor who teaches in Halifax Humanities 101. In an exchange that is all the more precious for its unlikely softening of the alienations that arise from our economic lives, teachers and students show each other aspects of the real world that they have not even imagined. Each helps to loosen the chains for the other. In that mutuality of gift offered and received, extraordinary friendships are discovered.

This essay began by asking the question, what if people gathered together to read great works of philosophy and literature, and to contemplate both ancient and modern art in all its forms, in order to learn how to know the world, to love the world, and to live fully within this world passionately and compassionately? The answer should now be clear. You would have *Halifax Humanities 101.*

ADVENTURE

VALEDICTORY ADDRESS 2012
Lisa Comeau

MY FIRST PARACHUTE JUMP
Gillian Webster

HITCH-HIKING
Barbara Whitby

"BRIGHT IS THE NOBLE WORK":
ABBOT SUGER AND THE CHURCH OF SAINT-DENIS, PARIS
Jannette Vusich

Moby-Dick AND ARISTOTELIAN TRAGEDY
Christopher Rice

DOING DESCARTES BACKWARDS
Steven Burns

FREE HUMANITIES:
TRUFFLES FOR THE MIND ARE THE NEW SOUL FOOD
Colin Starnes

Valedictory Address
2012

LISA COMEAU

THE LAST TIME I spoke to a group of people in church I was delivering my Mother's eulogy. This feels maybe just a tad easier! But not much.

I am thrilled to have been involved in this programme and to be graduating from it. I have never graduated from anything. I got pregnant in my last year of high school and did not finish. I entered university as a mature student and had to quit because of ill health.

I came to this class just after emerging out of a rough situation. Over ten years ago there was a furnace oil spill in my flat. I lost all of my possessions, my son was dislocated, and I became extremely ill, allergic to everything, and homeless. Because of my low income and the severity of my sensitivities, I stayed sick, homeless, and "underhoused" for over ten years, sleeping on people's floors, on decks, in bathrooms, and spent a total of 45 days living in a car. I stayed in places where I was not wanted—some places where really crazy, nasty things occurred. I had to keep my mouth shut for fear of ending up on the street. I kept my mouth shut for over ten years.

Now, with my health improved enough to go back into the world a bit and with safe housing under my belt, I was able to attend this programme. It felt great to speak out loud without any repercussions. No one told me to shut my mouth although, at times, they probably wanted to. Mary Lu was so accommodating around my health issues. The kindness and respect I received were healing for me.

It took all my energy to read the material and to come to class twice a week. I felt a sense of accomplishment to be able to do so. The readings energized me. I grew fond of my classmates. They were lovely. I appreciated their support and encouragement and I loved the chats we had after class. It felt good to be in a room with other people who had been through difficult things too. I consider us all real warriors.

I did not always like everything I read but I loved reading, loved the challenge. Darwin's suggestion of mutability reminded me that nothing ever really stays the same. Emerson reminded me to pay attention to what's right in front of me, not to reject my own experiences, that they have value. Mary Shelley reminded me to appreciate and integrate my dark side. R.C. Lewontin, in *Biology as Ideology*, asserted that biological organisms are interacting with their environments all the time in many unconscious and unseen ways. This made me feel that I was not alone and that maybe I had some kind of agency, that I really did affect things around me. In our last reading, an Alice Munro story called *The Beggar Maid*, Rose, the main character, compared her working class family to her rich boyfriend's family. She wrote: "Billy Pope and Flo were not protected. Things could get at them." I understand this lack of protection and the groundlessness and uncertainty that comes with just basic survival.

I am so grateful for this class, for its shoring up of my dignity, for reminding me that the universe is immense, for reawakening my curiosity, and for taking me to a place that is beyond survival.

I want to thank all the teachers who were a part of this programme— thank you for your time, your passion, for answering my questions, and for stimulating my brain. And Mary Lu, thank you so much for your consideration, generosity, encouragement, sense of fun, and, most of all, your kindness.

My First Parachute Jump

GILLIAN WEBSTER

WHEN I FINISHED school in Dublin, I qualified for a university grant. It seemed to me a small fortune. I chose Edinburgh University. I loved Scotland—I had visited in 1970 when I had gone to visit our pet dog. He was in quarantine near Edinburgh. My imagination was full of images of a happy—for once—family holiday.

I love a bargain, and when I was in my first week at Edinburgh all the societies were looking for new members. I joined the vegetarian club. That was easy as I was a vegetarian already. I joined the Christian group, since I reckoned I belonged there. They were both free. The parachute club offered a day long course, with a jump, for six pounds.

You had to be eighteen to take a "Static Line jump." I wouldn't even have to open my own parachute. The first available day was October 31, a day after my eighteenth birthday. I thought, wow, more of a bargain than I dreamed of! I would be just eligible. Perhaps it came down to doing something entirely different. It couldn't be that hard since there would be three hours of instruction. I had been on commercial planes and always took great pleasure when the plane lifted off and landed. That was really exciting! On the other hand, I had never seen anyone jump out of a plane. I laid my six pounds on the table.

I had real money for the first time in my life. I could spend it on myself. Maybe that had gone to my head? During a difficult childhood I became a bookworm. When my father asked me if I'd like to join the Brownies at age eleven, I refused. I was scared of making mistakes. Not much had changed by the time I went to university. I was still a loner. But perhaps I was so used to reading heroic animal stories where the dogs and horses performed great deeds in the face of terrible adversity that I developed an adventurous imagination.

I slept soundly the night before the parachute jump. I knew nothing about it so I wasn't scared. If I had known, I might not have gone. But once I'd signed up, I went about the day as usual and made myself a sandwich to take for lunch. The next morning, I peacefully climbed aboard the bus. I didn't feel curious about the others. I was excited about the free bus trip into the country but I didn't think about jumping out of a plane.

During the training, I focused on the instructor. I could not see the other trainees, all male. I was kitted out with a big jumpsuit, helmet, and two huge parachutes. I was trussed up like a diminutive spaceman! The two army parachutes (one round my tummy for emergencies) made me feel heavy and weak. I felt nervous, for the first time, on the way up in the six seater Cessna. For one thing, I didn't expect to climb into a stripped down plane. There were no seats or windows for us, and no passenger door! We sat on the bare metal floor. The instructor clipped the static line onto my parachute. Then, crouching beside the doorless exit, he yelled for the first jumper. He disappeared over the side of the plane. I was very anxious.

I braced myself to crawl onto the right wing strut. When it came to my turn, I scrunched forward and for the first time saw out of the plane. It banked left and right, making a long loop to drop me. I watched with amazement. I made myself look out of the plane and not think about jumping—I did not expect such beauty. The October light was shining in stained glass rays all over the countryside below me. Three thousand feet below. I reasoned with myself—how could I be afraid when I felt such awe and wonder?

Next thing I knew, I was out on the strut. A fierce wind was trying to push me off so letting go was not as hard as it might have been. I plopped off the strut in an undignified way. I hurtled backwards from the stalled plane, somersaulted, and fell uncontrollably—terrifying. After three very long seconds, my chute popped open and I was whisked right side up. I stopped falling. My mind went blank. I was floating. Forwards, slowly, weightless, alone—and alive. How loud the silence was! Drum rolls of blood pounded in my ears. The October light was shimmering through me. I didn't think about the sky or the parachute. I was part of the universe and it was vast, beautiful, full and empty all at the same time.

It was noisy and silent. I knew I must be moving but I felt totally still inside. How do I express such amazing feelings and what do they mean? How could I feel so totally safe? That first terrifying hurtling sent my soul to meet Something magnificent. I had committed to the unknown when I jumped out and I had been met with a safety that was not rational. I didn't expect what I experienced in the euphoria of the in between. I was too short to reach either toggle. I couldn't steer so I peacefully left off trying and relaxed, marveling at the view.

Then the ground became real and I was headed for a forest far from the landing zone. The trees grew larger and came up towards me. I watched them calmly. I closed my eyes as I flew into a tree and straightaway the canopy of my parachute embraced the branches. I was hanging twenty feet up. I kicked my legs in glee while I waited for rescue.

I went on to do another jump and then another, fifty-two in all, but the first jump was the best.

HITCH-HIKING

BARBARA WHITBY

JUST AFTER THE end of World War Two and the end of the bombing, it became relatively safe for teenagers to hitch-hike. My friend Brenda and I had both developed a hunger to visit many of the ancient sites throughout England. We were dirt poor and the only way we could reach most of these was by thumbing a ride. We fantasised that we were modern gypsies.

Sitting side by side on the grass by the highway, we played our recorders to tune into the mood of the trip. We became totally absorbed in the music. Brenda played bass, I accompanied her on treble. We rarely waited long as cars stopped out of sheer curiosity.

We travelled haphazardly, not taking much note of hours or distances. We slept in barns or haystacks, or wherever we could find permission to shelter. There was usually someone who would give us food in exchange for chores. If not, we went hungry. We travelled on our wits.

On this occasion we set out from London for a tiny Saxon church several hundred miles away near the Scottish border. It was in this region that Bishop Aidan of Lindisfarne conducted his mission to convert the Northumbrian Saxons to Christianity in the seventh century A.D. Brenda and I both became fascinated with the Venerable Bede's account of Aidan's life in *The Ecclesiastical History of the English People*. Aidan himself, originally from Ireland, was a tireless traveller throughout his English bishopric. A church associated with Aidan's work still remained and we wanted to touch the original beams of the building, if they still existed. We yearned to identify with him and the spirit of his times.

We travelled for three days before we got to our destination, a remote area of Northumberland. By now it was past sunset of the third day. Our current driver did not want to drop us off in an isolated spot on the country road. He did not think it likely that we would get another ride at this hour; he worried that we might stray in the dark and get sucked into one of the many surrounding bogs. In the cold, moonless evening, heavy mists were rolling in from the moors. He insisted on dropping us at a nearby village.

We scarcely had time to wrestle our knapsacks out of the car and say "good-bye" before a cottage door opened a few yards down the village street and a woman called out, "Well, ye've got here then, hinnies," she shouted, "and almost on time. Come ye in, I'm waiting!"

We assured her that she must be expecting someone else but she interrupted; she had *seen* our arrival and had prepared our supper and bed for us in advance.

I had heard that it was common to be *fey* (the northern word for second sight) in this area but it was still a shock to experience it this dramatically. She prodded us ahead of her and held her arms wide like a conjuror: "See!"

To our astonishment, a hot meal for two—mountainous helpings of roast beef and Yorkshire pudding with potatoes and vegetables, strong cheddar cheese, and home-bottled pickled onions—was indeed laid out on the red and white checkered cloth of the kitchen table. "Eh, lassies, ye must be hungry. There's meat, taties. Start on that lot on the table. Sit ye down and eat," she ordered.

Once she saw that we were tucking in, she turned to a large tea caddy on the mantelpiece. "I'll mash the tea," she called over her shoulder and began to bustle about hospitably. She heaped more coal from the brass scuttle on to the kitchen fire and blew on the reddest embers with a pair of worn leather bellows. The light of the brisk flames blended with the candles. Taking the simmering kettle off the hob, she made tea at the table in a large brown pottery teapot and sat down with us in the flickering room to share the pungent dark brew. "Eh, lassies," she said, beaming, "Now that ye're here at last, everything's plummy." She said that her husband would be away until tomorrow. "He won't put his neb in the door until it suits him," she remarked cheerfully.

She chatted away, questioning us about all sorts of facts from our lives that were astonishingly correct, but that we had not mentioned. She was engrossed by what she described as the gall of two young girls travelling the road in this way. Taking first Brenda's and then my hands in hers, she turned them palms up and looked closely at the lines. "There be no great harm coming to 'ee at this time," she said, looking us each straight in the eye.

She underlined that we took unwise risks. When she put the dangers to us explicitly, we saw our hitch-hiking in a new light.

At last she noticed how our eyes were drooping from the heavy meal and the warmth. "Ye must be ready to hit the sack, and here am I keeping ye up 'till all hours. Bed's yonder." She took up a heavy brass candlestick to light the way—there was no electricity. (We later found out that the most modern amenities in the neighbourhood probably dated back to the Roman occupation of Britain. At that time some fine plumbing had been installed in the commander's villa, though it had gone into disuse before the Romans' departure from Britain around 400 A.D.).

She guided us down a narrow, low-ceilinged corridor. The candle flame constantly wavered and stirred the shadows, making everything eerie. The guest room was almost completely taken up by an ancient four poster bed. The bed was so high that we had to climb a set of wooden steps. We sank into a thick mattress, surrounded by the feathers of birds that we somehow felt had been deeply loved. Two antique copper warming pans, stuffed with hot embers, radiated warmth between the sheets, drawing out the fragrance of the fresh lavender in which the linens had been stored. Before she left, our fey Northern hostess gestured towards the bed skirt. "Po's in that bit hidey hole. Empty it in t'morning."

We woke to the sound of birds and the fragrant smell of bacon cooking. I was the first to dress and our hostess met me with a warm hug as soon as I made it to the kitchen. I asked where I should empty the overnight potty. "Good lass, there's t'outhouse," and she pointed to a small shed some distance from the house. Pouring the brimming slops into the pail she handed me, I set off for what I expected to be the usual kind of ramshackle urinal with a smelly Isan container. Instead, there was an immaculate blue and white china toilet with twin seats. It was so large that it took up almost the entire space and the bowl was decorated with entwined hearts and lovers enjoying an amazing variety of scenes of erotic bliss. I left the door of this fantasy retreat ajar so that I could also enjoy a view of wild birds tugging worms from the earth for an early breakfast. A light breeze moved among the leaves of the tall bushes that had been planted nearby for privacy and scattered the sweet scent of flowers.

After breakfast, when it was time to leave, we tried to pay for her hospitality. "Nay, lassies," she insisted, "'Tis not right to take payment for the Gift. Get yourselves away, then. And God go with ye."

As so often in my life, I felt as if I had been absorbed into a fairy tale. From the first, we had been transported into an alternative space and time. When we reached the small village which had grown up around St. Aidan's church we felt a satisfying sense of completeness in our journey—we had travelled full circle, but in many dimensions. "True Travellers!" we said, poking each other in the ribs to dispel the strangeness, "though we still need to find our gypsy wagon."

At that moment I would never have guessed that I would one day seriously study St. Aidan's time on a different continent, across the Atlantic Ocean, in Halifax, Nova Scotia, Canada. Sixty years after my adventure with Brenda, as I quietly listened to Professor Colin Starnes discuss the early Christianity of Britain in the Halifax Humanities, I was privately carried right back into those first days of freedom after the War. In my mind I reverently touched the thousand-year-old beams of Aidan's ancient church and I wondered if our fey hostess was still alive and whether she had perhaps foreseen this treasured moment in my future. "Oh aye, lassies!" I heard her say, "The wheels go round and round." I was still a gypsy at heart.

"BRIGHT IS THE NOBLE WORK":

Abbot Suger and the Church of Saint-Denis, Paris

JANNETTE VUSICH

The Abbey Church of Saint-Denis in Paris, France, is critical to the history of art. Its importance is partly due to the fact that it was the royal church: its nave housed the tombs of the French kings, its treasury guarded the crown and other coronation regalia, and its school educated princes. Continuous royal patronage certainly raised the church's prestige, if not its coffers. Yet Saint-Denis is also considered the birthplace of Gothic architecture as its Abbot, Suger, utilized the most innovative techniques and artistic experiments of his age when renovating what had become a rather dilapidated Romanesque building. This renovation is remarkable both for its ambitious effects and because it was informed by contemporary theology, key strains of Christian Neoplatonism above all.

Abbot Suger was born to humble parents in 1081. A small and rather frail child, at the age of ten he became an oblate at the abbey of Saint-Denis in Paris. In the Benedictine Order of Monks, the term oblate was used to describe the children vowed by their parents to the monastic life. As Saint-Denis was a Benedictine abbey, we know that Suger began living under the Rule of St. Benedict as a child and that he took the habit as a monk as a young man. He spent several years studying at university and traveled extensively on missions for the abbey. He was consecrated Abbot in 1122. In addition to leading the monks of Saint-Denis, Suger also became a favoured counselor to kings Louis VI and VII. With the support of the French kings, he began his renovation of the abbey church in 1140. It is for this work that he was renowned then as now. As one of his biographers wrote a century after his death in 1151, though Suger was "Small of body and family, constrained by twofold smallness, he refused in his smallness to be a small man."

Some of the hallmarks of the new Gothic style that Suger initiated include: ambulatories articulated by radiating chapels, meant to accommodate the thousands of pilgrims who traveled to pray before the relics of Saint Denis; the longitudinal division of the nave into uniform spatial units called 'bays' or, in more technical terms, the articulation of the church's space as a system of linked arches and cylindrical shafts; sharply pointed arches whose upward-thrusting dynamism stood in marked contrast to the serene, rounded arch of the Romanesque style; and larger and more complex clerestory windows, filled with stained glass. Together, these elements produced the elaborate linearity, soaring verticality, and brilliantly coloured light that are the defining characteristics of Gothic architecture.

In addition to providing the basis for a new style of architecture, Abbot Suger's renovation of Saint-Denis also provided a new model of fully integrated church decoration, as its gilded bronze doors, elaborate altar frontals, and lavish stained glass were all conceived concurrent with its architecture—Suger imagined all these elements as being mutually beneficial; none was secondary to or put in service of another. He provides full descriptions of these furnishings in the two treatises he wrote on the renovation project. The treatises recount not only the practical aspects of the church's renovation, such as its financing and modes of production, but also the meaning of its decoration.

Suger was obviously proud of the church and his patronage. In addition to writing the two treatises on the project, he also had himself pictured in two very prominent locations in the church: first in the sculpture of Christ that tops the central portal into the church, and a second time in the apse, at the sacred east end of the church, in a stained glass window featuring the Annunciation scene that marks the miraculous moment of Christ's Incarnation. While the prostrate posture Suger assumes in both the sculpture and the stained glass is certainly humble, his decision to place himself alongside the holy figures reflects the high esteem he attributed to himself and his project.

Suger's personal account of the renovations is recorded in the *De Administrationae*, known in English as "The Book of Abbot Suger of St. Denis On What Was Done Under His Administration." This treatise charts the improvements made to the church's financial holdings as well as to its physical structure. Suger begins with a preface justifying the grand project on the grounds that it was done out of care for the church of God—"not," he claims, "with any desire for empty glory nor with any claim to the reward of human praise." He then begins his account of the church's decoration by listing the subjects found on the three main portals. Together, the three sets of doors represent the Passion of Christ (the suffering Jesus faced in the events leading up to and including his Crucifixion). Next, Suger turns to the great expense of both their materials and their execution. Most interesting, however, are the verses that Suger ordered to be inscribed on the central bronze doors themselves, for posterity:

> Whoever thou art, if thou seekest to extol the glory of these doors,
> Marvel not at the gold and the expense but at the craftsmanship of the work.
> Bright is the noble work; but, being nobly bright, the work
> Should brighten the minds, so that they may travel, through the true lights,
> To the True Light where Christ is the true door.
> In what manner it be inherent in this world the golden door defines:
> The dull mind rises in truth through that which is material,
> And, in seeing this light, is resurrected from its former submersion.[1]

There are two passages we should take special care to note here. The first is this:

> Bright is the noble work; but, being nobly bright, the work
> Should brighten the minds, so that they may travel, through the true lights,
> To the True Light where Christ is the true door.

---

1   Passages taken from Abbot Suger, *On the Abbey Church of St.-Denis and its Art Treasures*. Edited, translated, and annotated by Erwin Panofsky, 2nd edition (Princeton, NJ: Princeton University Press, 1979)

In these lines Suger seems to claim that the gilded bronze doors have a *spiritual* value, one that exceeds both their financial and artistic values and extends beyond the simple categories of form and content. He does so by asserting that the sheer beauty of the church furnishings will "brighten minds." The second line to note is the last:

> The dull mind rises in truth through that which is material,
> And, in seeing this light, is resurrected from its former submersion.

Suger's claim that the study of *material* things can act as a sort of stepping-stone on the path to enlightenment and the contemplation of *immaterial* concepts reminds us of Plato's Allegories of the Sun and the Cave. Much like the physical light of the sun makes ordinary things visible and enables them to grow, Plato explains, the abstract light of the Good makes intellectual matters intelligible and enables *us* to grow by acting purposefully. In the Allegory of the Cave, Plato's most well known and powerful image of the human condition, seeing the light of the sun, as opposed to the artificial light of the fire, is an important first step on the path out of the cave that closes out the light of the Good and replaces it with unhealthy illusions.

Suger imagines the ascent from material to immaterial conceptions of light much as Plato does—as a resurrection from a submersed state. However, the passage still more closely recalls the Christianized Neoplatonism advanced by his contemporary theologians: like them, Suger never rejects or demeans the material world but rather claims that one might recover the transcendent essence by retracing the divine "signatures" present in particular beings. Note, for example, how the quote says that looking at *these* true lights—meaning the stained glass windows—will lead to the *one* True Light that is Christ. The claim here is that the material world of multiplicity *is* true, as a manifestation of God's will, even if its truth pales in comparison to that which belongs to the essence of the divine *one*. The verticality of the church reinforces this reading as it offers us a symbolic manifestation of the spiritual ascent. The walls become increasingly attenuated and insubstantial—that is, immaterial—as they rise towards the heavens, with more and more space given over not only to windows but to light itself.

Though nothing can replicate a first-hand experience of the church, we only need to look at images of the apse of Saint-Denis to understand Suger's Neoplatonic claim that taking the time to contemplate it might enable the mind's passage from material to immaterial things. The masonry, while elaborate, all but dissolves: the elegantly elongated shafts create a lightness that belies the true weight of the stone. Our eye skims easily past these vertical punctuations, focusing instead on the almost unbroken circuit of large stained glass windows illuminating the radiating chapels and making the ambulatory and chapels register as a single space. Read in this way—as an expanse of pure colour and light rather than as individual windows or subjects—the stained glass is all about generating affect; we notice only the way it heightens our senses and works upon our emotions. Taken together, the windows provoke a sense of wonder and awe and, Suger would claim, encourage us to adopt this same standpoint toward the divine. As the light streams through the vivid, joyous colours, it draws our gaze ever upward: as a result, the windows are both metaphorically and literally uplifting.

Suger describes this mode of aspirational viewing, which aims to transfer the mind from seeing the material to contemplating the immaterial, as an "anagogical" process:

> When—out of my delight in the beauty of the house of God— the loveliness of the many-colored gems has called me away from external cares, and worthy meditation has induced me to reflect, transferring that which is material to that which is immaterial, on the diversity of the sacred virtues: then it seems to me that I see myself dwelling, as it were, in some strange region of the universe which neither exists entirely in the slime of the earth nor entirely in the purity of Heaven; and that, by the grace of God, I can be transported from this inferior to that higher world in an anagogical manner.

Anagogy is a term used to refer to the spiritual or mystical interpretation of a word or a passage—or, in this case, a work of art. It is a mode of interpretation that seeks to move beyond the literal, moral, or allegorical mode and, in doing so, aims to elevate one's self to a higher consciousness.

A century after Abbot Suger, the Franciscan Saint Bonaventure more fully articulated this anagogical process of interpretation in a treatise called the *Journey of the Mind towards God*. He offers us a beautifully evocative description of what Suger calls "the anagogical manner," writing that:

> All created things of the sensible world lead the mind of the contemplator and wise man to eternal God ... They are the shades, the resonances, the pictures of that efficient, exemplifying, and ordering art; they are the tracks, simulacra, and spectacles; they are divinely given signs set before us for the purpose of seeing God. They are the examples, or rather exemplifications set before our still unrefined and sense-oriented minds, so that by the sensible things which they see they might be transferred to the intelligible which they cannot see, as if by signs to the signified.

In the *Journey of the Mind towards God*, Bonaventure argues that sensible objects are not to be abhorred because they are "divinely given signs." He even calls God the "Supreme Creative Artist" of the visible world. He argues that the power of the divine thus "shine[s] forth in created things" and criticizes those who would reject the sensible world, sharply stating that "... whoever is not enlightened by such great splendor in created things is blind ... " In his view, the body does not distract from but rather serves the intellect.

Abbot Suger's great insight was to recognize that stained glass offered a particularly effective means of initiating man's shift from potential to actual, of lifting man from the material to the immaterial. Stained glass was especially appropriate to this project because its tangible substance is secondary to its purpose of conveying light and illuminating the world with its beauty. By opening the walls of his church to great expanses of coloured light, Suger aimed to create a vision of paradise on earth.

When Suger expressed his hope that the medieval visitor to Saint-Denis would view the light that streams through its stained glass in an "anagogical manner," he meant that one should look to the stained glass not for moral instruction but for a mystical *experience*. Stained glass spoke directly to the medieval imagination because it inspired wonder: it is, quite literally, wonderful to behold—*mirabile visu*. The concept of the wonderful or the marvelous was crucial to the medieval conception of God. For as much as medieval theologians encouraged the faithful to enter into an understanding or knowing relationship to the divine, they also acknowledged that the human's essential standpoint is one of wonder, and, as Dante would argue, of love.

Moby-Dick and Aristotelian Tragedy

CHRISTOPHER RICE

The great writer and literary critic Alfred Kazin once wrote that Herman Melville's *Moby-Dick* "is not so much a book *about* Captain Ahab's quest for the whale as it is an experience of that quest" (8). It is important, then, when addressing Ahab's tragedy, to remember that it appears within the context of an earlier subjectivity established in Ishmael—a crew member who refers to his role merely as the "shabby part of a whaling voyage" (22). In this sense, Ishmael's acceptance of his captain as a tragic hero, and his reimagining of Ahab in these terms is central to the experience of Ahab's quest; Ishmael's experience of Ahab *is* the tragedy of *Moby-Dick* and any attempt to speak of the aesthetic effect of Ahab's tragedy "taken in itself" must be misguided in this sense. For example, Sedgwick asserts that Ahab's tragedy "inspires terror as does no work in the language outside of Shakespeare. But it fails to inspire pity" (134). Yet Ishmael experiences both pity and terror in Ahab. The condition for Ishmael's pity lies in his deepseated intuition that the cosmic questions that his captain demands of the seemingly godless universe are in some sense justified. While Ishmael may never be able to understand why Moby Dick was the receptacle or "pasteboard mask" for all the malignancy and abandonment of the world, he cannot shake the sense in which Ahab may have come into contact with vital truth: "It was the whiteness of the whale that above all things appalled me. But how can I hope to explain myself here; and yet, in some dim, random way, explain myself I must, else all these chapters might be naught"

(159). In his constant fluctuation between everyday experience and insistent philosophizing and speculation, Ishmael shows himself to still be caught up with the irreconcilable challenge Ahab invokes. Ishmael is neither an isolated Ahab, nor contented land-dweller, but stuck between two worlds. He cannot simply dismiss the questions that Ahab's act has generated or release himself from their obsessive demands. His linear narrative breaks off and circles around Ahab's tragic action as Ishmael attempts to understand it.

It is beyond question that *Moby-Dick* incorporates many diverse elements of tragedy. The use of soliloquy, stage directions, oracular figures, the persistent invocation of fate or destiny, the "satyr play" performed by the crew, and the plot arc tracing a doomed hero's fall—all of these contribute to the tragic aura of Melville's book. Milton Millhauser notes that "The term 'tragic' is applied to aspects of the book by many critics, but generally in a more or less metaphorical sense—attributing gravity and profundity to the manner of its telling—rather than as a definition of form" (528). This more or less informal use of the term in one way is not so far off the mark. For instance, Melville viewed his own work as involved in a shared enterprise with Shakespeare, particularly in terms of what he understood to be the "dark interiority" of tragic truth. And certainly, Shakespeare's influence can be felt in the sheer verbosity, if not the penetrating insight, of numerous dark soliloquies throughout the narrative. Yet, there is a deeper and more concrete connection to tragedy that is not adequately discussed in the scholarship. As Patricia Robertson rightly observes, "The profound influence of Shakespeare and of Elizabethan tragedy on the structure, language, and development of character in *Moby-Dick* has been well established by critics such as Olson, Matthiessen, Sedgwick, and Rice. But Melville's use of the chorus derived from Greek drama" (61). Moreover, the function of the chorus which Robertson describes relies on something even more fundamental: the action itself can be understood in terms of ancient Greek tragedy. Millhauser contends that

> the pattern of tragedy is realized with a curious exactness. I
> speak here not merely of the temper, the tone and movement
> characteristic of tragedy, but of the formal classic definition [...]

> The action of the book, for all its wandering course, is, broadly
> considered, single; it stems from Ahab's character and leads to his
> destruction. (528-9)

Ishmael's imaginative recreation of Ahab's singular action is what constitutes
the essential tragedy of *Moby-Dick*. For not only is Ahab's action single but it
is a special kind of action; it accords in a profound way with what Aristotle
prescribes for the making and proper delineation of a tragic action in his
Poetics. It is also Ishmael's focus on this action which is marked by the fullness of drama: it is his crucial experience; it is his living encounter with
tragedy.

I do not claim, however, that Melville read or followed Aristotle's advice
in this regard. If anything, Melville was likely more immersed in Shakespeare's tragic imagination than any theory of tragedy during *Moby-Dick*'s
composition. Rosenberry argues that both Shakespeare and Melville "were
profoundly indifferent to the theory and practice of genres and profoundly
concerned with the theory and practice of life" (128). This much may be
true, yet while Shakespeare has sometimes been understood to have little
regard for the classical rules of drama (being one of the worst offenders of
the once sacrosanct "three unities"), scholarly work has been done recently
to vindicate the enduring power of Aristotle's principles *through* Shakespeare (Baxter 8-19). In other words, though Shakespeare may not have
paid much attention to the questionable rules touted as Aristotelian wisdom
which were floating around his England, the actual principles found in the
Poetics can help to illustrate why some of Shakespeare's plays are so powerful. In the same way then, Aristotle proves to be quite helpful in articulating
the effect of Ahab's tragedy. The first clue is that Ahab's action, unlike the
narrative that precedes it, is indeed singular.

William Faulkner once responded to the question "what book would
you like most to have written?" with *Moby-Dick*, praising its "Greek-like
simplicity" (640). Now, anyone who has read Faulkner side by side Melville, might not immediately see "simplicity" as Melville's great strength in
the comparison. But what Faulkner saw in *Moby-Dick* was its fundamental
action and substance and this he rightly expressed as possessing a "Greek-

like simplicity." Thus, while there are many tragic trappings to speak of in Melville's book, the primary sense in which it is a tragedy is in its tracing of a single action, which is announced by Ishmael in his role as a tragedian. Though he spends time raising the practice of whaling to what I would call "epic stature," this is a preliminary move in a larger plan to raise the crew of the Pequod to tragic stature. It is as he moves to discuss the "Knights and Squires" of the crew, that is, as he introduces the major actors, that Ishmael signals his intention to speak on the nature and destiny of man through the crew itself by "weav[ing] round them tragic graces" (103). At this juncture he reflects:

> Men may seem detestable as joint stock-companies and na-
> tions; knaves, fools, and murderers there may be; men may have
> mean and meagre faces; but man, in the ideal, is so noble and
> so sparkling, such a grand and glowing creature, that over any
> ignominious blemish in him all his fellows should run to throw
> their costliest robes. (103)

And though the crew is a part of Ishmael's attempt to speak on the nature of man through tragedy, it becomes clear that the focus of this tragedy is on its hero Ahab.

What is most interesting about the full dramatic rendering of Ahab is that it occurs precisely with Ahab's declaration of his ill-fated course. Though Ahab appears on deck before this dramatic revelation, it serves mainly to bring out his isolated and troubled cast of mind. As Stubb remarks in the "Quarter-Deck," "the chick that's in him pecks the shell. T'will soon be out" (137). There is substantial build up to Ahab's action; he gives the unusual order to send the whole crew aft, "an order seldom or never given on ship-board except in some extraordinary case" (137). It is here where Ahab announces his intent to hunt the white whale, riling the crew up into frenzy, and initially endeavoring to persuade them to raise the whale through a Spanish ounce of gold. But Ahab's ravings soon descend into sobs of suffering, and he exclaims:

> Aye, aye! and I'll chase him round Good Hope, and round the
> horn, and round the Norway Maelstrom, and round perdition's

flames before I give him up. And this is what ye have shipped for,
men! to chase that white whale on both sides of land, and over
all sides of earth, till he spouts black blood. (139)

Ahab discloses his intent, and his suffering which leads to it, but his real declaration is of something more like a "metaphysical act"—one commentator
refers to the tragedy in this sense as an "ontological drama" (Wenke 709).
The true nature of Ahab's action is revealed as not merely a hunt for the
white whale that took his leg but an attempt to "strike through the mask"
(140) at whatever thing might lurk beyond the "unreasoning" surface that
the white whale embodies:

> Sometimes I think there's naught beyond. But 'tis enough. He
> tasks me; he heaps me; I see in him outrageous strength, with an
> inscrutable malice sinewing it. That inscrutable thing is chiefly
> what I hate; and be the white whale agent, or be the white whale
> principal, I will wreak that hate upon him. (140)

The white whale embodies the impenetrable seeming malice of nature
itself and it is in this sense that Ahab's action is cosmic in its scope. Ahab's
enemy is not a whale but the situation he finds himself in. His act is an attempt to extinguish the source of human suffering and metaphysical evil in
the cosmos. This very declaration of Ahab's metaphysical act coincides with
the fullness of Ishmael's visionary world which is marked by the dramatic
use of stage directions. Like earlier figures of reading, Ishmael is so struck
by Ahab's challenge that to some extent he relives it and rereads it. But he
also transforms his encounter with Ahab into the "conjured objectivity" of
tragic form in an attempt to understand his ill-fated captain.

I want to claim that the "Quarter-Deck" not only declares but
constitutes the fundamental action or "mistake" of Ahab's tragedy. This might
not be readily apparent since Ahab's action can be seen as stretched over
time, culminating, one would think, in his actual attempt to slay the white
whale. However, it is with his declaration of action that Ahab brings about
his own binding to it (as well as the crew's). After delivering his metaphysical challenge to the cosmos, Ahab cries for "The measure!" (141) and the
scene turns into an eerie ritual where the crew and the mates perform the

binding of oaths. Ahab cries, "Death to Moby Dick! God hunt us all, if we do not hunt Moby Dick to his death!" (142). It is here where the crew commit themselves to Ahab's quest and it is precisely this oath he refers to much later in the narrative when he proclaims in response to a "half mutinous cry" (383): "All your oaths to hunt the White Whale are as binding as mine; and heart, soul, and body, lungs and life, old Ahab is bound" (383). An oath is an odd sort of thing: you can freely take up an oath, but subsequently your relationship to this free choice is one which is bound. And perhaps this was the "pact of souls" that Elijah had warned Ishmael about on shore. As has been said, it is this revelation of Ahab's action, and its mystic binding, that requires tragedy. The singularity of this action seems captured aptly in the gruesome harpoon that Ahab has forged especially for it. Ahab's impossible action—and even he on some level understood that his "object [was] mad" (157)—implies its necessary and fateful end. Thus, Starbuck can warn his captain: "I ask thee not to beware of Starbuck; thou wouldst but laugh; but let Ahab beware of Ahab" (362). In the end, Ahab is pulled under the sea by the rope of his own harpoon. Indeed, it is not simply a play on words to say that this action is a "missing of the mark," or a serious mistake.

Yet although I could not agree more with Millhauser that the essential tragedy of *Moby-Dick* consists in the singularity of its action, I am dubious of his contention that this action "stems from Ahab's character" (529). While Millhauser's claim seems to jibe with a widespread understanding of the "fatal flaw," which is often said to preside within tragedy, George Whalley explains that, for Aristotle:

> if the protagonist had by nature a "flaw" that steered him more or less inevitably into a fatal situation, he would be a mechanism and predictable to us, incapable of inducing terror or recognition; he would be repulsive or pathetic merely; he would no longer be a man-of-action in action shaping himself towards his telos in this action, but a man who—having fallen into mechanism—was no longer capable of discovering his 'form' in and through action. (27)

In Ahab's case, his character can be seen to stem from his action rather than the other way around. Ishmael pictures Ahab alone in his cabin declaring, "What I've dared, I've willed, and what I've willed, I'll do!" (143). Ahab's action before the "Quarter-Deck" remains hidden, but clearly it has been well set in motion. The action from the point of its declaration onwards only intensifies to a fever pitch. Ahab is said to sleep with "clenched hands," sometimes "burst[ing] from his state room, as though escaping from a bed that was on fire. Yet these, perhaps, instead of being the unsuppressable symptoms of some latent weakness, or fright at his own resolve, were but the plainest tokens of its intensity" (169). Interestingly, Ishmael depicts this tortured Ahab not as "the scheming, unappeasedly steadfast hunter of the white whale," but as an embodiment of the "eternal, living principle or soul in him," remarking that "the mind does not exist unless leagued with the soul" (169). It is this determination to pursue the white whale relentlessly, which Ahab attaches himself to through oath, such that Ishmael can describe the transition thus: "before living agent, now became the living instrument" (157). Directly following the crew's ritual oath is a soliloquy from Ahab in which he reflects on the now willed character of his action. It is at this point when he can speak of it as already set in motion by the binding of oaths: "Swerve me? ye cannot swerve me, else ye swerve yourselves! [...] The path to my fixed purpose is laid with iron rails, whereon my soul is grooved to run" (143).

But this oath, or these iron rails, should not belie—rather they should emphasize—the very real sense in which Ahab is making a moral choice and, indeed, Ahab's mistake is to be found in his action itself rather than merely in his person. Yet in what sense exactly can we say that this act possesses a "moral quality"? If we take Aristotle seriously in this context, we would first need to believe that Ahab is *capable* of making a moral choice—that he is not simply demonic or mechanistic. In this context, Ishmael actually pre-empts any dismissal of Ahab's action which would see it simply the result of madness by saying quite carefully that "in that broad madness, not one jot of his great natural intellect had perished" (157). But Ishmael also wants to present his captain in such a way that prevents any simple judgement which renders him evil and, in that, invites no further reflection. In a similar context, Harold Bloom remarks that most do "not come to love Ahab, and yet there is a serious disproportion between the reader's awe of, and admiration for, Ahab, and the moral dismissal of the monomaniacal hero by many scholarly critics" (3). The academic tendency Bloom describes is certainly at odds with Ishmael's tragic presentation. One way to think about tragedy is to say with Joe Sachs that "it washes our pity clean of sentimentality and our fear clean of self-righteousness" (13). For Sachs, Aristotle's *Poetics* demonstrates a sense in which these conflicting emotions are held in tension and proportioned towards the tragic hero's action so that it remains balanced between excessive aversion or partiality. This process is not one that finds its source in a "fatal flaw," but which is entirely dependent on a figure that is "both responsible agent and an innocent victim" (9). Thus, Aristotle remarks that disaster befalling an exceedingly virtuous or capable individual "is not terrible or pitiful but [simply] repulsive" (1453a). It is clear in Aristotle's account that the kind of action required for tragedy to be effective depends upon it happening to the "better kind of person," and tracing an arc "from good fortune to bad, [...] not because of depravity but because of a serious mistake" (1453a). Ishmael sees Ahab's tragedy in just these terms. He continually attempts to underscore the way in which his captain's act arouses both pity and terror in his heart.

To suggest that Ishmael is invested in Ahab's action in this way should be no special revelation. Yet the many interpretations of Melville's work that render Ishmael as a hero and foil to his captain make it sound as though Melville was having a good laugh at the romantics and not much more in his whaling book. *Moby-Dick* would be the story of that ridicule through the broken figure of Ahab. Insofar as commentators represent him in these terms, they highly underestimate the force of romanticism in Melville's own writing. As Yu remarks:

> Scholars have often noted that Melville [...] reacted against the Romantic spirit in general. But the truth is that Melville was basically Romantic as much as he was counter-Romantic. And precisely because of this he was more acutely aware of inner con-

flicts in Romanticism and more than other Romantic[s] dived deeply in quest of survival and almost succeeded. (111-112)

Ishmael's recreation of Ahab's act in tragic terms shows how deeply affected he was by the object of Ahab's madness. In this sense, Melville's novel is a serious attempt to grapple with the problem of evil—an effort that, for him, required the tragic form, and which remained unresolved.

Bibliography

Aristotle. "The Poetic Art." *Aristotle's Poetics.* Trans. George Whalley. Ed. John Baxter and Patrick Atherton. Montreal: McGill-Queen's UP, 1997.

Baxter, John. "George Whalley and a Way of Thinking about Shakespeare." *Animus* 15 (2011, 4-19.

Bezanson, Walter E. "*Moby-Dick*: Work of Art." *Moby-Dick*. Ed. Hershel Parker and Harrison Hayford. New York: Norton, 2002, 641-57.

Bloom, Harold. "Introduction." *Herman Melville's Moby-Dick*. Bloom's Modern Critical Interpretations. Ed. Harold Bloom. Revised ed. New York: Infobase Publishing, 2007, 1-6.

Cambon, Glauco. "Ishmael and the Problem of Formal Discontinuities in *Moby Dick*." *Modern Language Notes* 76.6 (1961), 516-23.

Faulkner, William. "I Wish I Had Written That." *Moby-Dick*. Ed. Hershel Parker and Harrison Hayford. New York: Norton, 2002, 640.

Kazin, Alfred. "Introduction to *Moby-Dick*," in Bloom, 7-18.

Lamb, Robert Paul. "Fast-fish and Loose-fish: Teaching Melville's '*Moby-Dick*' in the College Classroom" *College Literature* 32.1 (2005), 42-62.

Melville, Herman. *Moby-Dick*. Ed. Hershel Parker and Harrison Hayford. New York: Norton, 2002.

Millhauser, Milton. "The Form of Moby-Dick." *Journal of Aesthetics and Art Criticism* 13.4 (1955), 527-532.

Olson, Charles. *Call me Ishmael*. San Francisco: City Light Books, 1947.

Rice, Julian C. "*Moby-Dick* and Shakespearian Tragedy." *Centennial Review* 14 (1970), 444-468.

Robertson, Patricia. "The Lesser Crew as Chorus in *Moby Dick.*" *Publications of the Arkansas Philological Association* 7.2 (1981), 61-82.

Rosenberry, Edward H. *Melville and the Comic Spirit.* Cambridge: Harvard UP, 1955.

Sachs, Joe. "Introduction." *Poetics.* Newburyport: Focus Publishing, 2006, 1-18.

Sedgwick, William Ellery. *Herman Melville: The Tragedy of Mind.* Cambridge: Harvard UP, 1945.

Sewall, Richard B. *The Vision of Tragedy.* New Haven: Yale UP, 1959.

Vogel, Dan. "The Dramatic Chapters in *Moby-Dick.*" *Nineteenth-Century Fiction* 13.3 (1958), 239-47.

Wenke, John. "Ahab and 'the Larger, Darker, Deeper Part.'" *Moby-Dick.* Ed. Hershel Parker and Harrison Hayford. New York: Norton, 2002, 702-711.

Whalley, George. "On Translating Aristotle's *Poetics.*" *Aristotle's Poetics.* Montreal: McGill-Queen's UP, 1997, 1-32.

Young, John W. "Ishmael's Development as Narrator: Melville's Synthesizing Process." *College Literature* 9.2 (1982), 97-111.

Yu, Beongcheon. "Ishmael's Equal Eye: The Source of Balance in *Moby-Dick.*" *ELH* 32.1 (1965), 110-125.

$\mathcal{D}$OING $\mathcal{D}$ESCARTES $\mathcal{B}$ACKWARDS

STEVEN BURNS

I HAVE OFTEN had the pleasure of reading, together with students in Humanities 101, parts of the *Meditations* by René Descartes (1594-1650). First we need to put those dates in perspective. In 1604 Champlain spent a winter in Nova Scotia and in 1605 the permanent Acadian settlement at Port Royal was established. In 1755 the Acadians were expelled from Nova Scotia but many came back and they've stayed another 260 years. So all Nova Scotians at least know somebody whose roots here go back to when Descartes was about 10 years old. Meanwhile, back in England, Shakespeare died when Descartes was 20.

Descartes wrote many books but this one, the *Meditations on First Philosophy*, which was published when he was 45 years old, is the one that everyone puts on their list of Great Books. Why is this one of the Great Books?

One reason is that it does not start with God. Unlike other philosophers of his day and previous centuries, Descartes is revolutionary in not assuming the existence of a Divine First Principle that makes everything else intelligible. Descartes starts with Descartes. Just himself. Alone in the universe, thinking to himself. It is true that he will eventually get around to proving the existence of the Christian God, and we shall speak of that later. But his starting point is a new and radical one.

Another reason why the *Meditations* is a Great Book is that its FORM is as new as its starting point. Plato wrote dialogues because he understood philosophy to be a conversation among several people arguing back and forth. So Socrates is always asking someone a question and the dialogue happens in a public space where others often listen in. Aristotle left his thoughts in the most boring form of all, his notes for university lectures. Augustine wrote a great confession in which he talked to God. After Descartes, the great Dutch Jew, Spinoza, would write his *Ethics* as though it were a geometry text, with axioms and proofs. Great philosophers have often written in surprising new forms. But the *Meditations* is just Descartes sitting in his study, thinking to himself, and writing down the progress of his thoughts without reference to God or anything else.

A third reason why this is on the short list of Great Books is that it has a new fundamental question for philosophy. Descartes' first question was, "How can I KNOW?" Other philosophers put questions about <u>being</u> first: what is there? Why is there something rather than nothing? and so on. Others started with questions about <u>goodness</u>: What is worth doing? What is evil? and so on. But Descartes is a scientist. He had been taught in school that the earth was the centre of the universe and the sun went around the earth. But he was reading works by Galileo and other new scientists who claimed that the earth went around the sun. How could he KNOW which was right?

He tells us in his *Preface to the Reader* that he plans to "narrate ... the very thoughts by means of which I seem to have arrived at a certain evident knowledge of the truth." And so we come to read:

Meditation One

Descartes' method is to DOUBT everything that he does not know for certain. This is sometimes called "Cartesian doubt" or "the Cartesian method." (The adjective "Cartesian" is made up from the Latin version of his name, Renatus Cartesius. He wrote the *Meditations* in Latin before he translated them into French.)

In this First Meditation, Descartes has withdrawn into solitude and begins to doubt everything he can possibly doubt. He gives three main reasons for doubting everything he thought he knew.

(1) His senses sometimes deceive him, and he should not trust anything that has deceived him even once (Descartes, 14).

(2) He has dreamed of things as convincing as his present experiences so anything he has learned from experience could just be a dream (14).

(3) There could be not a supremely good God but rather "an evil genius, supremely powerful and clever, who has directed his entire effort at deceiving me" (16).

These three thoughts leave him with doubts about everything he once thought he knew. But now he is tired, and so gives up for the day.

Meditation Two

He returns to his study on the second day, picking up where he left off. "It is as though I had suddenly fallen into a deep whirlpool" (17). He doubts everything that he can see, or believe, or remember. He doubts that there are any physical things at all; he doubts that he has a body.

But then he has a revelation: there is something after all that he cannot doubt, namely that he is doing all this doubting, he is thinking. As he puts it in another book, "I think, therefore I am." In Latin this is "*cogito, ergo sum*," and it is often called Descartes' *cogito*, his "I am thinking" argument.

We notice that he still does not think that there is space, or a world of material objects, or that he has a body, and so on. He is just a thinking thing. But as long as he is thinking, he can be certain of something. He does exist. He does KNOW something.

So this is the remarkable new starting point for philosophy and for science. There is one thing that I can know for certain, that cannot be doubted. And it is not God, or anything else; it is just ME: "I know that I exist" (19). But just as a thinking thing. Nothing else.

At this point Descartes' mind begins to wander and he starts to think that "corporeal things," bodily things, physical things, are much more distinctly known than this "thinking thing" that is he. To stop this wavering, he introduces another famous argument: the Piece of Wax argument (21). It turns out, he claims, that, when we stop thinking about the sensible qualities of the wax and think about the wax itself, we discover that "I perceive it through the mind alone," not through the senses or through the imagination. So it is really his own mind that he knows clearly and the external things remain subject to doubt. And here Descartes ends his second meditation.

Now he still has a long way to go. By the end of the Sixth Meditation he will have re-established the possibility of knowledge about the external world as well as knowledge of himself as a thinking thing. Then he will be able to show how he can know with certainty whether the sun moves around the earth or the earth moves around the sun, and so on. He will then have achieved the goal that he set out to reach at the very beginning.

But Descartes thinks that he must first show that there is a good God who does not set out to deceive us, rather than the evil genius that he thought of in Meditation One. So that will be the job of the Third Meditation.

Descartes is often called "The Father of Modern Philosophy." One of the main reasons is that he puts the individual subject, the "I," first; it is the starting point of his philosophy. But he is not an atheist. When he does get around to discussing the existence of God, he offers one of the most complicated arguments in the history of philosophy. [If you doubt me, take a look at Bernard Williams' analysis of the argument in his book: *Descartes: the project of pure enquiry* (1978). He shows just how complicated it gets in Meditation Three.]

One of my happy discoveries in reading these three Meditations with students in Halifax Humanities is that it can help to read this Meditation BACKWARDS. It is an important part of the whole project because Descartes is now trying to prove the existence of something other than himself. We got the *cogito* established in Meditation Two. Now he needs us to agree that, just working by pure thought from the starting point of being a purely thinking thing, we can argue our way out. We can know that something other than our thinking self also exists.

Reading Meditation Three Backwards

So here is my attempt to show how the proof works, starting at the back of the chapter, and avoiding the worst of the complications.

(1) "The greatest pleasure of which we are capable" (35). Clearly it is not pleasant to be aware of painful or ugly things. The better the things that we are aware of, the more pleasure we feel. But then the greatest pleasure that a purely thinking thing could have would be the result of our being aware of the very best things there could be. That would be to have an idea of perfection.

(2) I know already that I am an imperfect being, capable of error and knowing very little. But I have in me the idea of a perfect being and this is an idea of God (a perfect, independent being and thus, by definition, the object that gives us the greatest possible pleasure). "[H]aving in me the idea of God" (35).

(3) I wonder "how I received this idea of God?" (34). For (a) I did not get it through my senses; God is not something I suddenly came across, or saw, or touched. Nor (b) did I get it by imagining it. [Earlier Descartes has a careful discussion of the limits of our imagination. We can form an image of a pentagon (a five-sided figure) and distinguish it from a hexagon (a six-sided figure). Perhaps we are even imaginative enough to form an image of a hendecagon (an eleven-sided figure, like a Loonie) and distinguish it from a twelve-sided figure. But no one's imagination is powerful enough to hold a clear image of a 1000-sided figure, and tell the difference between it and a 999-sided figure. So our imagination is not powerful enough to be the source of our idea of God.] So it must be (c) an idea that is <u>innate</u> or inborn in me (34).

(4) But here is a possible objection to that conclusion. Perhaps, although I am an imperfect being, I have (d) made up the idea of God by using my reason: I know a little bit and I can, by thinking of adding more know-ledge to me, eventually get to the idea of infinite knowledge. Similarly with power and goodness. But here Descartes has another clever defense. There are two kinds of infinite, he maintains. "It is true that my knowledge is

gradually being increased ... , [but] this gradual increase is itself a most certain proof of imperfection" (32). There is <u>potential</u> infinity: I can always add
another number to the number series and can never reach the last or biggest
number. But a different kind of infinity is the <u>actually</u> infinite: God is <u>actu-
ally</u> infinite, "nothing can be added to his perfection" (32). So I might have
constructed the idea of a potential infinity but an actual infinity is beyond
my senses, my imagination, and even my powers of construction.

So, having worked backwards through the last four pages of Meditation
Three, we see how Descartes has argued. (1) I, as a purely thinking thing,
have an idea of perfection. (2) It could not have come from me (or my
parents, he adds) or from some other imperfect thing in the world. So (3)
"the mere fact of my existing and of there being in me an idea of a most
perfect being, that is, God, demonstrates most evidently that God too exists"
(34).

Finally, armed with this conclusion that perfection, God, actually exists,
Descartes can say that there cannot be an evil genius after all, for "fraud
and deception depend on some defect" (35). God is perfection and, thus,
not a deceiver. And it must be this perfect being that both created me and
gave me the ideas of both perfection and imperfection, without which I
could not have reasoned my way to the *cogito*. I think that this can serve as a
relatively short and simple version of the long and complex argument that
you find if you read Meditation Three from the beginning.

In Meditation Four, Descartes will investigate the sources of error. If
God does not deceive us, we must be deceiving ourselves, he thinks. But
that discussion, and his final defense of scientific methods as the way to get
knowledge of the physical world, will have to wait for another discussion
at another time.

Bibliography

Descartes, René. *Meditations on First Philosophy.* Trans. Donald A. Cress. Indianapolis/Cambridge: Hackett Publishing Company, 1993.

Williams, Bernard. *Descartes: the project of pure inquiry.* Atlantic Highlands, NJ: Humanities Press, 1978.

$\mathcal{F}$REE $\mathcal{H}$UMANITIES:
Truffles for the Mind are the New Soul Food

COLIN STARNES

Our experience over the past decade with Halifax Humanities 101 and HalifaxThinks has revealed two unlooked-for things. Against all expectation we have found a powerful craving for the pleasure and interest of the ancient, ongoing conversation of the Humanities. This intense desire is shared between those with low incomes and high, those with university credentials and those who never completed high school, with professionals and unemployed, and with young and old.

The second discovery is an equally strong enthusiasm for teaching these courses for free. Halifax Humanities has more than enough volunteers to staff a small university. This is the kind of teaching many professors dreamed of when they started but were never quite able to realize in their university classes.

Three ingredients distinguish this way of teaching and learning. These classes *must* be free for the learners, they *must* be unpaid for the teachers, and they *must* be not-for-credit. Taken together these three simple things ensure that this activity is purely voluntary on all sides.

In the university proper the Humanities have been in a long slow decline. Because there are few jobs for which they are still thought to be directly relevant they appear to many as a useless anachronism. The terrifying cost of university education and the need to tie it directly to the economy have pushed the study of the Humanities out of the curricula of our universities. This has not squeezed the life out of the Humanities but it has made them pop up in unusual places which could turn out to be even more suitable to their nature than their traditional place at the core of the university.

By leaving to the university the economic considerations about what we need to know to control the world outside of us the Free Humanities have banished those ulterior motives. Its classes are open to anyone who is interested rather than to the members of a tiny privileged class. Our students consider these subjects for their own sake. This opens the possibility of surprise and discovery—to teachers who are still learners and to learners who can teach the teachers through their questions. Both seek contact with those realities of the intelligible universe that guide and govern us instead of learning techniques to control external realities. The goal is to know oneself in the context of differing notions of right and wrong, beauty and ugliness, faithfulness and deceit, through the splendid works of our ancestors. We consider the first definition of human purpose and friendship in the *Epic of Gilgamesh*, the quality of Abraham's faith, the ghastly wrath of Achilles, Oedipus's strange arrogance, Socrates' insight into the depths of justice, Aeneas' devotion to duty and Mohammed's realization of a stable universal community—to mention only a few of the ancient guideposts.

Coming together for this kind of inquiry is far from the kind of communities *Facebook* encourages. In virtual "friendships" we don't so much open ourselves to the chances of embodied friendship as we limit our connections to virtual people whose ideas are just like our own. Halifax Humanities is the precise opposite of this. The adult learners who come to HH101 and HalifaxThinks classes are looking for what they *don't* already think and they bring to the task a refreshing scepticism not generally found in undergraduates. Their lived experience of difference produces an unexpected curiosity, gentleness and courtesy. The noncompetitive setting—with no papers, no tests or exams, and where no questions are stupid—allows for a free interchange not often found in hypercompetitive universities driven from the top down by professorial knowledge.

Finally, we have been astonished to find that at the end of these classes, which offer nothing beyond themselves, the people who have taken them immediately look for more of the same. A new kind of voluntary community has begun to build. It is centered on a shared engagement with the questions, insights and dilemmas of these foundational Western texts. Such studies are nearly impossible without university-trained and employed scholars. But who knew that the Humanities and their most dedicated scholars could flourish at ground level *beyond* the ivory tower's secluded walls?

These Free Humanities classes act as truffles for the mind. Like the rare and delightful underground fungus, they grow in this spot one year, there the next, fragile but persistent, rich and pungent. Tucked away in community halls, church basements, and college classrooms after hours, they can neither be cultivated nor suppressed, yet a few morsels are enough to enliven a whole plate of nourishing but otherwise tasteless intellectual fare.

I think we are seeing in all of this the outlines of a new, more complete and adequate kind of university taking shape. It is one that takes nothing away from these institutions but adds back something. The oak tree of the existing university must recall its roots in the soil beneath it and rejoice in the wondrous truffles that soil can produce.

Universities have become the victims of their own success. They produce reliable credentialed workers and are the storehouses and purveyors of the world's non-proprietary knowledge and research. This requires large investments from the state, philanthropy, and their students. Yet people who lack entrance credentials, money or time are cut off from this collective good. For a time the Internet seemed to provide a solution by digitally re-duplicating everything and making it openly available. Its problem, however, is just that *everything* is here. Terabytes of data are a boon to those who know how to use them and an insurmountable obstacle to those who don't. The ability to distinguish good from bad information on the Internet depends on the prior education of the people who access it, so while a Harvard Massive Open Online Course may have 10,000 registrants, typically less than 3-4% finish it.

As high schools have also turned from the Humanities it has become more and more difficult for people to read them with pleasure or understanding. Almost the only people who are now able to do this are the formally trained scholars who have learned the languages and lived and worked with these texts for decades. These people constitute a vast reservoir of interpretive wealth and expertise that has no way to express itself in civic life.

In free Humanities courses, taught by volunteer faculty in not-for-credit classes, we see the beginnings of an open university that welcomes anybody who wants to join the conversation and is prepared to do the reading. This development could provide the solution to a whole lot of increasingly serious, and so far intractable, problems both in our economy and in society as a whole.

The Halifax Humanities Society is a tiny part of an international ferment in both humanities and sciences education but it also turns out to be at the leading edge of these experiments. World-wide, there are many free, high-quality, online offerings, such as those of the Kahn Academy. These have concentrated on math and science topics like biology, chemistry, and physics and they are now tentatively reaching into the humanities with playlists on finance and history. The Seniors College Association of Nova Scotia in Halifax is part of the truffle field, although its offerings are only for seniors. How can this all be paid for? While the teaching must be voluntary, the incidentals can also be donated. These include a room, bus passes, books, tickets to shows, daycare, a website, printing, and a coordinator to make it possible for faculty to focus on the discussion. We are still trying to figure this out. It is tempting to look to either the province or the universities for funding but perhaps the best way to raise these relatively small amounts is through some form of voluntary donations on the part of the users such as we find in religions or with Public Broadcasting. This has the advantage of bringing together small sums from those who can afford it so as to make it possible for others to take part in these discussions that belong to us all. Their presence at the table strengthens and improves the whole community.

Free, not-for-credit undergraduate level education available to anyone who wants it, and especially in the Humanities, alongside the for-credit and for-a-price offerings of the established universities, is a small change that could change everything. It points towards a brave new world in which any taxi driver who wants it can enliven his or her days and nights with the rarest, the most prized, and the most delightful mind truffles found on earth.

VIGILS

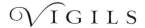

VALEDICTORY ADDRESS

2011

LAMONT DOBBIN

Congratulations! To all of us! It was a wonderful experience but it was a real challenge as well, wasn't it? Several weeks into the programme, when a few folks dropped out, I realized how valuable my fellow students were to me. It wasn't just words and ideas. It was the human voices expressing those ideas. There was a psychological, emotional, and spiritual energy circulating in that room and most of that energy came from you. Thank you for sharing this year with me.

What a magnificent programme you folks have created! Every week, not just a new subject but a new professor, a new face, a new voice, a new tone—a new atmosphere. Three quarters of the way through the year and I'm on my way to a class that is just as fresh and unpredictable as the very first day! I never got used to this. I never got tired of it.

It seems to me that we all have a little door in our mind that we can close off and allow the words and ideas we don't like just to pass by without touching us. In order to open that door and invite in those ideas, in order to engage those ideas, we need two things: a safe environment and an idea worth engaging. Week after week after week this programme provided both. Several times during this course I've heard discussions about the value of a humanities course as opposed to a more practical, pragmatic programme.

The problem with practical instruction is that the role of giver and receiver never changes. If you are teaching someone math, it is highly unlikely that you will learn something new about math from your student. In the humanities, however, the role of giver and receiver is constantly shifting. Whoever is speaking at the time becomes the giver. This can be a very empowering and validating experience for people in low income situations like us. We are used to being seen as the receiver and are rarely valued for our life experience or our opinions. Being able to share something of ourselves and being validated for this can change our minds about who we are and this change will manifest throughout our lives.

Part way through the course, our director left to visit a university in Ontario that is thinking about starting up a free Humanities programme and I remember thinking to myself at the time, "Even if they obtain the funding, recruit the professors, and have detailed instructions on how the programme runs, they are still going to need a Mary Lu to make it work." Mary Lu, you have been a bridge between some of the finest minds and biggest hearts in Halifax and ourselves and, the way our society is structured, we really need that bridge because these people would not normally be a part of our lives. Day after day, you created an atmosphere of academic excellence and warm welcome. I could never figure out how you did it, I could just observe the results in every class. I know I speak for the entire class when I say, "Thank you so very much."

IT COMES IN

BONITA SHEPHERD

My pain is so much a part of me it's like my evil twin.
I try not to let it bother me but, it comes in.
Daytime or night I can't seem to fight it and win, it comes in.

So prevalent these days and, what they say, is just grin and bear it;
it comes in.
It's like some awful smell that won't go away, or a constant bad memory
that won't cease today, it comes in.

What can I do, it reminds me of you; there have been ups and downs
like a circus clown.
It's so strong and free to adversely affect me;
I try to avoid it but it won't be denied, it comes in.

It gets harder with age, it insists on taking center stage.
I wish it would go somewhere else and play,
but again it's here with me, it always stays, and, it comes in.

I may be quite busy and try to say, I don't have time for you today,
to be held hostage this way but, it comes in.

It is persistently permanent as my color is to me, sort of
concentrated there, I don't think it's fair, it comes in.

Does it knock or say please; like anything that does not ask for permission
it arrives like some unwanted guest would be received, it comes in.

Sometimes I want to say, ouch, or not so tight, or to rub it there,
it does not care, it's always here and, it comes in.

When I first wake up just for a moment the evil is not there,
and then I raise my head to get out of bed and, it comes in.

GILGAMESH AND MORTALITY

JOHN B. COX

THIS IS AN article about death—how we fight and, in some cases, ignore the inevitable.

We are all going to die. We have for centuries tried to explain and/or justify our own mortality. Plato talks about a soul, most religions talk about the afterlife in absolutes: Heaven and Hell. Christianity gives us a list of ten rules to follow to get into heaven. Dante, in his *Divine Comedy*, describes seven deadly sins that lead us to hell.

I know this is an oversimplification of organized religion because that debate has been going on for centuries. But I am fascinated by the fact that, no matter how much we try to prepare for death, we can never accept it. The first great work of literature, *The Epic of Gilgamesh* (from around 2000 BCE), illustrates this point.

Gilgamesh is a king who exploits his people until the gods create Enkidu to be his equal and his friend. When Enkidu becomes ill and dies, Gilgamesh mourns his friend, then starts obsessing over his own mortality. When he meets Siduri—the wine maker—she warns him about the futility of seeking immortality and she advises him to enjoy the pleasures of this world.

Looking to gain immortality, Gilgamesh travels to find Utnapishtim, who survived the flood and was granted everlasting life from the gods. Utnapishtim tests Gilgamesh by asking him to stay awake for seven days. He cannot. When he fails, Utnapishtim sends Gilgamesh away, but not before he tells him of a plant that will restore his youth. A snake steals that plant.

When Gilgamesh arrives home, he finally accepts his mortality.

This is a story that mirrors the lives of many people even today. We are obsessed with slowing our own aging. Like Gilgamesh obsessing over his mortality, we tend to gravitate towards anti-aging products, diet fads, exercise to extremes—we obsess over our body image. We can't turn on the TV or open a magazine without being bombarded with images of what people think we should be. We are seeking our own immortalities. And, as Siduri tells us, that effort is futile. We should enjoy our time on Earth with family and friends.

We spend so much time trying to stay alive with all these fads that we fail to enjoy life.

Like Gilgamesh, we hunt for this elusive immortality, ignoring the simple fact that death is inevitable. We can't avoid death. We may think we've achieved eternal youth only to have it stolen from us. Whether by our own hand, some accident, or old age, we are not preventing anything by running away from death. It's been my experience that grief is equally strong, no matter how or when we go.

Many stories have been told about the afterlife. We try to express life after death because we can't understand why life is so short. Like imagining life on other worlds, we refuse to accept that our short time together is all there is. What happens after I die I'll leave to others to decide.

Like Gilgamesh, I have finally accepted the fact: I am dying.

THE *L*ENGTH OF THE *C*OURT[1]

ROSE ADAMS

In the twisted sheet hours
I unmuffled my head
to decipher my son's sleep talk
knees banging against his walls   *uuugh (a grinding growl)*

The doctor says I take notes
at every appointment
just like my mother,   *maaaaaaa*
a lurching as she is lost
to me, a longing like when my son
said Mama, his first word   *maaaamaaaaa*
when his stroller couldn't fit
in my bathroom stall

Three days ago
I crafted a short letter
about my daughter's health
enclosed a two page report
sealed the envelope and in cursive   *fuuuuuck*
wrote a name

The letter passed from the palm of my hand

---

1   "The Length of the Court" was originally published in the Spring 2014, issue 3 of *Understory* online magazine.

to my son's and then to his father's
at the basketball game
where my daughter ran
the length of the court
between her two parents
and poured water
from the bottle in my hand
down her throat

I saw him sink
the unopened envelope
into the recycling bin   *Yuh! (with an intake of air)*
as if I was sucking the words back
Silenced

The other team
a humiliating
slam-dunk

THE *P*ROCEDURE

BRENDA DELORENZO

It was five and thirty years ago.
She was ushered into a grey sweaty room.
People were gathered around a wooden table.
Everyone was clad in green robes.
A small radio hummed tunes.
Nobody uttered a word.
A woman checked her hair for bobby pins.
She examined her mouth for dentures.
Gurneys were stretched down a long corridor.
It was a fearsome day.
A tall anemic man in a white uniform tried to becalm her
In her tempestuous storm.
The room blackened. She became dizzy.
She plummeted down a turbid tunnel.
It was a terrifying day.
She woke up and it was five and thirty years ago.
She was ushered into a grey sweaty room.
People were gathered around a wooden table.
Everyone was clad in green robes.
The procedure was over.
We ate cold toast and boiled eggs.
Nobody uttered a word.

$\mathcal{E}$ M P T Y $\mathcal{E}$ Y E S

DAWN HALE

I REMEMBER SO many pairs of empty eyes that sometimes they haunt my dreams. There are degrees of empty eyes. I think age has a lot to do with how empty they become but then again maybe it's how beaten down they've been. The emptiest eyes show no emotion at all, no anger or pain, no joy or excitement. To show an emotion runs the risk of being ridiculed or humiliated, to have anything good beaten out of you. I have met many pairs of empty eyes in my life.

The eyes I love best in the world are the ones newborn babies open as they see for the first time. I fall in love with those beautiful eyes. Those beautiful eyes can even keep the empty eyes at bay for a while.

I dislike winter intensely, and I finally figured out why a few years ago. There are no bright colours, no smells or birds singing joyfully in winter; no flowers, bees buzzing, bright colours of clothing on happy people, children running and laughing, squeezing the last bit of fun out of the day before they're called in for bed. Their eyes fall shut no matter how hard they try to fight it—they are not empty eyes.

The empty eyes belong to the children who were brought to us to fix. Someone had decided they were broken. It could have been a family, a doctor, a teacher or social worker, someone who decided the child didn't fit into their definition of "normal." We would try to talk to them to find out what had hurt them, what had drained the life out of their eyes. There were many reasons, and none of them you'd want to hear about.

Each drained a little life from my eyes and replaced it with fire. Angry eyes. Of course I couldn't show those eyes to the ones who had hurt them;

that would be a "judgment call." Judgment calls are not allowed when you work with people, even when you know they are abusing a little seven-year-old girl. I guess I was supposed to close my eyes to the bruises on her little genitals, and her empty eyes.

There are the empty eyes of the chronically mentally ill who have lived most of their lives locked up in institutions: a hallway, a kitchen, a couple of bathrooms, a television room, and sometimes a few hours outdoors in a yard with a ten foot fence around it. There were no surprises in the kitchen either, even though the most important thing in their days was food. So many empty eyes there: eyes that stared into nothingness unless their keepers made an effort to create some fun for them. Then again, many of their keepers had empty eyes too. It's called "burnout" they told us and suggested we move to another unit. To forget the empty eyes?

There were lots of empty eyes in the city housing building I lived in. People abandoned by society who had little hope of life improving and gave up trying long ago. You could see it happen to them from the time they moved in. Eyes of hope and relief, of being safe from homelessness, of trying to make friends—to connect with—the empty eyes. Slowly the life drained from the hopeful eyes too as they realized there was not enough money to buy food to last the month. It didn't take long before they spent most of their time sitting in their box of an apartment staring at the television with their empty eyes.

There were a few lucky ones who still had family and friends who came to visit or take them out to do fun things. Their eyes were not always empty but the shadows were never far away. Some managed to keep their bright eyes no matter what life threw at them. I marvelled at their ability to find joy in the simplest things in life. I also wondered if it was a role they played and if, inside their hearts, they hid their empty eyes.

My father's eyes slowly emptied as Alzheimer's wove its tangled roots through his brain and choked out the light. My mother's eyes emptied when the love of her life died and left her alone. She can't seem to find the life to bring back the light. My sister's eyes have emptied watching what has happened to our parents under her roof.

My eyes have been empty so many times in my life. I have fought to keep every little ray of light I could. I learned that "things" can't keep the light burning but a little bird singing in a tree can give some light. Friends can open your eyes as well as family. Reading wonderful books, listening to beautiful music, creating something from the heart can bring joy too.

After several years hiding from the empty eyes in my box of an apartment, I read a little community paper one day. A course was being offered—free! The paper said we would study "some of the truly great treasures of our heritage: Plato, Homer, Dante, St. Augustine, Shakespeare, Machiavelli, Descartes, Kant, Nietzsche, Alice Munro, and F. Scott Fitzgerald. You will also be exposed to opera, live theatre, and classical music concerts." All the books would be provided. Here was a chance to open my mind and do something I had longed to do for so, so long: to study for the joy of learning. I could meet others who felt like I did and open our eyes together. I called the number provided with fear that I might not qualify to attend but I met with Mary Lu in a few days and she told me I was accepted.

It turned out to be so much more than I ever imagined. Mary Lu became such an important part of helping us in so many ways: from making sure we had all the books we needed, keeping our spirits up when we felt overwhelmed, right down to teaching us Jane Austen. Without her we never would have made it and might have starved without her wonderful coffee and snacks!

The professors were amazing and it wasn't long before we found ourselves discussing Homer's *Odyssey*. They never made us feel that our opinions or questions were unworthy and there were even times when we challenged them. I felt and saw the light rekindle in our eyes as we realized we could do this. The fear that we might fail disappeared and our little worlds that had beaten us into a corner opened up. We saw the limits we imposed on ourselves. We could go to operas, plays, visit art galleries, and read the classics just like everybody else and hold our heads high.

I have grown in my thoughts and ideas of the world historically and presently in so many ways. I am hungry to learn more. Being introduced to the great thinkers who held true to their beliefs no matter how many times their peers told them they were crazy gives me the courage to pursue my own writing and art. The Empty Eyes have been gently put away but not forgotten. I hope to make a difference to others who just need a chance like I was given, a chance to bring the light back to their eyes.

ℋORSES, 𝒟OGS AND 𝒪THER ℋEROES

GILLIAN WEBSTER

BY THE TIME I was nine, I had read a lot of illustrated books starring animals. My favourite series, *Silver Brumby*, followed the adventures of a band of wild horses, or brumbies, set in Australia's back country. These were noble animals who kept to the rugged ranges—people were treated with suspicion. For family reasons, we didn't own a car or telephone so entertainment was mostly watching *Star Trek* and reading. There wasn't much after school play—my older sister and I had to do housework, while my father worked in the city and brought the groceries home for supper, along with animal supplies. We had wanted guinea pigs and budgies and we got them, but my father insisted they not be caged. He was very pro-animals and said it was cruel to coop them up in cages. We did agree, even though there were an awful lot of droppings to clean up.

I remember going to a Hobart city department store with my older sister, Julie, when I was about nine or ten and, with my pocket money, I bought a palm-sized china horse. My father pronounced it cheap. I didn't care; I loved my statuette and named it Helena. I also had an adorable wooden figurine—part horse, part dog, and part elephant. It had a silly expression. I named it Ross after a boy I'd met at a summer camp. I'm sure I wore a silly smile whenever I looked at him.

My family moved back to Wales from Tasmania and I couldn't find my Brumby books. I wasn't very good at making friends all over again. I turned for company to stories such as Jack London's *White Fang* and *Call of the Wild.* Then I found *Old Yeller* written by Fred Gipson. Half a century later, these titles are still magical to me. Some words or phrases catch in your mind and stay there. Themes and plot lines were eerily similar—the dog heroes lived in remote places, in the manner of brumbies. Persecuted by people, surviving on their wits, these silent heroes rescued only those who deserved help while deserting the evil doers. Justice was clear and swift and satisfactory. Living in the wilderness, battling with the elements, their animal lives were full of freedom and adventure. Despite disasters, I knew the novels would end happily. The libraries I went to selected their children's titles with care. I didn't know that what I was reading was award-winning material and the authors well-regarded.

I lived in a world of make-believe. I did not want to accept the real world where I would have to grow up. The signs of my maturing body showed it was pointless to try to avoid this fate. Now I felt adrift. Dogs and horses did not cry. I would not cry. They gritted their teeth and got on with it. They set their muzzles to the wild wind, uncomplaining in rain or fire. They did not have difficulties with handling conflicts with real children, as I did. I grew more alone and lonely. I ran to my books where I felt understood. There, the codes of contact did not seem complicated and yet they were meaningful. Somehow, these books comforted me and taught me courage to go on during this difficult time.

I could not put my feelings into words but I could recognize them in my animal tales. There were so many moves; I was having trouble figuring out the current one and then there would be another move. My father was very restless. When our mother died, my older sister and I began a series of moves that seemed full of promise to him. I think he lived in a world of make-believe, too. In our own way, we were scared by life; I had a difficult childhood and I felt lost.

When I started high school at eleven, we read *Jamaica Inn*. I loved it. The heroine, Mary, was lonely and scared in the madness that was synonymous with the terrible Jamaica Inn, where she was forced to live. She was brave, intelligent and virtuous. Here was a world set back a hundred years ago on the desolate Bodmin Moor in Cornwall. The ancient moor held secrets in its quicksand that sucked in living things and never a ripple would show that there was anything wrong. It was a romantic world, spiced with secret contraband. Jem, the hero, was devil-may-care and confident. Mary fell in love with him despite herself. I could be courageous and wily like the heroine and wait patiently for the difficult life at home to get better. I got comfort and inspiration from my books.

Mary was trapped in a big, dark, dirty house where no corner felt like her own. I too felt like this. Just like the settings in my animal stories, the drama of *Jamaica Inn* was heightened by the unpredictability of the outdoors, a living character in itself. Smuggling and murder were normal to this environment. There was little ambiguity about the Inn and upstanding people avoided it. I read it over and over again. My house in North Wales was full of people but so silent I could hear the church clock strike every quarter hour. What a dismal sound! I had a sense of foreboding whenever I heard it. I was absorbed in my stories. I pretended that nothing bad was brewing in my home.

My heroine mostly survived on her wits—she, too, hid behind doors to avoid the large, authoritative figure. Her wicked uncle could read her thoughts. My heroine had left a nice home in another land, and so had I. We were disoriented together and I identified with the mystery and misery of *Jamaica Inn*. My heroine was determined to survive. Her character was so well drawn. She started out looking forward to an easy life in her home village and dreamed of marrying a farmer. By the end, she ran off with the intrepid Jem with whom she would live a wandering but full life. She gambled away dull safety and rose to her fullest potential. She wasn't born to be stuck in a predictable life. I was fearful of her unknown life ahead with Jem but I knew at the same time her heart chose him.

Midway though that first year, my teacher asked us to write an English essay and I wrote mine inspired by *Jamaica Inn*. My fictional heroine overcame her circumstances through the steadfastness of her heart, just like Mary. I poured every romantic word I could think of onto paper. A week later, my story was brought back personally by the headmaster who said it was very mature. I was thrilled. I took it home. My father was surprised Mr.

George had praised it. Mr. George had poor taste—he should know since he had been at the same school thirty years before. I don't know if my father ever read the essay. I pretended that nothing had happened.

We continued to move often and I rarely got to say goodbye. Closing a book wasn't so hard when you knew how to find more but gradually I became very shy of new schools and new towns. I wasn't very good at making friends all over again. There was no stability in my life except school work and my world of reading.

Fast forward to 2012. I read a lot of great literature; the classic ones that publishers often put out as series. Dismay and urgency enveloped me when I walked past high schools. I felt I had wasted my education and who would give me a second chance? I was past fifty and needed to find more meaning in life if my self-worth was to rise.

I joined Humanities 101 in the fall of 2012. The Humanities 101 program highlights the development of thought in the Western World in five chronological sections. Students are encouraged to read further— the director stresses that this programme gives only an overview and that participants will come away with a solid base on which they can build. Here was my second chance! Towards the end of the programme, we studied Ralph Waldo Emerson's 1842 public lecture on transcendental idealism. It was a passionate essay on the need to explore our individual potential by leaving common, everyday activities behind. This was reading I would never have discovered on my own. My newest hero is Emerson.

I first read "On Walden Pond" thirty years ago. I didn't understand why Thoreau's account of his "2 years out" of civilized society drew me—I was smitten by it and felt great respect for the author. My hero found a harmony with nature and the universe by taking time (two years!) and just "be-ing." He reveled in appreciating everything he hadn't found in society. He appreciated nature and gave it respect. He spent time exploring every aspect of Walden. He listened to the loons; he watched ants fight under his hand lens and microscope. He thought his time with the Divine on his doorstep was delightful and deeply rewarding. Thoreau died at the age of forty-five, but he crammed a full life into his years.

I went to Concord one year. I loved Ralph Waldo Emerson's home nearby; it had a well-worn look. But I was disappointed at the little pond called Walden. It looked dull; Thoreau's cabin hadn't survived. There was a replica but it had no sense of habitation. It was a riddle I couldn't solve. It was only when I followed up with my own reading of these philosophers' biographies that I understood that Thoreau shared Emerson's philosophy. Then I was able to put the pieces of the puzzle together. This philosophy reminded me of Jesus' Biblical exhortation (Luke 12:27): "Consider the lilies how they grow: they toil not, they spin not: and yet I say unto you, that Solomon in all his glory was not arrayed like one of these." Jesus tells people not to worry about how they made money for clothes, etc., but rather to live their lives fully. The light bulb that illuminated these three sources helped me understand transcendental idealism. I would not have been able to link the Biblical verse with any philosophy before this. Each work shone light on the other two.

When I started 101, I didn't always know how to engage with the texts. When I needed help to decode them, I got it. These authors supported my personal growth. I felt more grounded in life. Mary Lu said if we could do this reading marathon for an intensive eight months then we would have a good literary foundation. I came away with lots new to think about and looked forward to renewing acquaintance with my favourite authors—at less than lightning speed! In addition to an expansion of learning material, I also felt a new respect and fellow feeling with my classroom neighbours. Discussing literature and ideas gave us something new to talk about every week. We have never grown stale with each other; we have a lot in common! All of us have a shadow in our past but with the class focus on growing I find myself more able to shut out the unwanted bits and realize other people have gone through very much the same difficult childhood as I did.

$\mathscr{P}$ATRICIA'S $\mathscr{S}$ONG

KATHLEEN HIGNEY

All your waves and billows are flowing over me
And I can no longer see the sun
There is no place left for me to run
All your waves and billows are flowing over me

I went to Boston trying to buy time
To spend on the ones I love
But even there—
Your waves and billows kept flowing over me

Now decided—
I'm going with the Lord
I and God in one accord
All your waves and billows are flowing over me

And I can no longer see the sun
There is no place left for me to run
Striving forever said and done
All your waves and billows are flowing over me

Deep calls unto deep
At the sound of your waterspouts
All your waves and billows are flowing over me

Patricia died in 2013. Waves and billows are from Psalm 42 which gave Patricia comfort as she faced death.

WHAT IS A VIGIL?

Reflections on December 6, 2014

SUSAN DODD[1]

WHAT IS A vigil?

It is a time of watchfulness, of being awake through the night.

As I edited some contributions to this book, I heard stories that Halifax Humanities participants deliberately did not write down. I realized that though I've known many of these people for a decade, I do not know details of the diverse ways that poverty happened to them. As well, because I've always talked with them about books from the curriculum, they don't know much about me, either. We agreed that this is one of the best things about the programme. When we come together to talk about books, we are liberated from some of the weight of our pasts. It's not that we escape the past or the differences between us, but that, for the moments when we talk about books, our pasts don't fully define and control us. While talking about their contributions to this collection, though, we shared some personal stories. The worst of our experiences cannot be conveyed in literal stories, and so they're encoded in analogies and metaphors, or hidden behind exegeses of other people's writings.

Our editorial committee for this anthology—Shari Clarke, Lamont Dobbin, Mary Lu Redden and I—met regularly to discuss this manuscript during some intense months: shootings on Parliament Hill, accusations of

---

1   Thanks for comments from Victoria Goddard, Nicholas Hatt, Shirley Tillotson, Angus Johnston, and for conversations with Melanie Frappier, Catherine Joudrey and Neil Robertson, and my co-editors Lamont Dobbin, Shari Clarke and Mary Lu Redden.

sexual violence against a once-beloved national broadcaster, the murders and disappearances of aboriginal women, increased Canadian bombing in Syria, increasing media coverage of atrocities by ISIS, and the coinciding anniversaries, on December 6, of the Montreal Massacre (1989) and the Halifax Explosion (1917).

Through all the public discussions of this violence, my discussions with my co-editors, with Halifax Humanities graduates, and my exchanges with established writers about their chapters helped me to clarify my thinking about the political uses and abuses of grief. I'm now convinced that the best ways for activists to carry out the crucial work of resisting apolitical sentimentality in commemorating violent deaths is by collaborating with religious communities. There must be two separate public moments—the call for political vigilance and then the silent vigil of remembrance.[2] I think that the sequence should be in this order—political vigilance first, a vigil in remembrance second—so that the traumatic energy tapped by remembrance is lovingly contained and not exploited.[3]

My question, "What is a vigil?" is about the relation between personal and political but it is more pressingly about whether it is currently possible for there to be a public mourning that is not always already geared towards some political end.

Could we publicly commemorate those who die through violence in two, connected moments—one of political vigilance about the structural causes of violence and the other a spiritual vigil of remembering the dead?

"Vigil" means, literally, a watchfulness through the night, and an

---

2   My position up to now about the imperative of refusing apolitical sentimentalization of loss is expressed most fully in The Ocean Ranger: remaking the promise of oil (Black Point: Fernwood, 2012), and in "Remembering the Ocean Ranger: The Weight of Memory and Injustice," Our Times Magazine, Labour Education Issue, Spring 2013, 35-39.

3   Though I have been immersed in literature about the politics of memory for a long time, I'm continuously rethinking. Much of what I say here is the subject of massive scholarly, psychological, feminist and theological literatures, but the question seems too pressing to me now for a research project and so, with trepidation, I offer this essay as a non-academic reflection on the power—and dangers—of releasing collective trauma into political arenas.

interruption of sleep in anticipation of some possibility.

For whom, or what, do we wait when we purposefully break our sleep? Is the excitement of trauma a true wakefulness? For whom, or what, do we hold our restfulness in abeyance?

My 24-year-old brother, Jim, was among the 84 men who died when an "unsinkable" oilrig sank off the coast of Newfoundland in 1982. Thirty-one years later, after I published a book on the social and political aftermath of this Ocean Ranger disaster, I was asked to give thanks on behalf at the families at the Gonzaga High School annual memorial service in Saint John's. Students and teachers of Gonzaga High School host the service at Pius X Roman Catholic Church. It is a beautiful ecumenical service where members of the whole oil production community gather.

My father had died the year before and my mother, Joyce, came with me to Saint John's for the service. Together, Joyce and I skidded along Saint John's steep, icy sidewalks, arm in arm. My mother's key chain says: "Joyce —the merry one"; my mom is unusually susceptible to the moods of her location and in Saint John's in 2013 that meant unpredictable energy surges. I had a fit of tears the morning before the Gonzaga service, but Mom waved it off: "Oh come on. You've got it written out and if you're crying too hard I'll read it."

The church was packed. On the altar, 84 candles waited to be lit. Students who weren't even born when the rig sank filled the pews and dodged around various religious ministers, preparing the sound system. Mom and I greeted other family members and took seats near the front. The "Royal Salute" heralded the arrival of the Lieutenant Governor, John Crosbie, and his wife, Jane.

I interviewed John Crosbie early in my research for the book. He almost cried talking about the Ocean Ranger disaster: "Your brother was one of the men out there that night? Poor devil." When my book came out, he became a very intimidating fan. At one of the big bookstores, the manager told me, "your book must be good—John Crosbie was here the other day making sure we had it out where everyone can see it." This endorsement from John Crosbie was disconcerting—we are hardly what you'd call obvious political allies. He personifies the Newfoundland elite who, I believe, realize that they failed to be vigilant about the risks the foreign oil companies took with their workers—our men—when they moved into Canadian waters. Of course, Crosbie also personifies a certain Newfoundland spirit. He is smart and he knows the story I tell in *The Ocean Ranger* intimately. As a Nova Scotian writing a very Newfoundland story, I took heart from his enthusiastic praise.

Even with my two fans—my mom and the Lieutenant Governor Crosbie—front and centre, when I rose to face the assembled students, the other Ocean Ranger family members and the oil producing community, I was thrown back into the grief and rage of my 16-year-old self. Still, I was determined to keep sentimentality from obscuring the corporate crime and governmental negligence at the root of our loss. I did all I could to parlay sadness into anger, passivity to action, comfort to political mindfulness. I wanted to remind everyone that Jim and the 83 others died because the oil companies' managers were paid to make profit and never to think about the rig as a place where humans work and live. I wanted everyone to face our past negligence and our current responsibility for keeping governments vigilant about regulating all corporate activity.

I wonder now if I was right.

I don't mean that I wonder if I am right in my analysis of the unpunished manslaughter at the root of the Ocean Ranger disaster. Those 84 deaths are manslaughter, perpetrated by the oil company managers, their bosses, and the government agents and elected representatives who set the stage for this loss. And that manslaughter was sanctioned by international capital and it is bound to happen again in some other form, as it did in Lac-Mégantic in 2013.[4]

I am sure about that.

What I am unsure about is what a vigil is, what it does, and what I think and feel about that.

_____

4   See Bruce Campbell, *Willful Blindness? Regulatory failures behind the Lac-Mégantic disaster*, Canadian Centre for Policy Alternatives, August 18, 2014.

★

THE GONZAGA OCEAN Ranger service has such gravity; it is a vigil in the religious tradition of being a public act of collective silence. My politicization could work there, if it worked at all, not in spite of the silence at the heart of the service but only because of it. While listening to the students read the 84 names and seeing them light the candles, I felt an intense opening of myself to the lost men in their particularity. One after another, these men, so many of them under the age of 30, presented themselves to my heart's eye. Once the names were read, we who remained sat together in the long silence with the enormity of the loss weighing upon us all.

People who die violently are vulnerable to the even further violence of having the grief over their deaths manipulated for political or even commercial ends. People who mourn violent losses are uniquely susceptible to having their emotions "triggered," and so of being subjected to uncontrollable flashbacks or blazing fury at unpredictable targets. We are vulnerable when we remember violence. We are even more vulnerable when we fool ourselves into thinking that redirecting traumatic energies is a simple act of will and that we can control the direction of any ensuing political action.

None of this is new thinking, but it's worth recalling.

Yesterday was the anniversary of the murder of 14 women engineering students at the Ecole Polytechnic in Montreal, 25 years ago.

The man who murdered those engineering students in Montreal didn't go to a mall to shoot; he went to a university, and not just any university. He went to a technical university because in his evil insanity he needed to reassert the prohibition against women going into engineering. So, while this was, undoubtedly, an act that expresses a misogynistic culture, the fingers that pulled the trigger were moved by a particular man who was shooting particular women. For him "feminism" was the choice of a woman to become an engineer. They broke into what he took to be his rightful place, and he was willing to shoot them for it.[5]

Now these dead students' names are a rallying cry and we take the

---

5   Thanks to Mélanie Frappier for helping me to clarify this point.

anniversary of their deaths as a chance to raise awareness of men's violence against women in all its forms. The personal *is* political, without question. But is mourning political? Should it be? What happens when days of mourning become only political?

Do we lose the particularity of the loss, and of the crime?

There arises, also, the question of who owns the event, that is, who organizes it and determines the balance between reflection and politicization. The Montreal massacre memorial is particularly difficult here. The attack was on women as women but also on universities and civil spaces generally. This commemoration is a civic act, and so a public secular service makes sense. But, so, too does a spiritual service of remembrance. The event seems to cry out to us to overcome all such divisions as well as we can, and so we have developed ecumenical services ...

Recent public discussions of sexualized violence have awakened us to the pervasiveness of male dominance, particularly in polite-seeming workplaces like the universities and the CBC. I have been in the Canadian university system for all of my adult life, and it is hard to imagine an institution of privilege in democratic societies that is more insidiously patriarchal. I do wonder, though, what will happen if we conflate the "systemic" violence of everyday patriarchy with rape and shooting.

The shock of picking up my newspaper on December 6, 1989 and reading that a gunman had shot 14 women engineering students in a Montreal university has changed over the decades, from a narrative memory into an emotional trigger. Because of this change, I now feel the need for a spiritual moment. That is, I need a prayerful silence in which I open myself to the presence of the dead where each name can present itself as a particular missing person. It is in contemplating the unknowable fullness of her lost life that we confront the evil of the gunman's crime.

The civic campaign against misogyny cannot achieve full power without the silent and, I believe increasingly, the religious apprehension of each individual's particularity and ultimate self-responsibility.

Haligonians are doubly reflective on December 6 because that is the anniversary of the Halifax Explosion as well as of the Montreal Massacre.

Commemorations of the Halifax Explosion are characterised by a sense of awe. It's impossible not to be impressed by the sheer magnitude of the event, the destruction of social infrastructure and the generosity of those who poured money and supplies—especially from Boston—into our devastated city.

Samuel Prince, a sociologist at the University of King's College, wrote one of the most important early works analyzing the aftermath of disaster: *Catastrophe and Social Change: Based upon a sociological study of the Halifax disaster.*[6]

He dedicates his work in this way:

> *Halifax*
> *is not a large city*
> *but there are those who love it*
> *who would choose to dwell therein*
> *before all the cities beneath the skies*

TO

ALL SUCH

CITIZENS, PAR EXCELLENCE,

I COUNT IT AN HONOUR TO DEDICATE

THESE LINES

For the Reverend Doctor Prince, writing in the scientific optimism of the earliest sociologists, the catastrophe of the Halifax explosion was an opportunity to further rational social progress; but it was a chance that could equally be squandered without timely studies and expert interventions. As he cautions: "… catastrophe always means social change. There is not always social progress."[7] For Prince, "social progress" means an ever-increasing rational order in human collective life. Prince's optimism about science and its application towards a better human life is astonishing considering that

---

6   Samuel Prince, *Catastrophe and Social Change: based upon a sociological study of the Halifax disaster,* Columbia University Press, 1920.

7   Samuel Prince, *Catastrophe and Social Change,* 21.

he was studying the devastation wrought by the development of weaponry, transportation, and chemical technology for the purpose of war.[8]

Prince describes the work of the harbour during the First World War:

> Hither the transports came, and the giant freighters to join their convoy. Cruisers and men-of-war put in to use its great drydock, or to take on coal. Here too, cleared the supply and munition boats—some laden with empty shells, others with high explosives destined for the distant fields of battle. How much of the deadly cargo lay in the road-stead or came and went during those fateful years is not publicly known. Certainly there was too much to breed a sense of safety, but no one gave the matter a second thought. All were intent upon the mighty task of the hour. Sufficient unto each day was the day's evil.[9]

Each year, we hold memorials to the thousands who died in the Halifax Explosion, and we send our Christmas tree to Boston in thanks for its incredible support. Of course, we don't emphasize that, as in most man-made disasters, we should have seen it coming. As well, we don't mention that part of Boston's contribution was to send a team of experts who studied the devastation and organized the relief effort according to the most up to date scientific practices of the day.

A few weeks ago, a mentally ill man shot a soldier whose job was to stand, in a military kind of vigil, at the War Memorial on Parliament Hill. The sounds of rounds of shots were played and replayed on radio and television, as the assailant was "taken down" by security forces. Meanwhile, we hear nothing of the sounds of Canadian bombs exploding in civilian territory in the Middle East in our news reports.[10]

---

8   Robert Oppenheimer studied the effects of the Halifax Explosion—then, still the largest man-made explosion in history—as he attempted to anticipate the effects of the bomb he was developing (Ray Monk, *Robert Oppenheimer: life inside the center*, Random House: New York, 2012, 961).

9   Samuel Prince, *Catastrophe and Social Change*, 25-26.

10   Gary Thorne made this clear in his interview on CBC's *Information Morning*, Halifax, Monday, November 17, 2014. http://www.cbc.ca/informationmorningns/ information   morningns/2014/11/17/why-we-should-ask-tough-questions-about-canadas-bombing-decision/

Patriotism and gratitude for Corporal Nathan Cirillo's "sacrifice" now excite support for further Canadian investment in bombings and these diversions of resources into the "fight against ISIS" go largely unquestioned out of respect for the Canadian dead. This closing down of critical reflection—especially our ability to ask who profits financially from the bombs and whether we endorse the civilian casualties that bombing entails—can only intensify with the videos of ISIS atrocities.

★

When you trigger a gun, you have a pretty good idea of where the bullet is headed. When you trigger an emotion ... well, there is no telling, is there?

When we revive traumatic memory, we are not necessarily reawakening to the humanity of others. Too often, we revive traumatic memory in order to keep ourselves comfortable, revisiting familiar grief and anger so we don't have to face new ones.

To commemorate deaths by violence we need two moments: first, a political moment, where grief and anger are focused on policy and cultural change; and second, a spiritual reflection where the ghosts are invited to speak to us in their particularity and the perpetrators are banished to obscurity.

In the second, traditional sense of "vigil" we can commit to being awake to the past, open to the future, and to asking the spirits of those who have passed to guide, comfort and inspire us.

Who, or what do we evoke when we refuse sleep by holding a vigil? If, in answering this we ever find ourselves replying to violence and exclusion with new forms of the same, then we have erased the particularity of the loss and the crimes behind it.

This Halifax Humanities anthology is itself a kind of commemoration and, as a friend reminded me, we should mark the goods that we create together and hold in common.[11]

---

11 Victoria Goddard is a Boethius and Dante scholar, the author of *Till Human*

Friendship is the vigilance of the every day.

What is a vigil?

It is a time of watchfulness, of being awake through the night.

Voices Wake Us (Halifax: Underhill Books, 2014) and the layout designer for this book.

MEMORY WORK IN THREE PARTS

SYLVIA D. HAMILTON

1

MEMORY IS A non-linear, non-chronological mobius strip; it is fluid, porous, a collage. Much remains unspoken about the historical fact that Nova Scotia was a slave society and the traces of its legacy haunt us still: in the names of prominent Nova Scotians, in street names, in archival records, and in churches. African people were present here from the earliest period of European colonization. I write about the traces, invisible to most eyes, that remain, the places carrying embedded memories of African peoples in Nova Scotia. Much depends on who is looking and what meaning comes with that look. Who remembers the people enslaved?

The interlocking themes of history, oral and written, memory, and location/space/place preoccupy me. I am interested in what memories have we failed to represent and what memories do we not want to represent and why? The enslavement of African-descended people in Canada sits at the cusp of these questions. I've faced silence when I explain that ministers, political figures, and business owners enslaved African people. There are wills on record bequeathing women, children, and men as part of household property to heirs and successors for ever and ever and ever; the women and girls were looked upon for their capability *to breed* more property as it were. The first enslaved people in what we now know as Canada were people of the First Nations who were enslaved by French colonists who later replaced them with African people.

When I walk along the Halifax waterfront I think of the young children who were bought and sold there—of a young African girl child sold along with hogsheads (barrels) of rum and sugar.

When I stand beside Halifax's St. Paul's Church, I think of the enslaved Africans who were baptized there to "save their souls" but their Black bodies were not their own. Many ran, took their lives into their own hands, took freedom, and escaped. I call them *Freedom Runners.* Early Halifax newspapers document their quest for freedom in the form of advertisements taken out by "owners" trying to reclaim their so-called property. They offered rewards for re-capture.

> *This is my history. This is our collective history*
> *whether we choose to remember it or not.*

My ancestors, the Black Refugees from the War of 1812, were Freedom Runners: they, like thousands of others, escaped from plantations in Georgia and Virginia, fought with the British, and sailed to Nova Scotia after the war as free people under the British Crown. 2014 marked the 170th anniversary of the Beechville Baptist Church, founded by families, including my own, who descended from the Black Refugees. The first name for our community was Refugee Hill. When I was a child, revival services at our church were emotional and exciting. The first voice rose to begin a spiritual. Quickly, as if on cue, other voices joined in until the whole congregation was on its feet singing. Within minutes, adults, and even the smallest children, hands locked together, were at the front of the church moving and swaying in a ring shout. We kids loved it—slipped in a few extra body moves from the Friday night dances whenever we could. We didn't know what the words meant. Or why some of the older people were so overcome they would weep. We knew nothing about slavery, its relationship to us, or its story echoed in those powerful, enduring songs.

> *I am on an exploratory journey, trying to understand, trying to unlock that*
> *trapdoor of memory. What does one do with memories, real or Imagined,*

of moments when the personal takes flight, converting itself into something, not quite, but still recognizable?

2

MY MOTHER, DR. Marie Nita Waldron Hamilton, was a school teacher. She became a teacher because Black women were not allowed to enter nursing. She took me with her sometimes when she went to other communities to teach. I used to think I was going to school. I remember sitting in a desk at the front of the class with a piece of paper and a pencil, listening to mom talk. The other kids called her "teacher" or "Mrs. Hamilton." But she was my mom. I thought I was doing schoolwork because I was there with the rest of the children. How I came to be there I can't remember. How old could I have been? Obviously not school age, otherwise I would have been at our segregated school in Beechville. Where was my brother Wayn? He was only two years younger than I. Was someone keeping him at home? Mom boarded with Mrs. Diggs in East Preston. I remember she had a store in the lower part of the house; we slept in the upstairs. I went to Upper Hammonds Plains with her too where we stayed with Cleo and Aubrey Whiley. He had a large sawmill where he and his family made barrels and crates. The Whiley Mill was one of many mills that operated in the community for generations. When time came to actually go to school, I was ready and eager. Mrs. Marion Skinner was our teacher. We had several grades in the one room. She was the authority, much to the chagrin of my older brothers and sisters. I would correct them with the "But Mrs. Skinner said" phrase. Whatever she said was right.

We learned our times tables and knew our spellings. When called upon we would stand straight beside our desk, hands by our sides, to answer her questions, or do her bidding.

Repeat your 5 times tables: five times one is five, five times two is ten, five
times three is fifteen, five times four is twenty, five times five is twenty-five ...

I liked twenty-five, not sure why. Just something about that number.

And we said the Lord's Prayer. Not sure if we sang *God Save the Queen* but I think so because otherwise how would I know it by heart? A curious memory fragment is this: when I went to Lakeside School, the white school, I encountered Catholic students for the first time. They were taken out of class for some religious reason. Catechism I imagine now. And there was a pledge that we all said in that school. I now know it was some modified version of the American pledge to the flag, the American flag. Why we said it, I have no idea; otherwise, how would I know it by heart. My oldest sister Ada remembers it too:

> *I pledge allegiance to this flag and to the nation for which it stands one nation under God with liberty and justice for all ...*

It is a puzzle to this day why it repeats itself so easily in my mind. I do not want it to. Worse than those musical earworms.

Now back to Mrs. Skinner.

She was proper. She was an African Baptist churchwoman. She made sure you did your homework, came around and looked at how you did your printing. You erased it if it was not to her standard, a goal hardly anyone could reach. Her handwriting was beautiful, flawless. She taught us to be polite and respectful. I remember one day we were given medicine on sugar cubes. For polio maybe. We lined up. We took cod liver oil on a spoon and were vaccinated. A nurse came to our school, rubbed a small swab on an arm, and stuck in a needle. A day or two later, a scab appeared and it left a mark. An oval shaped one but not a perfect oval. You were not to pick at the scab because it might get infected. *Leave it alone*, we were told. Well tell a kid not to do something. So there were a few who had second visits with the nurse when she came back because the scab was oozing something awful. Those kids emerged with a bandage on their arms and were told, *do-not-take it off*, the nurse will return.

We did memory work, memorized poems, then stood to recite them.

> *Abou ben adam may his tribe increase, awoke one night from a deep dream of peace. And saw within the moonlight in his room ... making [something, something] a wish ...*

In Flanders Fields the poppies blow, beneath the crosses row on row, that mark our place and in the sky, the larks still bravely singing fly ...

I think that I shall never see, a poem lovely as a tree ...

At Sunday School we memorized the Psalms and passages from various chapters of the Bible, especially the book of John, Chapter 14. Segregation in education meant that many people in the community had limited formal education. The Bible they knew and taught it to us with care and conviction. We knew the books of the Bible, both the Old and New Testaments. When I entered Acadia University, one of the required courses was English Bible 100, the study of the Bible as text (King James version, of course), as literature. I was taken with the complexity of the Book of Job. I began to understand some of the underlying meaning of the phrase "to have the patience of Job" in the face of unrelenting suffering.

3

Waiting for God

Walking in Shelburne where the graveyard sits
eyeing the Court House. Where the Anglican Church
looks from the other side of the road:
Come to worship, Leave to serve.
In Paradise or in Hell, Who can choose?

Voices rise, echoes of time interrupted.
Job asks shall we accept
good from God and not adversity?

Here are the dust-caked children of Palestine,
digging in the rubble to find Grandma's book of stories,
the baby doll and carriage, the old football, the radio.
They look to God asking where is our state of grace.

In Chibok, Nigeria, a father sits
clutching her torn picture. He wept
like they said Jesus did. The shortest
verse in the Bible. Why did they steal his girl?
He longs for her life in the Sambisa Forest.
Beside his bed he keeps her name on a lined
page torn from her scribbler. Repeating her name
every night in a whisper until sleep overtakes him.

He would not eat, his wife said.
Every morning he sits on a small chair
stationed outside beside the door.
Last night, she said, he gave up.
When he went to bed he called a truce,
made peace with death.

We were young together once
alone against the sky.
Which side of the road
do you want to be on you asked:
the history side or the other?
Which side of the road
are you on, you on, do you want to be on?

Wait until that bend where the roads meet
at the switchback. Sure, it's never easy, I said,
Do we reject wrong only to think about right?

Let us not compare atrocities,
Let us not be consumed by guilt,
Let us press our faces to the wounds of history,
Let us open our hearts to the songs of justice.

EARL SHORRIS:
Sophos *and* Agape *in Halifax Humanities*

ANGUS JOHNSTON

> No moment in the teaching of philosophy will equal that of
> the decision by Socrates not to take Crito's offer of escape from
> death, but the end of the *Nicomachean Ethics* leaves the students
> awed at the discovery of their own possibility as reflective be-
> ings.[1]

DURING ONE OF his visits to Halifax Humanities, Earl Shorris taught
a seminar on Cervantes. The students and the rest of us had been looking
forward to the class for a month and it did not disappoint. In his version of
the "Socratic" manner, Earl asked question after question about the term
"irony" used by a contemporary writer in reference to *Don Quixote*. Laura
Penny, one of our most dedicated volunteer profs, had sat quietly with the
students. But now she asked the group about the term "ambiguity" in the
same text and its possible relation to irony. Earl turned on her abruptly
and asked "And who made you a student in this class?" All went still. Then
Bonita Shepherd, a student sitting beside Earl, brought her passionate fist
down on the table, startling all of us once again, and said "Ah, that's just
Laura. She sits with us, argues with us, all the time. She is one of us." Earl
accepted this in the midst of nodding heads and went on to lead a very fine
seminar.

That incident points to hard questions about teaching, especially in

---

1   Earl Shorris, *Riches for the Poor: The Clemente Course in the Humanities* (W.W.
Norton & Co., 2000). Location 2759.

programs modeled on Earl's groundbreaking "Clemente" programmes. Earl Shorris stressed the joy, equality, and community that resulted from reading great texts. At the same time, he wrestled with the dangers of making the class an end in itself. For Earl, the free contemplation outlined by Aristotle in his *Ethics* is not as important as moral autonomy for the development of political personhood.

In *Riches for the Poor* Earl argues that the poor in America are kept poor by a "surround of force" which keeps them always "reacting" to life as against "reflecting."[2] For Earl, "power" stems from the ability to reflect on one's situation sufficiently to become "political," and this means to have the "autonomy" to create the conditions for communal life instead of being subject to, determined by pre-existing social conditions.

Earl always taught with purpose: he aimed to bring autonomy and responsibility out in students. Earl saw dangers in the Halifax Humanities' confusion of teacher with student, with the lure of potentially endless contemplation, and the possibility that our course would become an end in itself, even a social escape.

Earl was a great friend of our program as well as our ardent critic. At this ten year mark, it is simply imperative to turn our attention to what he found troubling, flawed, as well as fertile and revealing in our Halifax adaptation of his Clemente Course in the Humanities.

I first met Earl at a conference in San Francisco in 2000. He gave a plenary address on the programmes he had founded or helped found in Manhattan in 1995 and in other cities in the years following. He spoke about the "surround of force." For him, various forms of aid, social programs, and generally "the war on poverty" simply substitute one form of force for another—what he sometimes referred to as "mobilization." His insight was that a study of the humanities can bring about a substantial change in a person: a moment of free "reflection" rather than incessant "reaction" to external necessity. This first taste of "autonomy" opens the possibility for the poor to enter into the "public space," the political.[3] Earl writes of his

---

2   L 1112.

3   " ... there is a simple proof of political thinking by most people in every cul-

"Clemente" program: "if there is a political bias in the course, it is against mobilization and for autonomy."[4]

This is a subtle and difficult notion. As someone who has spent his life teaching the humanities, I was intrigued, especially by the notion of sharing the joys of great texts with those outside of educational institutions. Earl and I fell in together after his address, ended up having supper, and talked well into the evening.

I came home to Halifax full of hope that we could do something here and with the beginnings of friendship with this remarkable man. (Aristotle calls this beginning *eunoia*, i.e., we were "well-minded" towards each other.) It turned out that Earl was way ahead of me in relation to doing something in Halifax. Through an article he had written in *Harper's Magazine*, Earl had inspired one of the pillars of our city: the Reverend Doctor Gary Thorne had already approached an academic department to try to organize a course along "Clemente" lines. In the end, Gary involved the remarkable fundraiser Susan Barthos, an independent board was set up by 2003, and we launched "Halifax Humanities" in 2005.

For news of us, advice for us, and continued support of us, Earl would call about once a month in the early years. He admitted to me that he fell into the habit of phoning Saturday morning because I was often out and that meant he could talk with my wife, Sandra Haycock, instead. Anyone who knows my wife will understand this. I would come home after chores and find them laughing on the phone. For much of one winter he tried to persuade me—not seriously I think—to go to Buenos Aires with him where they wanted to set up a Clemente program. As if I could be much help! He did end up going to a number of cities in South America and across the globe. In *The Art of Freedom* he narrated these encounters and especially the people he came to know. He became close with many here in Halifax, and he wrote especially of his affection for Gary Thorne and our Director, Mary Lu Redden.

Earl believed that much that we did in Halifax Humanities was right,

ture in the United States: they are not poor." (*Riches for the Poor*, L 1244)

4   L 145.

but he did raise significant concerns. In the following, I treat aspects of his critique which seem to me to circle round the central question of "rigor."

Governance

EARL JUDGED THAt our board did not represent our community, especially the segment of it we particularly sought to serve. We have had too few African Canadians serving on the Board and have recruited only a few black students in our ten years. Earl found Halifax "more divided along racial lines" than the American south.[5] He saw in the Board and especially in the founding chair, Gary Thorne, a spirit of *agape*, of fellow spiritual love, which moved him deeply and disturbed his assumption that the courses he founded were focused on *sophos*, wisdom, brought out by "rigor." Earl found that the Halifax course was "different," even from other Canadian programmes, and that it was not easily understood. Earl Shorris affirmed Halifax Humanities heartily, but as an alternative, even an aberration, from his standard Clemente Course in the Humanities.

Teachers and Director

EARL ADMIRED THE Director, Mary Lu Redden, but again found a spirit of *agape* which, again, gave him pause. Not that *sophos* was left out. Our course, compared to more standard Clemente courses, was, he thought, "a softer version, designed to accommodate students wounded by nature as well as by society."[6]

At his first meeting with some Halifax Humanities teaching staff, Earl outlined the normal Clemente standards: the teachers should be well paid, widely published, and distinguished in their fields. Halifax Humanities faculty are different: we are volunteers, at various stages in our careers, and we happily teach outside of our expertise. As Dr Neil Robertson, a leader

---

5   Shorris, *The Art of Freedom*, L 1716.
6   Shorris, *The Art of Freedom*, L 1707.

among us, blurted out: "So none of us is qualified to teach in this course!"

Earl's Clemente model depended on American assumptions about funding and the specialization implied in his five-course, highly focused curriculum. For our faculty, university employment was already a kind of public position and so, while this was work done freely, it was made possible by our partially publicly-funded collegial life. In the end, Earl affirmed enthusiastically the quality of teaching by academic volunteers in this interdisciplinary great texts course.

Curriculum

EARL ALMOST ALWAYS included Sophocles' *Antigone* in his Clemente courses. Anyone who has encountered that text knows its beauty and its stark focus on clear issues. It strikes an immediate chord with most students. Our students in Halifax debated whether the girl, Antigone, had the divine right and responsibility to bury her traitor brother in contravention of the King's edict forbidding it. "Suppose she had wanted to honour Hitler in this way, that he was her brother?" one student snapped during the debate. In *Riches for the Poor*, Earl tells of a woman who revealed that she had lived the tragic conflict between family and state, as she explained: "I had to turn my daughter in to the FBI."[7]

For Earl, the reaction of the student to *Antigone* expressed the rigor and focus of applying the ancient Greek questions of the tragedy directly and immediately to today's dilemmas. The great texts of the past speak directly and immediately to our own conditions, in Shorris' view. The curriculum should always bring the texts to bear on our current situation. That being said, the merely practical should, in his view, never be the direct end of the courses: the transition from "reaction" to "reflection" will be a "by-product of taking possession of some significant part of the riches of the humanities."[8] "Significant" is perhaps the central term here.

---

7 Shorris, *The Art of Freedom: Teaching the Humanities to the Poor* (W.W. Norton & Co., 2013)., L 2131.

8 Shorris, *Riches for the Poor*, L 2619.

One of the inspirations for Earl's course is Niecie Walker, a woman Earl met in a prison in New York State. He spoke of her the first night I met him and referred back to her and consulted her as he developed the Clemente programmes. Niecie spoke of the liberating "moral life of downtown" by which she meant the great art pulsing from Lincoln Center. In Earl's view, Niecie "followed the same path that had led to the invention of politics in ancient Greece. She had learned to reflect."[9]

The American Clemente curriculum follows the five parts of humanistics set out by Petrarch in the late medieval period: philosophy, literature, art, history, and logic, taught as five separate courses. Common to the courses, speaking perhaps over-generally, is the focus on the students recognizing their "autonomy." American history is set out to enable students to see their situation and to move from "reaction" in the "surround of force" to a moment of freedom in their situation. To go from "reaction" to "reflection" is the key. So, for instance, in philosophy there are definite steps—Hobbes' individualism, Kant's rational self-governance, Mill's utilitarian liberalism—which give the students three clear ways of analyzing present and pressing questions. A clarity concerning the number and nature of these steps allows for a defined "rigor" on the part of the teachers and students.

The Halifax Humanities 101 curriculum is more Hegelian in character.[10] A single sweeping course treats the art, literature, history, and philosophy of the West in the form of primary works. These texts Earl Shorris admired and in general he was happier with our curriculum than with those of many developing Clemente-type programmes. But because our emphasis is on the independence of moments in Western developments as well as their mutual dependence, we work first to distinguish between reflection in Athens and reflection in Manhattan, and then relate them. Our demand is that students step out of their own time at each point of the curriculum. Once you make that your aim it becomes more of a question how they are to step back into their own. The "byproduct," political autonomy, is

---

9   Shorris, *Riches for the Poor*, L 1493.

10   In the courses on Art History Shorris comments that a Hegelian model is often used, but the historical "end of art" teaching is avoided.

in no way assured when the curriculum itself and its historical moments are the focus for both teachers and students. And there is a passivity built into the curriculum: I am sure we include much of the "insignificant" part of the riches of the humanities, the part that does not relate to "saving politics."

This may be a central point in understanding why our "outcomes" are not as clear as in so many of the Clemente programmes. And, because our end is less defined, so is our excellence and our "rigor."

Students

ACCEPTANCE INTO THE American Clemente programs differs from pro-gramme to programme. "People are poor when they concede that they are poor, when there is no saving politics in their lives. That became the criterion for selection."[11] The desire to do the course, the ability to read a newspaper, and some level of need are really the prime criteria for our programme. Our students are older on average and more affected by mental and physical problems—as Earl put it, wounded by nature and society. We have accepted students who have done substantial university work, even graduated. We have also had students who were taking the course because they had recognized aspects of "saving politics" rather than because they were in need of it. Although students—not a large percentage—have gone on to university work, our course is not for credit, nor in its present state could it be. We have no objective requirements, no formal written assign-ments, no exams. We do indeed lack the formal rigor that Earl stresses: "Rigor is the truest measure of respect."[12]

---

11   Shorris, *Riches for the Poor*, L 2029.
12   Shorris, *Riches for the Poor*, L 2443.

The Irony of Rigor

I BEGAN WITH the contrast Earl drew between the moral decision of Socrates to die and the contemplation of truth as expressed in Aristotle. Moral courage was more primary than contemplation for Earl. The way in which he brought out that central contrast most clearly in his own writing was through reflection on three ancient thinkers: Socrates, Protagoras, and Plato. For Earl, when Protagoras says that "man is the measure of all things," he is expressing the heart of Socratic teaching. In contrast, Plato's interpretation of Socrates is as searching for an objective "Good" which unites the human with an absolute measure, a higher realm, and a hierarchy of being. In Earl Shorris' view Plato opens the door for hierarchical authority and thus submission of our selves to another.[13] Earl judges that we can find the good in the self directly.

The Hegelian approach of Halifax Humanities sides more with Plato than with Protagoras. The contemporary self is an end in itself, the Good, because the history of the West has brought the self and the objectivity that Plato demanded together—in modernity. Our curriculum seeks, in my view, to go through the cultural journey which can remind us of this profound modern self—rooted in, but radically different from, the ancient.

In Plato's dialogue, *The Protagoras*, the arguments on behalf of a human measure of virtue and those which make that problematic are brought out. Protagoras holds that virtue can be taught—it is his life's work—and Socrates (in this Platonic portrayal) is skeptical. The argument turns, at the end, on whether "courage" is a form of knowledge or something beyond that. The irony is explicit in the final arguments. Socrates states that the "argument" itself addresses the two interlocutors: Protagoras, who has argued that virtue can be taught, is now arguing that "courage" is beyond knowledge and teaching; and Socrates, who has argued that it cannot be taught, is now arguing that "courage" is a form of knowledge, and thus teachable. I judge that "the argument" between Earl Shorris and the Halifax

---

13   Shorris all too readily sees Plato through the work of Alan Boom—an unfortunate and partial view of Plato, in my view.

Humanities programme could address both sides in a similar way.

Shorris is most confident of the direct value, the Goodness, of the contemporary self and yet his course is designed not to affirm that self but to transform it: to inject the "courage" to be autonomous.

The Halifax Humanities programme is skeptical of the value of a contemporary self that has lost sight of the development of the tradition, yet we trust that self to find its own way if the material is presented to it: we count on the "courage" of our students. The first position leads to a focus, to the defined steps towards autonomy and to a notion of "rigor"—one can define success or failure in the clarity of the steps.

For the Halifax program, the steps are presented in a "rigorous" curriculum but really are there to wait upon the students. This waiting is not easily measurable in terms of progress. Our "outcomes" are not as clear as in many of the Clemente programmes. This may also help to explain why our recruitment is by no means straightforward and why funding (which is often directly related to outcomes) is so problematic. And because our end is less defined, our students are less "rigorously" trained.[14]

Sophos *and* Agape *in Halifax Humanities*

THE LATE KING'S professor, Robert Crouse, used the image of solar systems to speak about education. "Teaching is not showing students what sun they should orbit but rather what sun they are orbiting." Using this image writ large in a "galaxy" of suns, I see our students and those of most "Clemente" courses to be akin to comets. They are indeed circling their suns but not in the usual "planetary" manner. When they enroll it is not clear to us or to themselves where their "sun" lies. The temptation I see in Earl Shorris' position is that teaching the humanities leads to rigorously finding one's "sun" but does so primarily in order to promote the final "byproduct"—in the image, the center of the galaxy. That is the universal

---

14   Shorris notes that all of the students in his first course were enrolled in colleges or universities or were fully employed upon completion save one; she had been fired from a restaurant for trying to start a union.

center they "should be circling." This is his notion of *sophos* and it will lead the way out of poverty.

In contrast, the temptation in our course, tending to *agape*, (or *philia*, as Gary Thorne suggests) is to reflect on the path the "comet" takes, but too readily to assume a relation to the center of the galaxy and never make clear the distinct solar system through which, for each individual, that relation is accomplished. Our work may bring out the "center" for students but we do not turn them towards it. We leave that to them.

From the start, Halifax Humanities has served our curriculum above all and that curriculum is rigorous and demanding for both those who teach and those who learn. Do we need to focus more on the students and "outcomes"? Are we demanding enough of ourselves and of them? Does our "rigor" or lack thereof explain why we do not attract younger and/or more diverse students?

Earl Shorris was a bit of a comet himself, rare, and a privilege to encounter. Understanding his "sun" started Halifax Humanities on its course more than ten years ago. Now that he has gone, it shines still, and I know will help us to see our own center for years to come.

HOME AND AWAY

VALEDICTORY ADDRESS 2010
Grace Morris

CHRISTMAS GROTTO
Bonita Shepherd

WEATHER PATTERNS
Laura Legere

FEELING ALONE
Barbara Whitby

ONE STAR
Rose Adams

TORN
Madeline Reid Comeau

DARKSIDE: THE GHETTO
Corrine Gritten

ALICE AND WONDERLAND
Howard Epstein

THE SONG OF ODYSSEUS: LIFE LESSONS LEARNED
Vernon Provencal

SIMON DUBNOW: JEWISH HISTORIAN, DIASPORA NATIONALIST AND
SOCIAL HEGELIAN
Roni Gechtman

THE SMALLEST OF KINDNESSES: 'THE SEMINAR' REDEFINED
Scott MacDougall

VALEDICTORY ADDRESS
2010

GRACE MORRIS

GOOD AFTERNOON EVERYONE, and welcome. Thank you for coming to show your support for the people you love. I have been given the honour of saying a few words on behalf of the class. I hope I don't disappoint them.

When I first began this course I wasn't sure that I could put two thoughts together, let alone express my opinion about anything. I have rediscovered my ability to think, the necessity to pause and consider how others think and feel, and to learn from that experience—to know that I'm more than just a mother or a wife but also a thinking thing.

My classmates have taught me to look beneath the surface, not to judge a book by its cover. They are the people I have depended on to refresh my batteries, the faces I have been glad to see every week, and I hope they have felt the same because I will miss them.

My time with this programme has made my life more enriched, more interesting, and definitely more busy. I hope to continue to learn and experience new things as I go forward and deal with life's ups and downs. This course has made me stronger just by making me realize that I can accomplish the things that I put my mind to—that I can grow and learn new things and grasp difficult concepts, if only I try.

As the new year begins and we are not there, it will be sad but it opens up opportunities for new experiences and chances to learn and grow. I truly believe that if you do not continue to learn you will stagnate and cease to be. I have gone through many changes in the time since I read the advertisement for Halifax Humanities, as I am sure my classmates have. It was like a window opening, a breath of fresh air. And now the door is open and we are ready to go through. I see great things for all of us if we choose to go through.

It has been a great experience with all of you but I'd like to thank Mary Lu, without whom it would have been near impossible to stay on track, for her gentle guidance and subtle directions. And to our most superb teachers—no one could ask for any better—our many thanks and praise: great minds who have come to give us pearls of wisdom, who have challenged us to think and feel, and who have given us great joy—we will never forget you.

CHRISTMAS GROTTO

BONITA SHEPHERD

THE REST OF the year, for three hundred and fifty eight days of the year, it's known as the living room. It's where we watched tv news, or soap operas, game shows, whatever the oldest person in the room wanted to watch. That is what the rest of us had to watch, like it or not. The other seven days of the year were spent getting ready for that one day, the one day when everyone smiled. There was toxic stuff to be sprayed on the windows, especially in the living room, in those days. We called it snow. It was stenciled all over the windows—festive, eh! The ceiling was decorated with streamers from corner to corner. The walls also didn't escape the shiny foil streamers. They may have been tacky, but they were durable.

Then, there where the decorations sat on the coffee table, this table made of metal rods that were bent in half and had a top that set inside of the metal frame. The top was made out of a small plank of wood, not a nice piece of glass. It probably would have ended up getting broken anyway, with five kids. It was a table that my older brother had made one year in wood shop at school—if you put a long enough table cloth over it, it looked normal enough.

As the week went on the intensity of the smile day grew. What would the big man fit down the chimney this year? We didn't know exactly what would appear, and if there would be batteries to run it—not usually.

There were usually clothes, some fruit and candy in a stocking that you hung up yourself the night before. There were some other toys. And then there was the dinner. This was a feast that would have made Henry VIII envious. There was turkey, enough to put everyone asleep after the meal.

There was duck, because that was what Bing (Dad's nickname) wanted. There was lobster or crab for salads, there were pickles, and at least two kinds of sweet jelly. There also were cranberries, dressing and just about any vegs that you could think of. There was gumdrop cake, pound cake, or mincemeat pie, with sauce, or, if you didn't want any of that, there was also the option of apple pie with ice cream. Are you full yet?

There was cherry syrup and gin for pink ladies, or eggnog if anyone wanted some, and finally, of course, to wash down all of this there was Baby Duck wine.

All this was to come on smile day; it was getting into the Christmas grotto to get the day started that was the challenge.

My father was aware of just how excited we would be so he stood guard at the entrance to the grotto until it felt like forever, and getting up in the night to go to the bathroom at night didn't work either. We just had to wait until the actual day to start, it was one time that we all seemed happy, and we all smiled.

WEATHER PATTERNS

LAURA LEGERE

For we don't have tornadoes here
The air is too cold and lazy to move that forcefully
Fog and damp is here to camp ...
    And moderate to stay

Fires, well we've had a few
They never last for long
An acre here, an acre there
    No catastrophic wrong

We've never had an earthquake local
This land is just too damn content to shake and heave
The wind it blows, oh heaven knows
    But shelter is all we really need

I know there's floods and mudslides too
I've seen them on TV
And although I don't know Mother Nature
She's been a friend to me
She has never pushed her weight around, just a little ocean sand
For where we live, it's safe to say
Is firmly in the palm of God's hand ... Amen

This poem is really about the power of words and was written for my son Nick who had to read a poem in the auditorium in front of the whole school at nine years of age (so it is really intended for children). But he got a standing ovation and was asked for multiple encores and it changed him in the most positive way ...

FEELING ALONE

BARBARA WHITBY

IT IS SEVEN in the evening, the time my parents usually leave for the pub. This is also the moment for me to beg silently that I will not cry or in any other way betray my fear. After all, I am nine years old.

Once the adults have disappeared into the darkness my attention sharpens. I listen, not just with my ears but with my entire body. When I touch the window with questioning fingers I can feel the distant thrum of engines that has set the glass to trembling. It declares the enemy presence long before the planes arrive.

The dim blue bulb overhead swings from its frayed cord in an ever-widening arc. My mother has swathed the shade with her paisley scarf as added blackout protection and this act of caring makes me feel even more abandoned.

I am suddenly horrified at being pinpointed by brilliant orange flares. They dominate the night sky and dramatize the crump after crump of exploding bombs. One lands next door but I do not hear it, I only know that my body is in shock, assaulted by a massive whoosh of energy. I cannot breathe: not in or out.

Walls are falling in slow motion. I fumble to lift my baby brother but I cannot release the catch of his crib and he will not let me pick him up. He screams and lashes out until I finally nuzzle his face against my shoulder. "There, there," I murmur, deeply comforted by his human presence in this chaos.

I snatch up a plate of cold fried potatoes and onions when we escape out the kitchen back door.

Our dog continuously yelps with terror as he crowds my heels. We make it to the Anderson air raid shelter in the garden. There is a stench, water has flooded in, but it still feels safer to hide there.

Sloshing my way in murky darkness I do not expect the dog to thrust his nose upwards. He knocks the plate from my grasp and the food is scattered. The sudden loss of the fried onions and potatoes, and even of their smell, seems a greater burden to bear than all the other experiences of the night.

At last there is a noise of alarm and indignation as the adults return and see the damage. I call out and they find me. With weariness, exhausted by managing the baby for so long, I lift him towards my mother's figure where she blocks the shelter entrance. Her flashlight, carefully guarded by her cupped hands in obedience to blackout regulations, illuminates first my brother, then my face, and finally the muddied plate.

I expect to hear my mother say how thankful she is to find we have not been killed and to receive a little praise for getting us out. Instead I find myself cowering at her angry accusation. "How dare you!" She is almost screaming at me. "You stole the supper!"

Finally overwhelmed, I appear defiant but inwardly someone begs: "hug me."

Mama leaves it to my father, once I climb shakily from the shelter with the scared dog, to show a greater tenderness. He pats the cowering animal and presses my cheek against his harsh tweed trouser leg. Then raising my chin with one finger he ruffles my hair and says in a bright tone, "Jerries didn't get you this time did they? Tough little monkey. Chip off the old block, aren't you? Eh?"

ONE STAR[1]

ROSE ADAMS

I stand in New York
drenched with the light from one star
in front of the dark cypress flames.
Refusing to move for photographers,
cell phones snapping a digital view,
I stand, slowly absorbing the light of
Van Gogh's cell of darkness.

Sky sprinkled
with cake decorations
yellow, greens and blues
in swirls of icing.

At the elementary school,
after a grade two study of Van Gogh
my son painted his memory
of the star. *Mommy, which one is mine?*
We stare at twenty blue sheets
each with a luminous shape of yellow
suspended in the corner.

I am dazzled
by sharp fragments
of the universe.

---

1   Based on the paintings"The Starry Night" by Vincent Van Gogh 1899 and "Response to The Starry Night" by Manuel Moncayo-Adams 2006.

Originally published in the online poetry journal, RHYTHM, (Dalhousie University), March 2008.

TORN

MADELINE REID COMEAU

I GOT TO leave home at the tender age of sixteen and it was none too soon as far as I was concerned. Any place had to be more exciting than the boring little place in Newfoundland where I grew up. I don't even remember hugging my Mom and Dad as I went out the door. I doubt I even waved to my three younger siblings as the car that was taking me to the train station drove away. I honestly don't remember shedding a tear or snatching a backward glance. I couldn't get away fast enough.

What was there to miss, really? Certainly not my last year of high school with Sister Mary of the rote memory for every subject. A rotund woman on a mission, her pedagogical style suggested that she had invented an eleventh commandment: *Thou shalt not exhibit any creativity.* And being a nice girl, except for those few occasions when that beast of my imagination escaped from captivity, causing Sister Mary's face suddenly to turn a deep shade of scarlet, I would mount a quick retreat, chanting in my head *Please God, make June come fast, please, please.*

June did, of course, arrive in due time, only to be followed by two months of summer boredom. It didn't help that, despite my teased hair and thick mascara-caked eyelashes, I could barely pass for thirteen. Not that there was a big supply of guys or that my mother would let me hang out with them anyway. For reasons I have yet to figure out, there were also no girlfriends on the scene. Maybe after so many years of not being allowed outside of my yard, I had missed the boat on that as well. My salvation, I knew this for sure, would start with university where I would find a nice guy and eventually get married. And, if I was really lucky, I might even end

193

up living on the mainland.

Most of my classmates, unlike me, eventually returned home to the Port au Port peninsula. I continued to pride myself on how lucky I was to have gotten away. For quite a while, that is. And then, as a young mother living on the mainland with time to kill when the babies took a nap, I suddenly got the urge to write poetry. As I arranged and rearranged words on scraps of paper, I was overcome by memories of home, warm loaves of bread ready for a coat of blackstrap molasses, juicy raspberries hitting my taste buds in quick succession, and the comforting, mellow aroma of Edgeworth pipe tobacco wafting through the living room.

Playing with words worked its magic. It started with a simple little poem called *Dactyls for Dad*. I didn't set out to go there, to revisit the place I was so eager to leave as a teenager, but neither did I resist. And more than thirty years later I can still revisit *home* whenever the mood hits me—word by word and line by line. I no longer feel torn.

Dactyls for Dad

Trotting to school on your coat-tails
Camel hair split at the back
Baseball while dinner is cooking
Homerun but the runner falls flat
Berries to pick midst the brambles
A bounty of bites empty pail
Lunch boxes filled for a picnic
Black clouds sad tears 'fore the gale
Trapped in my sandpail 'til noon hour
A soldier who's scared as can be
Kicking my way from the pantry
No bogey-man's gonna get me.
Slow down you'll trip and you'll stumble
But an inner voice won't let me be.

$\mathcal{D}$ARKSIDE: THE $\mathcal{G}$HETTO

CORRINE GRITTEN

Darkside
city glide
life will take *you* for a ride
old folks
poor blokes
rich men think you just a joke
hooker stroll
strollers roll
teenage mothers on the dole
street fights
turf rights
gunfire in the dead of night
ill health
night stealth
tie it down or lose your wealth
arson car
culprits are
not so really very far
johns cruise
girls lose
shards of soul and pay their dues
death toll
honour roll
score another murd'rous goal
boombeat
summer heat

young guns race cars down the street
take down
cops frown
black men hand-cuffed on the ground
dumpster dive
half alive
you can't pay me for this jive
siren wails
hard as nails
inner-city urban tale
bedbugs
street drugs
sanity pulls at the plug

and me.

ALICE AND WONDERLAND

Halifax Humanities 101—Alice lecture— April 15, 2014

HOWARD EPSTEIN

THANK YOU FOR the opportunity to talk a bit about one of my favourite books, Lewis Carroll's *Alice's Adventures in Wonderland*.

There is a huge amount of writing about *Alice*. There is literary analysis. There are biographies of its author. There are references to it wherever you turn—from newspaper articles to novels. In discussing it at all, I feel hesitant. Dissection is what occurs to something deceased: there is an element of attempting to pin down things, which is not my intention. I hope to stimulate thought rather than confine it.

There are many editions of the book, which was first published in 1865. The different editions vary primarily as to the illustrators, though there are also shortened versions intended for very young children. Carroll used Sir John Tenniel as his illustrator. Carroll himself drew pictures for the very first version of the book which he offered as a gift to the original Alice, Alice Liddell, who was one of the daughters of the Dean of the Oxford University college where Carroll (as Charles Lutwidge Dodgson, his proper name) taught mathematics all his life. Since then dozens of illustrators have taken up *Alice* and its characters, including Sir Arthur Rackham (1907) and Salvador Dali (1968). But Tenniel's drawings seem just right for the book. Certainly they have persisted in the popular imagination, perhaps reinforced by the popular Disney animated film from 1951 that based its characters on the Tenniel drawings.

The edition I hope you use is one with Tenniel's drawings. They are easily available. *The Annotated Alice* with the glosses of mathematician and science writer Martin Gardner is a particularly useful edition. And it contains the companion piece, the sequel, *Through the Looking Glass* (1871). We are going to look only, or primarily, at the *Wonderland* book, though.

Alice is a classic. This is measured by popularity as demonstrated by how often it is quoted, how often its characters are referred to (the Queen of Hearts, the Mad Hatter, the Cheshire Cat, Alice herself). There are influences on other writers (James Joyce, Vladimir Nabokov, Paul Auster). There are all the translations (more than sixty other languages, including a 1923 translation into Russian by Nabokov writing as V.V. Sirin) plus films and plays.

But is it read? There is something of a sad statement about *Alice* as a classic: "no educated person's library would be complete without it, and so the book is never taken out of the library."[1] This suggestion that *Alice* is not actually read so much as known about might well be accurate and, if accurate, a bit depressing. Because the book reads well. *Alice* is especially a classic of English literature, a part of English self-definition or self-consciousness. This is in part because of the independence of mind that Alice shows and in part because of the abundance of eccentrics in the *Alice* books, characters bordering on madness: both of these seem to speak to something the English see in themselves.

Alice is also, of course, a children's book. Its hero is a child. It is full of pictures and conversations. It is treated, though, as also a book for adults. It is also a particular kind of children's book. It is not a fairy tale or a book of folklore. It is not sentimental, or only occasionally. It celebrates and is respectful towards children—Alice is a strong character: curious, thoughtful, logical, polite. The book makes fun of sentimentality and strict moralizing, which had characterized some earlier children's books, such as Charles Kingsley's *Water Babies* or the poetry of Isaac Watts. In fact, it treats the adult world as arbitrary, emotional, illogical, pompous, and as generally ill-

---

[1] A paraphrase from G.K. Chesterton, *A Handful of Authors* (New York: Sheed and Ward, 1953).

equipped to deal well with child-rearing. So it offers a perspective that might well appeal to child readers.

What happens in *Alice's Adventures in Wonderland*? On a warm Spring day, sitting by a river bank in company with her older sister, Alice falls asleep. She sees a white rabbit dressed in clothes and with a pocket watch. Curious, she follows the rabbit into a hole where she tumbles down and finds herself caught in a room where she changes size after drinking from a bottle. Swimming in a pool of tears, she meets a mouse and recites poetry to it, with problematic results. The white rabbit appears again, taking up his dropped fan; she shrinks as she waves it. She meets up with a variety of talking animals who are wet from being in the pool. They dry themselves by having a "caucus race." Alice manages to frighten or insult some of them. The white rabbit appears and sends her to get him some gloves. Arriving at his cottage, she eats and grows so large she fills the house, only shrinking again when she is tossed some cakes to eat. She runs off, now three inches high, and meets a caterpillar sitting on a mushroom and smoking a hookah. Following his advice she eats some of the mushroom, grows very tall, then shrinks. She visits the home of the Duchess where an invitation is delivered from the Queen of Hearts to play croquet and where a chaotic kitchen (with a grinning cat) endangers a baby. Alice rescues the baby which turns into a pig. As she walks through a wood, she meets the grinning cat which is in a tree; she is advised to visit the Mad Hatter or the March Hare. Arriving, she joins their tea-party. After a barbed conversation, she leaves, sees a door in a tree, enters, and finds herself back in the original hall. Adjusting her height, she is able to go through a small door and arrives in a garden, that of the Queen of Hearts whose court consists of playing cards. Offending soldiers are to have their heads chopped off (though the King quietly pardons them). A game of croquet is played with flamingos as mallets and hedgehogs as balls. The cat appears, though just its head. Alice leaves and meets the Gryphon and Mock Turtle by the sea where they dance the lobster quadrille. Then the trial of the Knave of Hearts starts. Evidence is taken, including from Alice who becomes enraged at the chaos of the trial, condemning the participants as nothing but a pack of cards. She is chased but then wakes up. She tells her dream to her sister who reflects to herself on Alice's future life, as a mother who might tell her own children this story.

I have left out some things, chiefly the reciting of poetry (which "comes out wrong") and which is so strongly a part of the book. What is apparent is that the story is very dream-like: it is a bit chaotic and repetitious and accepts very unusual things as normal. Carroll was one of his own best readers and the sequel, *Through the Looking Glass*, takes up all of the themes of *Alice's Adventures in Wonderland* in a more disciplined, structured, conscious way. Just as a small example, though both stories are dreams, *Through the Looking Glass* adopts the orderly layout of a chessboard to guide Alice's movements rather than the unstructured meandering of *Alice's Adventures in Wonderland*.

What are some of the themes of *Alice*? There is the interaction of adults with children. There is the ridiculousness of the adult world and its institutions (family, education, monarchy, the law, parties and other gatherings). There is death. There is the aspect of philosophy of finding morals in experience or tales. There is the problem of personal identity. There is language and logic. There are games and puzzles. There is the problem of emotions.

Death? Yes, indeed. There are constant jokes and references to death. The very first joke in the book is about death: as Alice is falling slowly down the rabbit hole, she says to herself that after the experience of such a long fall she would say nothing about it if she fell off the top of the house; to which the narrator adds, "which was very likely true," meaning she would probably die. The references abound: "Off with his head;" animals eating each other ("my cat Dinah loves to eat birds and mice"); unknown liquids might be poison; Alice's fear of being eaten, when she is very small; her fear for the baby being murdered by the chaos in its home. Death for Carroll is thematically related to eating, change, and growing up. Thus, the book is painfully aware that childhood is a transition phase; that it passes quickly, that adulthood comes inevitably, followed by extinction. Indeed, that children might not make it beyond childhood is a part of this preoccupation. Obliquely, to take this gloomy view gets at any religious theology of an afterlife. Religion is not satirized directly as are the law or family etc. but the implication is there to be drawn out.

Adults fare poorly in *Alice*. They are boring (reciting history lessons as a way to get dry); authoritarian, moralistic, and hypocritical (always scolding children; trying to teach them proper behaviour but not behaving well themselves); threatening ("off with her head"); angry (the Queen of Hearts); rude (the Duchess saying "You don't know much, and that's a fact," the Hatter calling her "stupid"); plagued by time (the White Rabbit fearing to be late); ageist (the Lory says "I am older than you and must know better"); easily offended (the caterpillar as to its height); conniving (the White Rabbit trying to get Alice in trouble with the Queen at the croquet game); and seemingly inebriated (the caterpillar smoking its hookah, the Frog Footman muttering to himself). Fundamentally, adults in *Alice* are unattractive, engaged in pointless activities, and seemingly incapable of conducting their business properly—the trial being a striking example.

The poetry that is recited, and that comes out all wrong, is mostly based either on traditional nursery rhymes like "The Queen of Hearts/She made some tarts"[2] or identifiable and popular (with adults) poems for children such as "Twinkle twinkle little star"[3] and "How doth the little busy bee,"[4] the poem that includes the lines "For Satan finds some mischief still/For idle hands to do." In Carroll's versions, the poems are just funny. But they are funny by taking the original message and twisting it. Thus Southey's "The Old Man's Comforts and How he Gained Them" (with the moral being "In the days of my youth I remembered my God/And He hath not forgotten my age," as if a bargain could be struck with the divine) becomes the story of the athletic old man Father William who enjoys life by eating, stands on his head, and avoids silly conversations. Or they dwell on the hard reality of life for animals (the turtle singing about turtle soup; the crocodile who "welcomes little fishes in/With gently smiling jaws!"). Or they are about

---

2   Date unknown (consult Opie & Opie, *Oxford Dictionary of Nursery Rhymes*) though in print 1782.

3   Jane Taylor, "The Star," *Rhymes For the Nursery*, 1806.

4   Isaac Watts, "Against Idleness and Mischief," *Divine Songs for Children*, 1715

abuse of children ("Speak roughly to your little boy/And beat him when he sneezes"). The undermining of an established Victorian order is enormous in this. Especially for *Alice*'s author, an ordained clergyman who came from an ecclesiastical family.

Language and logic are played with. Indeed, this is usually what is meant by casual references to something being "like Alice in Wonderland": the idea is that everything is topsy-turvy, illogical, nonsense. Alice herself is rigorously logical, even in baffling circumstances. Thus, at the tea party where she is told that everyone just keeps going on to the next place when the dishes are dirty, she wants to know what happens when they get back to the beginning again ("suppose we change the subject," says the Hare). Or she tries to work out the rules in her new universe: do eating and drinking now immediately change her size? Or there is play with language such as "Do bats eat cats? Do cats eat bats?" regarding which we are told that, since she did not know the answer to either question, it did not matter which way it was posed. Other aspects of philosophical discourse appear as when Alice struggles with her identity, wondering, since everything is so strange, if she is now someone else. She tests this hypothesis by trying to remember things (poetry mostly) and she is open to the possibility that the world is now something other than she had previously thought (animals talk; she might have become her friend Ada).

As with other dreams, the *Alice* story has often been analyzed as sexual allegory. The critic William Empson says it is only necessary to tell the story to see how blatant this aspect is. Alice goes down a hole into a confined space. An exit is available to an outside but the exit is small. She swims in a salty fluid. Later, in the garden she sought, she carries a flamingo, a pink bird with a long neck. While she holds it, the Duchess makes overtures to her, re-marking, "I dare say you're wondering why I don't put my arm round your waist: the reason is, that I'm doubtful about the temper of your flamingo."

And so on. It hardly seems likely that this view of *Alice* is incorrect. Undoubtedly there is a strong element of sexual preoccupation. It is, how-ever, hardly the whole story. Knowing what we do know of Carroll's life, it seems reasonable to suppose that the sexual element was unconscious, though likely related to the theme of the passage of time, growth, maturing, and death, along with the idea that remaining a child is a desirable thing.

Another modern view of *Alice* is to think of its drug implications. The most obvious episode is that of the caterpillar sitting on a mushroom and smoking a hookah. The eating of mushrooms and smoking of intoxicating substances are both now commonly known. To some extent they were in Victorian England as well. There is no compelling evidence to think Carroll was directing our attention to such activities. What does add to the Cater-pillar chapter as suggesting drug use is the overall dreaminess of the book, its alteration of a normal state to one of uncertainty. It is not, however, nec-essary to conclude that Carroll was pointing to drug use. Such a state can arise from a powerful imagination, or from rigorous thought, or from stress, or from some forms of mental illness. The modern fascination with Carroll shown by musicians known to have used drugs[5] indicates an identification with Carroll's writing but tells us nothing about Carroll himself.

Which brings us to Lewis Carroll—the Reverend Charles Dodgson—himself. Biography is far from a reliable way to approach works of fiction but investigation and speculation about an author's life is a field of its own that is interesting. For Carroll, biographers have always linked his life with his works. Born in 1832, Dodgson was one of eleven children of a clergy-man in rural England (a family of thirteen, like a pack of playing cards). He was educated at a boarding school, Rugby, and at Oxford. He took holy orders although he never took a living as a priest; he taught mathematics from 1851 to the end of his life in 1898, residing in Christ Church College. He never married. He had a stammer, suffered from migraine, and had some epileptic fits. In 1856 he took up photography and became a noted portrait photographer. Because of his fame as author of the *Alice* books, he was able to get other well-known and eminent people to sit for him. He also photographed children, often in costumes and sometimes nude. He loved the theatre and was friends with the actress Ellen Terry. He carried on an enormous correspondence and indexed his letters so that he had a record

---

5   The Grace Slick song "White Rabbit" or the inclusion of a photograph of Carroll on the cover of the Beatles' *Sgt. Pepper's Lonely Hearts Club Band* album.

of what he had written to whom. He travelled with games and puzzles to entertain children he met. He invented games, especially word games (word ladders, in which one word becomes another by replacing one letter at a time, which he called "doublets"). He travelled outside of England only once, an 1867 visit to Russia. He supported his sisters, and died of pneumonia age 66.[6]

Alice Liddell was one of the daughters of the Dean of his college; their family also lived at Christ Church. There is speculation that Carroll fell in love with Alice who was some twenty years younger. There is also speculation that he had an unhealthy fixation on pre-pubescent girls since he sought them out all his life. In neither case is there any serious evidence of improprieties. Still, it is impossible not to see the underside of Carroll's situation and interests. One Canadian writer, John M. Gray, has written a novel, *White Stone Day*, which centres on a Victorian-era Carroll-like figure who is involved with child prostitutes. I make no such suggestion about Carroll who seems to me more likely to have lived a repressed life. What can be said about him is that he lived through a time of social transformation, the height of the industrial revolution, that was characterized by extremes of poverty, child labour, child prostitution, and the first documentation of the science of evolution, yet there is little to show his awareness of much of this.[7] Beyond the written documentation, there was the evidence available to anyone just by being present in London. What does seem to have registered is Darwin. There is apparent reference to *On the Origin of Species* (1859) in the caucus race, especially a monkey in Tenniel's drawing, and the character of the Dodo, an extinct bird. Instead of being on the record about any of the important social and intellectual issues of his century, Carroll-Dodgson seems to have dedicated his life to middle-class comforts,

---

6   For bibliographical information about Carroll, see Robert Phillips, editor, *Aspects of* Alice, Penguin, 1971; Derek Hudson, *Lewis Carroll*, Constable, 1954.

7   Evidence was not lacking. Chadwick's *Royal Commission on the Poor Laws* had appeared in 1834; Dr John Snow reported on the cause of cholera in 1854; the four volumes of Henry Mayhew's *London Labour and the London Poor* were published between 1851 and 1861; Engels' *Condition of the Working Class in England* (1844) appeared in translation in 1885.

the demands of his teaching, some interesting sidelines of thought (e.g. a preoccupation with establishing an international dateline), games and puzzles. And yet ...

And yet, he gave us *Alice*. For this we all should be hugely grateful.

THE SONG OF ODYSSEUS:
Life Lessons Learned

VERNON PROVENCAL

> One narrow strait may take you through ...
> denial of yourself, restraint of your shipmates.
>
> —*Odyssey* (11.189)[1]

THE HOMERIC EPIC of the homecoming (*nostos*) of Odysseus offers lessons in life that are as valuable today as they were for the ancient Greeks more than 2500 years ago.

The central part of the *Odyssey* (books 9-12) is the "song of Odysseus," the account Odysseus recites for his hosts, the Phaiákians, of his journey homeward from Troy. He tells of how, immediately after finally leaving Troy in ruins after a ten-year siege, they raided the Kikonês for plunder to add to the riches of war-spoils taken from Troy. It was a costly venture: "Six benches were left empty in every ship ... And this new grief we bore with us to sea: our precious lives we had, but not our friends" (9.147). After weathering a three-day storm sent by Zeus, they set sail once more for home but were dragged away by a strong sea current and ten days later landed among the Lotos Eaters, where those who ate of the Lotos "longed to stay forever, browsing on that native bloom, forgetful of their homeland" (9.148). Driving his men back to the ships, they set sail once more and came to the land

---

1   Homer, *The Odyssey*, trans. R. Fitzgerald (New York: Vintage Books, 1990). (11.189) refers to book 11 of the *Odyssey*, page 189 of this edition; subsequent citations in parentheses adhere to this format.

of the "Kyklopês, giants, louts, without a law to bless them" (9.148).

Odysseus' encounter with the Kyklopês is the most famous episode of the *Odyssey*, as popular among the ancient Greeks as with us today (Odysseus blinding the Kyklops, Polyphemos, is depicted on the earliest example of classical Greek pottery—and think of our depiction of Odysseus escaping the clutches of the blinded Kyklops by clinging to the underbelly of his favorite ram on our "Odysseus Live 2012" t-shirts). By this time, we realize that Odysseus is a master storyteller and his tale utterly enthralling—no wonder Homer's *Odyssey* is a classic! And what a hero! How brave and daring—and, above all, how *clever*! But just as we are preparing to celebrate the heroic greatness of "that man skilled in all ways of contending" (1.1), we learn from Odysseus that when he offered Zeus the sacrifice of Polyphemos' ram to give thanks for their escape from the man-eating Kyklops, "Zeus disdained my offering; destruction for my ships he had in store and death for those who sailed them, my companions" (9.161).

The *Odyssey* begins with a council of the gods on Mount Olympos in which Zeus tells Athena that the only god who still bears a grudge against Odysseus is Poseidon "since he poked out the eye of Polyphemos" who is the son of Poseidon. "Naturally," Zeus tells us, "the god, after the blinding—mind you, he does not kill the man; he only buffets him away from home" (1.3). But it turns out that it was not only Poseidon Odysseus offended but Zeus as well. Zeus does not tell us why he refused Odysseus' sacrifice of Polyphemos' ram, but we can guess that it had to do with his boast:

> "O Kyklops! Would you feast on my companions?
> Puny, am I, in a Caveman's hands?
> How do you like the beating that we gave you,
> you damned cannibal? Eater of guests
> under your roof! *Zeus and the gods have paid you!*"
> [1.159 (emphasis added)]

Why did Odysseus take it on himself to declare that he was acting as an agent of Zeus—that his act of blinding the Kyklops was an act of divine justice? What was he thinking? Nor was that the only boast he made. Despite his men's plea that he shut up lest his shouts give the blind Kyklops a target for the huge boulders he was launching at their ship as they made their get-away, Odysseus confesses that "I would not heed them in my glorying spirit, but let my anger flare and yelled:

> Kyklops, if ever mortal man inquire
> how you were put to shame and blinded, tell him
> *Odysseus, raider of cities, took your eye:*
> *Laertes' son, whose home's on Ithaka!"* [9.160 (emphasis added)]

At long last learning the name of this self-proclaimed "Nohbody"—who proved himself not so smart as to keep his identity to himself—Polyphemos uses Odysseus' own boastful words to pray to his father, Poseidon, to avenge him:

> "O hear me, lord, blue girdler of the islands,
> if I am thine indeed, and thou art father:
> grant that *Odysseus, raider of cities, never*
> *see his home: Laertes' son, I mean,*
> *who kept his hall on Ithaka ..."*
> In these words he prayed, and the god heard him.
> [9.160 (emphasis added)]

Well, what, then, is this heroic tale really about? Clearly not, as so often thought by those who only hear about it from others, the tale of a man boasting of his many triumphs; rather, the song we hear sung by Odysseus himself is that of a "man of constant sorrow" (the magnificent choice made by the Coen brothers for the theme song of their re-telling of the *Odyssey* in *O Brother, Where Art Thou?*). The song of Odysseus is a song about heroic *hubris*. It is really a confession by Odysseus of the wrong he committed in blinding Polyphemos and boasting of it as an act of Zeus, utterly oblivious to the unbreakable fraternity between the god of divine justice who dwells on Olympus and his brother, the god of "earthly necessity" (Thank you, Angus, for that remarkable insight into the divinity of Poseidon) who dwells in the sea.

Because he didn't see things that way at the time, he went on to one disastrous encounter after another, "buffeted away from home" by Poseidon's wrath. As with his encounter with the Kikonês, Odysseus sailed away from the Kyklopês "sad in the vast offing, having our precious lives, but not our friends" (9.162), and came to the island of Aiolos, warden of the winds, who gifts them "a mighty bag, bottling storm winds" enabling the gentle west wind to carry them within sight of Ithaka. Yet he did not make it home. "No luck: the fair wind failed us when our prudence failed" (10.166). Trusting only himself and not his comrades, Odysseus failed to keep the bag closed and was blown back to Aiolia. Driven away by Aiolos as "a man the blessed gods detest," they spent another "six indistinguishable nights and days" at sea with "no breeze, no help in sight, by our own folly" [(*hubris*) (10.167)] before landing at Laestrygonia. "In that land the daybreak follows dusk"—the sun never sets—"and he who never slept could earn two wages" (a curious reflection by a man who just proved his inability to stay awake). Laestrygonia is a strange land—indeed, if we hadn't noticed before, all these adventures occur in places quite foreign to Odysseus, "Laertes' son, whose home's on Ithaka": a land where people care only to browse on the Lotos, forgetful of all else; an "isle unplanted and untilled" (9.148) whose one-eyed inhabitants "care not a whistle for your thundering Zeus" (9.153); the home of "a brute so huge … he seemed rather a shaggy mountain reared in soli-tude" (9.150); Aiolia, "an isle adrift upon the sea, ringed round with brazen ramparts on a sheer cliffside," whose king's twelve children—"six daugh-ters and six lusty sons"—are married to each other (10.165). Strange places whose inhabitants are shut in upon themselves in isolation from the rest of the world—none of them a place that could ever be home for Odysseus, no place that Odysseus belongs. But it would seem that having once glimpsed and once more lost sight of his beloved Ithaka, of *home*, Odysseus becomes ever more lost in the world that is *not*-home. Escaping the nightless land of the Laestrygonians, who prove to be monstrous man-eaters, they come finally to the isle of Kirkê, the sorceress, where Odysseus realizes they have now lost all sense of time and place:

> "Shipmates, companions in disastrous time,
> O my dear friends, where Dawn lies, and the West,
> and where the great Sun, light of men, may go

under the earth by night, and where he rises—
of these things we know nothing ..." (10.171)

Just where it seems that Odysseus has gone as far as it possible to go
under sail in the realm of Poseidon—for now we have reached the point
where the earthly dimensions of time and space are themselves utterly lost
sight of—he learns from Kirkê that he must venture even further away from
home. Odysseus must venture to a place beyond time and space, beyond the
land of the living, to the realm of Hades, where dwell the shades of those
who have departed this life for the life after.

This seems a good point to pause and put to ourselves the question:
What life lessons has Odysseus passed on to us thus far? What could we
possibly learn from these thrilling adventures in strange places of Homer's
mythic hero? What are they even about? To answer our question, we should
consider the context in which Odysseus recounts his homecoming to the
Phaiákians. Beginning with the Phaiákians themselves, they are, we may
have been surprised to learn, distant kin of the Kyklopês. Phaiákians and
Kyklopês are unlike in almost every possible way except one: both are children of Poseidon, lord of the realm in which all of Odysseus' adventures
have so far taken place and which he only escapes when he journeys on to
the realm of Hades. So how was it that Odysseus came to Phaiákia?

The *Odyssey* is so constructed that when we first meet Odysseus it is
on the idyllic isle of Kalypso, whose home is a cave nestled in the woods
among luxurious flora and fauna: "Even a god who found this place would
gaze, and feel his heart beat with delight" (5.83). Here we find Odysseus
stranded for seven long years in exile from rocky Ithaka, living in a natural
paradise with a goddess, groaning his heart out on the shore, no longer de-
sirous of the goddess' bed, cold even to her bribe of immortality. We begin
with Odysseus' rejection of a place not unlike biblical Eden, the life of the
golden age, an earthly paradise. We begin with his longing to be home in a
home which is not the home of Kalypso. The home of Kalypso is much like
the home of Kirkê; there is an important difference, but each is a natural
paradise, where the temptation is to forget who you are as human—neither
god nor animal—and live in nature. Nature is Poseidon's realm (which is

not to say Poseidon is a nature god; he is an Olympian, like Zeus, but he resides and exercises his dominion in the realm of nature). The song Odysseus relates to the Phaiákians has three parts: what happened before he went to (the house of) Hades, what happened in Hades, what happened after he returned from Hades. The two-thirds which take place outside Hades are about Odysseus' relationship to Poseidon as the god of "earthly necessity," before and after learning from the shades he meets in Hades how he has offended Poseidon and what he must do to appease him. When we first meet Odysseus, *after* his return from Hades and his escape from Kirkê's isle, it is at the point where, you might say, he now *knows* his *desire* to be home. But what he understands in the first place is that *he is not at home in nature.*

Because he is not at home in nature, he must leave Kalypso's isle, which he does by building a raft with his own hands with the kind of craft (what the ancient Greeks called *technê*, from which we get our word "technician") of which the Phaiákians are supreme masters (with the help of Hephaistos, god of *technê* and Athena, goddess of reason). But once adrift from Kalypso's paradise, once out of *harmony* with nature, Odysseus finds himself in a *hostile* relationship to the natural. Poseidon whips up a storm and Odysseus clings to his [c]raft; unexpectedly, our hero is offered salvation from certain death by drowning by the goddess Ino—the gift of a mere scarf. But it's only when the god of necessity smashes the raft with a Peggy's Cove-like wave that Odysseus is *forced* to let go and clings to the scarf, the gift of divine grace, as his only hope. The lesson here seems to be that *we would not survive in a nature that is hostile to our needs without the aid of the gods.* That is our first lesson. (And it is also the last lesson to be learned from the Song of Odysseus, the lesson of allowing starvation to compel us to feast upon the untouchable cattle of the Sun—our very survival depends on recognizing our utter dependence as humans upon the gods: first and last, *we must honour—fully honour—the gods.*)

And so Odysseus washes ashore on Phaiákia, naked, bruised, and battered, but mindful to loosen the gift to wash back to the goddess. As humans we do not exist, like other natural creatures, in a paradisiacal relationship with nature such that our needs are provided for naturally. We don't grow fur on our backs or hooves on our feet; our bodies are not big enough, strong enough, or quick enough to feed ourselves; we neither can (nor wish) to eat our meat raw, etc. It is with our human ability to reason, which sets us apart from all other animals, our innate capacity for *techne* that we take what we find in nature and by use of "fire" (technology) we adapt it to our needs. With *techne* we *make* the tools—axe, hammer, saw, spear, hoe, plough, wagon—by which we hunt, plant and harvest crops. We *build* our homes, we exchange goods in markets, and we develop communities around those marketplaces (the Greek *agora*, physical and spiritual center of the *polis*), places of talk and trade—trade in goods, trade in ideas, trade in ruling and being ruled in turn. We have washed up on the shores of Phaiákia—*utopia*—the master builders, the hyper-civilized kinsmen of the uncivilized Kyklopês: the antithetical children of Poseidon. For what we build, we build in relation to nature, with what we take from nature. And we can rest in the wondrous palace of King Alkínoös and Queen Arêtê, parents of the beautiful princess, Nausikaa, whom the King would like Odysseus to marry. But Phaiákia, an utopia free from necessity, a life of pure leisure, of feasts, games, and songs, is *not*-home to Odysseus, either.

What is missing is not easy to find: but it comes out in the sorrow of Odysseus—a man too sick at heart to take pleasure in the games, to whom songs of the Akhaians bring tears, having a different meaning for him than for the Phaiákians. What is mere entertainment for the god-like Phaiákians is *life* for the all-too-human Odysseus—these are his lost friends that they sing of! His experience in Phaiákia is not unlike that of Telêmakhos in the wondrous palace of Menelaus, home of Helen: where a joyous feast becomes an occasion of untempered sorrow as the memory of loved-ones-lost falls upon them. The Phaiákians seem to know nothing of sorrow; they are blessed by the gods—Poseidon, Athena, Hephaistos—with a life of leisure that is utterly removed from the hardship endured by Odysseus, by what makes up his song. By the divine gift of *techne* they live free of necessity in harmony with the divine reason of the gods in another kind of "golden age," another kind of paradise. As humans, we neither live in unbroken harmony with nature nor with the gods. The Phaiákians, moved by Odysseus' sorrow, will bear him home to Ithaka—and their lives will be forever changed by their forgetful act of disobedience, their failure to remember the prophecy that such a man as Odysseus would someday come to bring upon them *human* sorrow.

And so we set sail with Odysseus, with the impossibilities of a life either at home in nature or free from nature firmly established in our wake, to work out how we must live—how we must build our home—in relationship to nature. We plunder the Kikones, get "stoned" on Lotos, and come demanding guest-gifts of the Kyklopês as our hosts, from creatures who care nothing for the law of Zeus Xenios (guest-host), which governs *human* relations. All three episodes involve the relation of the human to nature as the external environment within which we must make—or lose—our way home. Odysseus' encounter with the Kikones and the Lotos Eaters teach us about the excess and defect of desire for what the world has to offer, lacking in the (ethical) reason which would curb one, cure the other. The problem is summed up in how Odysseus regards the land of the Kyklopês. In hindsight, it is depicted as a pastoral paradise where Kyklopês live peacefully among themselves, *without need of* agriculture, ships, merchants, laws, or assemblies that constitute a *human* community. Kyklopês are creatures who drink milk and eat cheese and are easily overthrown by wine, the fruit of human *technê*. But Odysseus tells us that at the time he could only see the land of the Kyklopês as another land for plunder, not for what it was in its own right.

The lesson we learn from the Kyklopês is one we know all too well: the *hubris* of our exploitation of nature as a *resource* for human development, as though nature existed *only* for us, as though it were only something for us to use for our ends. We disregard the beauty of the forest in calculating its potential board feet of lumber; we greedily deforest the planet, our home, placing our own well-being in peril. ("Eco" in "ecology" is derived from the Greek *oikos*, "home"). Odysseus cannot see what the Kyklopês are, he only sees them as what they are *not*—as the "other." The whole problem is that Odysseus does not understand how, as human, he is not only *apart from* nature, unnatural (just as the Kyklopês are *in*human), but how he is *a part* *of* nature, *natural*—a human *animal.* He would include nature within the limit of the human; what he must learn from Poseidon is how the human is included within the realm of the natural. Like the Phaiákians, we are unlike the Kyklopês, except in one crucial respect: we, too, are part of nature—children of Poseidon—and we must to learn to live in nature in that context. We must learn to respect the natural environment as our "ecos," our "home."

And so the next three episodes, the winds of Aiolos, the sleepless Laestrygonians, and the isle of Kirkê, take Odysseus beyond his external relation to nature as "out there," as the "other" that is not-him, to discover nature at a deeper level of relationship as "in here." The move inward to see how nature is within us is also a move inside nature itself, inside the outside— and thus the increasing loss of our sense of time and place, of orientation in nature as external, as landscape. The winds bottled in the Aiolian bag is an image of harnessing the power within nature which I liken to how power is stored in a battery (except, as a student pointed out, it's the unbagged west wind that drives the ship toward Ithaka). Odysseus proves unable to keep the winds harnessed, to keep nature under control, because he is not able to stay awake. He is not so much like Zeus on Olympos that he can go without sleeping; he is subject to Poseidon's earthly necessity. As human, he is natural; as natural, he has limits—all natural things need to sleep.

Ah, but if only he could stay awake! Well, then he could work 24 hours every sleepless, nightless day on Laestrygonia where the human is the battery (the "Matrix," "Neo?"), power, energy, abstracted from any end that would limit it. We move beyond the particular forms of nature, of things that we make, to the power by which things are made—the potency of nature, its plasticity, and the plasticity of human nature. On Laestrygonia, men are eaten, suggesting that there is something self-devouring about losing sight of what distinguishes between one thing and another, one activity and another, one end and another. There are no ends in Laestrygonia, land of the workaholic—the monstrous life where we lose ourselves in work and work becomes our end—something unknown to the animal kingdom.

We are being drawn ever deeper into the ceaseless, protean activity of nature, of the waves ceaselessly pounding the surf, where things are battered into other things ("Those are pearls that were his eyes," *The Tempest* I. ii, quoted in *The Waste Land*)—and so we fall under the potency of Kirkê's power to turn us into beasts. On Kirkê's isle it is possible for a whole year to go round unnoticed as we feast on the pleasures of her palace, what is really Pleasure Island. Plato will later pose as a question foundational to human ethics, *the* ethical question of happiness: is pleasure the good? For Plato, this question is actually posed by nature itself, insofar as nature *pretends* to be the good. Nature even has the power to *seduce* our unguarded reason and persuade us to believe that it *is* what it *appears* to be: all that is. The great temptation on Kirkê's isle is, having been drawn wholly into nature—into our own nature as natural and naturally part of the natural—to regard ourselves as only that: as though that were all that is, all that we were. Our only escape is to go to Hades, to the place beyond the natural, to the potency that is prior even to that of the protean plasticity of Kirkê's isle.

Ironically—as we learn to expect of all things "Greek"—it is in Hades, the place furthest from home, that Odysseus learns what he needs to learn to get home. In some sense, by escaping nature to the pure potency of Hades' realm that underlies all of nature (all natural things live and die), Odysseus does come home. Hades is the final resting place of the human. There he meets his mother, and the fallen Achaean heroes, and the only subject of conversation, really, is the *oikos*, home. From Achilles and Agamemnon he learns that there is no happiness known to humankind greater than that which awaits him in the arms of reunion with his loyal servants, his son, his wife, his father—and let us not forget the significance of recognizing and being recognized by his dog Argos—by all that he belongs to and all that belongs to him as human, his *home*.

And the wisdom taught to Odysseus by Tiresias in Hades, does it not sum up perfectly the hard-earned lessons forced upon him by the wrath of Poseidon? "One narrow strait may take you through his blows, denial of yourself, restraint of your shipmates" (11.189). Perhaps you would agree: that is a lesson still worth learning today.

SIMON DUBNOW:
Jewish Historian, Diaspora Nationalist and Social Hegelian[1]

RONI GECHTMAN

The ideology of Jewish diaspora nationalism was Simon Dubnow's exclusive brainchild.[2] Dubnow was born into a religiously observant family in a *shtetl* in Byelorussia. As an adolescent, during the optimist years of Alexander II's Great Reforms, he rebelled against tradition, rejected religion, and taught himself Russian to be able to study in a state high school. The young Dubnow adopted the progressive principles of the Hebrew *haskala* (Enlightenment) and was influenced by the positivism of Auguste Comte. Materialistic atheism—the rejection of all forms of *a priori* reasoning and notions of a supernatural origin of nature—and utilitarian morality—an ethical system not based on divine revelation—merged in Dubnow into a progressive conception of human history and staunch confidence in the liberating effects of science.

By the mid-1880s, however, the optimism of the Great Reforms era had turned to despair under the reactionary Czars who succeeded Alexander II whose reigns were marked by anti-Jewish popular violence and renewed

---

1   This essay is a section from an extended article on Jewish non-territorial autonomies forthcoming in the journal *Ethnopolitics*.

2   On Dubnow's life, see Sophie Dubnow-Erlich, *Diaspora Nationalism and Jewish History: The Life and Work of S.M. Dubnov* (1950), ed. Jeffrey Shandler., trans. Judith Vowles (Bloomington and Indianapolis: Indiana University Press, 1991). On Dubnow's intellectual method, see Jonathan Frankel, "S.M. Dubnow: Historian and Ideologist," in Dubnow-Erlich, *Life and Work of S.M. Dubnov*, 1-33.

restriction of Jews' civil rights on the part of the authorities. These changes affected Dubnow personally: he was not allowed to settle in Saint Petersburg where he had sought to start a career as a writer. As a result Dubnow underwent a psychological and philosophical crisis; he experienced "doubts about the moral progress of man" and distanced himself from the emotionally detached principles of positivism.[3] While he never regained his former religious faith, Dubnow embraced Leo Tolstoy's romantic, ethical populism as an alternative to positivist detachment. Dubnow admired Tolstoy for having rejected established religion while dedicating himself to ethical self-perfection.[4] Besides Tolstoy, Dubnow was also influenced by the method of historian (and French nationalist) Ernest Renan (1823-1892), in particular his struggle to find a balance between reason and faith and his attempts to treat religion as a proper subject of historical study.

By the age of twenty-seven, Dubnow had concluded that his "path to the universal lay expressly through the field of the national" in which he was already active as a writer of cultural essays on Jewish topics for the Jewish intellectual press; it was around this time, too, that he turned himself into a professional historian.[5] He found the solution to his dilemmas in what he called "historism" (not to be confused with historicism): the assertion that the development of the individual's character, tastes and convictions are strongly shaped by collective (national) historical experience. The answer to the injunction *Gnothi Seauton* (know thyself, the aphorism inscribed in the temple of Apollo at Delphi) was to be found in the study of the collective, historical past. Historical consciousness became for Dubnow the essence of the Jewish national ideal.[6] Historism served Dubnow with a dual purpose:

---

3   See Robert M. Seltzer, "Coming Home: The Personal Basis of Simon Dubnow's Ideology," *Association for Jewish Studies Review* 1 (1976), 284–292; the quotation, from Dubnow's memoirs, is cited on page 292 of Seltzer's article.

4   Seltzer, "Coming Home," 297.

5   Dubnow's memoirs, quoted in Seltzer, "Coming Home, pp. 293-294.

6   Dubnow published his "historical credo in miniature," *What is Jewish History*, in 1893. Dubnow's diary, cited in Seltzer, "Coming home," 295. Dubnow's essay was first published as a series of articles in the journal *Voskhod* between October and December of 1893; English translation: *What is Jewish History: An Essay in the Philosophy of History* (Philadelphia: The Jewish Publication Society of America, 1903).

on the one hand it allowed him to write social, empirical history with intellectual rigour while on the other it reinforced his Jewish identity under a secular guise.

Dubnow articulated his views on politics and history in his *Pisma o starom i novom evreistve* (Letters on Old and New Judaism), published and revised in the years 1897-1907—yet another turbulent period in Russian history, which climaxed in the 1905 Revolution.[7] Jewish political life in Russia was also revolutionized and ushered into modernity with the creation of the Jewish Labour Bund, a workers' revolutionary party, and the Zionist movement, both in 1897, and of a myriad other political parties and movements after 1905—not least among them, Dubnow's own Folkspartey, founded in Saint Petersburg in 1906.

Dubnow's Jewish nationalism and his political views derived, to a large extent, from his historical theory and analysis. At the same time, unlike other politicians or political theorists who pay lip service to history, Dubnow was *the* preeminent Jewish historian of his generation, whose major historical works became accepted by scholars and laypeople (including his political rivals) as authoritative in his and subsequent generations in most quarters of Western Jewry. Dubnow's historical interpretations were often informed by his ideological preconceptions nonetheless.[8]

Like other nationalists, Dubnow not only traced the existence of his nation to ancient times, but also judged the historical actors positively or negatively according to the evaluative criterion of whether their actions

---

7   An English translation of the *Letters* is in Simon Dubnow, *Nationalism and History: Essays on Old and New Judaism*, ed. Koppel S. Pinson (Philadelphia: The Jewish Publication Society of America, 1958, 73-249). However, this version is abridged, and therefore the numbering of the letters is different from that in complete editions. For the full text of the *Letters* in Yiddish, see *Briv vegn altn un nayem yidntum* (México D.F.: Shloyme Mendelson Fond bay der Gezelshaft far Kultur un Hilf, 1959), and in French, *Lettres sur le judaïsme ancien et nouveau* (Paris: Cerf, 1989). Unless noted, all references to Dubnow's *Letters* are to the English edition and by letter number (e.g., *Twelfth Letter*).

8   I discuss this to some length in "Creating a Historical Narrative for a Spiritual Nation: Simon Dubnow and the Politics of the Jewish Past," *Journal of the Canadian Historical Association* 22:2 (2011), 98-124.

matched what he perceived as the true (and eternal) spirit of the Jewish nation. Those who followed this spirit were veritable (and commendable) nationalists. According to Dubnow's account of Jewish history, the Jewish nation developed in three progressive phases: tribal, political territorial and cultural-historical or spiritual.[9] In this historical scheme, the nation of Israel achieved its natural maturity at some point in late antiquity and thanks to a series of "rigid tests" to the spiritual energies of the nation: the loss of political independence to alien rule, the loss of the homeland and the scattering of the people in alien lands, and the loss of a unifying language. "If, despite the fact that the external national bonds have been destroyed," Dubnow asserted, such a nation still maintains itself for many years, creates an independent existence, reveals a stubborn determination to carry on its autonomous development—such a people has reached the highest stage of cultural-historical individuality and may be said to be indestructible, if only it cling forcefully to its national will. ... This unique people is the people of Israel.[10]

According to Dubnow, the true source of the vitality of the Jewish people consists in the fact that, after developing "through the states of tribal nationalism, ancient culture and political territory," the Jewish nation "was able to establish itself and fortify itself in the highest state, the spiritual and historical-cultural, and succeeded in crystallizing itself in a spiritual people that draws the sap of its existence from natural or intellectual 'will to live'."[11] Dubnow did not see this pattern of development (tribal, political-territorial, cultural-spiritual) as particular to Jews; it was historically inevitable that all nations would develop according to the same historical teleology. As it happens, Dubnow claimed that Jews were the only nation that had achieved so far the highest stage of a purely cultural or spiritual entity that does not depend on a state or territory (but he did not claim a special status for Jews as God's chosen people).

---

9 Dubnow, "The Survival of the Jewish People: The Secret of Survival and the Law of Survival," in *Nationalism and History*, 328-330; originally published in *Heatid* 4, 1912 (this journal was edited by Sh. I. Hurwitz).

10 *First Letter*, 80.

11 *First Letter*, 84-85.

The theoretical presuppositions of Dubnow's historical method bear a strong resemblance to Hegel's dialectics. Dubnow's discussion, in the *Fourth Letter*, of the historical phenomenon of the autonomy of the traditional Jewish community as a justification for his autonomist political program, is organized as a dialectical triad consisting of thesis, antithesis and synthesis. According to Dubnow's analysis, the isolation of the traditional community, embodying the "old fossilized order of Jewish life" (the thesis), was challenged during the Age of Revolutions of the early nineteenth century by the idea that dominated West European Jewish communities at the time: that Jews would achieve full civil rights and equality through assimilation (the antithesis). Dubnow claimed that historical experience "has demonstrated that both the thesis and the antithesis [were] one-sided."[12] It was therefore a historical necessity that the synthesis (autonomism) be a suppression and elevation (*Aufhebung*, Hegel's term, not Dubnow's) of thesis and antithesis. In other words, Dubnow's imagined future (a national-cultural autonomy for Jews in the context of multinational states, or the synthesis) would not seek to reverse the civil rights Jews had achieved, or were striving to achieve, in the countries where they lived. Nor would it mean a regression to the isolation of the medieval Jewish community. Rather, Jewish culture would be invigorated by new meanings and modern secular contents that would emerge in the renewed, secular autonomous communities.[13]

Unlike Hegel's, however, Dubnow's history, though teleological, was free of theodicy, that is, the belief that, despite the concrete historical accidents and evils that individuals may suffer, history is guided by providence to an ultimate higher end. Dubnow's own national teleology did not rely on

---

12   Dubnow, *Fourth Letter*, 134-135. See also Hillbrenner, *Diaspora-Nationalismus*, 107-115.

13   Dubnow warned his readers that his use of dialectics differed from the pure idealism of Hegel, since his historical approach was based on sociological facts rather than ideas; *Fourth Letter*, 131-132, note. Historian Raphael Mahler agreed with Dubnow's assessment of his method as non-Hegelian, and characterized it instead as national, secular, "sociological-realistic and scientific-evolutionary." Still, Mahler criticized Dubnow's historiography for paying little attention to economic factors; see "Shitat Dubnow umif'alo bahistoriografia hayehudit," in *Simon Dubnov: L'homme et son oeuvre*, 61-63, 66-67 (quotation from page 62).

divine intervention; in this sense, his views differed from those of most other Jewish nationalists (and orthodox Jews) for whom, in one way or another, God's promises to ancient Israel acted as a justification of its nationalism.[14]

Furthermore, the technical use of dialectics is not the only aspect of Dubnow's method that echoed Hegel's. Dubnow's phases of development of the nation (discussed above), from tribal to political to spiritual, were also imbued with a Hegelian logic. For Hegel, reason governs the world, human history is a manifestation of spirit, and world history "represents the development of the spirit's consciousness of its own freedom and of the consequent realization of that freedom."[15] The state was central to Hegel's philosophy of history as the manifestation of spirit in human society and the embodiment of rational freedom. Its most advanced form was to be found in the modern German states where all citizens enjoyed freedom and were conscious of being free. In Dubnow's historical system, the Jews had gone one step further than the Germans by having abolished and elevated (*aufheben*) the state, thus becoming a pure, *spiritual* and stateless nation.[16]

The Jewish nation was, for Dubnow, a world-wide living organism whose existence spanned the entire world and all of history.[17] According

---

14   See, for instance, the debate on "the essence [*mahut*] of Judaism" that followed the publication of Hurwitz's "Lish'elat kiyum hayahadut (hegiyonot vehirhurim)" in *Ha-shiloahh* 12 (April 1904), 287–303, which provoked responses from some of the most renowned Zionist thinkers of the time (M.L. Lilienblum, A.M. Brukhov, Yosef Klausner, etc.). In this debate, justification was sought by recourse to traditional (religious) sources of authority, concepts such as "essence" or "organic nation," and metaphysical or supernatural laws, all of which are virtually absent from Dubnow's works.

15   Georg Wilhelm Friedrich Hegel, *Lectures on the Philosophy of World History* (1837), trans. H.B. Nisbet (Cambridge: Cambridge University Press, 1974), 43.

16   The theme of the Jews being a spiritual nation pervades Dubnow's writings and is a constant thread throughout his life, from his earlier works of the early 1890s; see Oscar Isaiah Janowsky, *The Jews and Minority Rights (1898-1919)* (New York: Columbia University Press, 1933); Pinson, "The National Theories of Simon Dubnow," 342-343.

17   Seltzer, "Coming home," 298-299 note 43. See also Veidlinger, "Simon Dubnow Recontextualized," 417-418. In his autobiography, Dubnow refers to his thorough study of Spencer's evolutionary theories during the "home university" period during which he developed his own historical and philosophical synthesis; see Dubnow, *Sefer ha-hayim*, 177, 179–180.

to Dubnow, each "generation in Israel carries within itself the remnants of worlds created and destroyed during the course of the previous history of the Jewish people." Every generation "builds and destroys worlds in its form and image, but in the long run continues to weave the thread that binds all the links of the nation into the chain of generations."[18] Nevertheless, what set Dubnow apart from other nationalists (and from social Darwinists) and prevented his ideology from developing into a destructive and aggressive form of nationalism was his conviction that what made the Jewish nation distinctive was precisely its spiritual and non-territorial character.[19]

Like other intellectuals formed in the period before the Great War, Dubnow was a firm believer in human progress. His study of history strengthened his faith that, despite the many human setbacks and calamities of the past, justice and freedom would ultimately prevail in the future. Already in 1901 Dubnow reckoned that despite "the present reaction, the course of history [was] directed, not toward the subjection of national groups, but toward their liberation." Just as the hegemony of one ruling church over the state had been eliminated after bitter struggles, so too the principle of a ruling nationality was bound to be discarded. If the nineteenth century was able to secure the legal recognition by the community of the principle of freedom of the individual, the twentieth century was faced with the task of establishing the freedom or the autonomy of the national individual.[20]

Dubnow's views on national-cultural autonomy in the context of a multinational state were elements within this teleology:

> In the same way that enlightened countries came to recognize that only a free citizen can be a loyal and useful member of the community, so the realization will slowly come that, in a state composed of different nationalities, a nationality enjoying internal autonomy is a stronger support for the commonwealth than a suppressed nationality made restless by constant oppression. The function of a "ruling nationality" in the state will be relegated to

---

18   Dubnow, "The Survival of the Jewish People," 326.

19   In Dubnow's words, "the Jewish national idea ... can never become aggressive and warlike"; *Third Letter*, 130.

20   *Fourth Letter*, 141.

the same position occupied today by a "ruling Church" in a free state. This is not just a myth, but a historical necessity.[21]

What worried Dubnow in the years leading to the Second World War, what he considered "the worst plague of our times," was that "the world is [was] returning once again to political unitarism"; nevertheless, he believed that Nazi and fascist insanity, which would "be remembered as one of the greatest catastrophes in world history," would not prosper in the long run. Despite these "volcanic eruptions," he insisted, human history develops according to laws founded in human culture:

> There are times when large masses of humanity are beset by the evil principle, by the beast in man. In such times all the others must organize themselves in order to strengthen the good principle, the human conscience, the categorical imperative.[22]

Dubnow kept his optimism and his faith in the eventual triumph of emancipation until the very end of his life. According to a witness, during the "terrifying night of 7-8 December 1941," the Germans "evacuated" the Jewish population of Riga, they loaded the sick and the feeble into dark blue buses. There wasn't enough room for everyone, and they shot many old people and pregnant women then and there, on the spot. When they drove Dubnow out into the street he had a high temperature—38.5°C. He hadn't the strength to climb the steps of the bus quickly. A drunken Latvian militiaman run up and shot him point blank in the back of the head. Dubnow fell dead. The next day they buried him in a mass grave in the old

---

21   *Seventh Letter*, 174-175.

22   From an article published in the *Zukunft* in 1935; quoted in Pinson, "The National Theories of Simon Dubnow," 341, 357-358. The "categorical imperative" refers, of course, to the central concept in Kantian ethics. Not all of Dubnow's disciples continued to share his optimism by the late 1930s, though. Some of them, like Elias Tscherikover, Yisroel Efroykin and Zelig Kalmanovitsh, the founders of the journal *Afn Sheydveg* in 1939, succumbed to deep resignation and despair in the face of the increasing power of fascism and Nazism and declared the whole emancipation project a failure; see Joshua Karlip, "In the Days of Haman: Simon Dubnow and his Disciples at the Eve of the WWII," *Jahrbuch des Simon-Dubnow-Instituts / Simon Dubnow Institute Yearbook IV* (2005), 531-564.

Jewish cemetery in the Riga ghetto.[23]

Simon Dubnow was 81 at the time of his death. According to survivors, as Dubnow walked to his death he urged his fellow Jews not to forget and to document what was happening, repeating: "Yidn, shraybt un farshraybt" (*Jews, write and record*).[24] Not only did Dubnow not survive the war, but the world that emerged from the Second World War had the nation state as the almost exclusive form of political organization, with little will to find other forms of non-territorial accommodation for cultural and national minorities. Nationalists opted for aggressive militarism rather than accommodation to solve conflicts. The state of affairs in Israel/Palestine today is a sad reminder of the tragic fate of Dubnow's optimistic ideas on national coexistence.

---

23   Dubnow-Erlich, *Diaspora Nationalism and Jewish History*, 246-247.
24   Pinson, "Simon Dubnow: Historian and Political Philosopher," in *Nationalism and History*, 11.

THE SMALLEST KINDNESSES:
"The Seminar" Redefined

SCOTT MACDOUGALL

Delicacy of mule deer, the sharp
    dry scent of spruce—
we have been grateful for the smallest kindnesses:
a shelf that holds up books, dry socks.

      —Jan Zwicky

I

"THE SEMINAR" HAS been an integral part of my life for the past four years. As I began to assemble notes for this essay on the weekly reading and discussion group that is open to all graduates of Halifax Humanities 101, my mind went to three places. First, to the fortuitous community that meets once a week for eight months of the year, where contingent circumstances yield bouquets of "the smallest kindnesses." Second, to our room at Alderney Landing and the sound of tables and chairs pushed into place by John and Lamont and Stephen and the smell of coffee brewed by Grace and cookies laid out by Jymy, Lillian and their friends and the sight of clouds over the harbour and light streaming through the large western window. Third, to the special joy with which the students greeted Angus Johnston, knowing that the Seminar might continue now that he had left the role of coordinator, but that it would never have the same light. Later, in the middle of the night, my mind turned to the image of water, just as it rolls into its first boil of innumerable small bubbles and then into larger bubbles that smile and burst.

II

"WHAT ARE WE going to do now?" Bonita Shepherd demanded of Angus in the closing days of the inaugural year of Halifax Humanities 101. Bonita was not asking about a next step towards a cashable goal. A warm, expansive woman with a powerful presence augmented by a Herculean cane, Bonita dismissed Angus' weak response: "This is a one-year programme." Backed against a bookcase, Angus reached into the lexicon of higher education and promised to start "a seminar."

The standard dictionary meanings of the term seminar range from the informal "meeting for the exchange of ideas," through the vague "any class of fewer than fifty students where the professor speaks for less than 90% of the time" to the more restricted "a small group of advanced students engaged in intense study under guidance of a professor." There are normally around twenty in our group, advanced due to their graduation from the one-year programme, and intensely committed. Normally a guest from one of the cooperating universities presents a text for about 30 minutes followed by 90 minutes of discussion. Unlike some undergraduate posturing, no one makes point-scoring displays of knowledge and no one holds back from speaking.

The first Halifax Humanities 101 graduates wanted more of Odysseus and, over three months in 2008, Angus and that small group read Homer's *Iliad* and *Odyssey* and James Joyce's *Ulysses*. The following year, the students chose Shakespeare. They read three of Shakespeare's tragedies supplemented by what Angus remembers as two thrilling days with Elizabeth Edwards on *Romeo and Juliet*. The third year students asked to consider "history." They read Herodotus, Machiavelli, and Hegel. Late in the year I attended a class on Nietzsche led by Peggy Heller. The following week we moved from readings in the "philosophy of history" to the practice of doing history, and I led a discussion of Jack Hexter's essay "The Historian's Own Day."

To this point Angus had single-handedly organized the Seminar. With each year it had grown in both the number of participants and in the frequency of meetings. I gladly accepted his invitation to share its coordination. Early in September 2010, sixteen of us met to decide on a theme for the year. After animated discussion that set aside Bonita's suggestion that we focus on the Roman Empire, Stephen's suggestion that we focus on Russia, and Scott Lynch's ardent demand that we focus on the literature of horror, we settled on the general theme of comedy. Angus and I then set about recruiting volunteers for seven months of classes. To effect this task we had to broaden our conception of comedy and put aside notions of systematic curriculum. The various interests of our volunteers compelled us to approach the theme from many perspectives. We read *Clouds*, *The Frogs* and *Lysistrata* by Aristophanes, "The Miller's Tale" by Chaucer, *Twelfth Night* by Shakespeare, Pope's "The Rape of the Lock," and Moliere's *Tartuffe*. The year ended with a viewing of "Philadelphia Story" and a discussion of Stanley Cavell's *Pursuits of Happiness: The Hollywood Comedy of Remarriage*.

In the academic year 2011–12 we agreed to experiment; we were keen to spend longer stretches of time with a single work. Persuaded by Scott Lynch, we began with a series of classes on the literature of horror that included Edgar Allan Poe and H.P. Lovecraft and a memorable day with Bill Barker reading Coleridge's "Rhyme of the Ancient Mariner." Perhaps our deepest glimpse into horror came when one of the students, Ben Van-Seeventer, read us the last lines of Robert Frost's "Out, Out—":

> Doing a man's work, though a child at heart
> He saw all spoiled. 'Don't let him cut my hand off—
> The doctor, when he comes. Don't let him, sister!'
> So. But the hand was gone already.
> The doctor put him in the dark of ether.
> He lay and puffed his lips out with his breath.
> And then—the watcher at his pulse took fright

No one believed. They listened at his heart.
Little—less—nothing!—and that ended it.
No more to build on there. And they, since they
Were not the one dead, turned to their affairs.

In the new year we devoted six weeks to both *Little Dorrit* and *Crime and Punishment*. The experiment with reading long difficult novels met with mixed reviews but it will be some time before we tackle *Moby Dick* or even *Don Quixote*.

In 2012-13, the students chose "Canadian History and Canadian Literature." We considered the early settlements, the Acadian expulsion, the politics of Confederation, Canadian journalism, the mid-20th century project to define our national identity, and the critiques of that identity by George Grant and Scott Symons. We spent two days with Emily Carr's paintings and read excerpts from her journals and from *Klee Wyck*. We read poems by Leonard Cohen and E.J. Pratt, P.K. Page and Jan Zwicky and fiction by Alice Munro, Ernest Buckler, Gabrielle Roy, and Marie-Claire Blais. As we moved through the seasons, the changing sky above Halifax Harbour helped us to think more clearly about place, its particularity in shared belonging, and its universality as idea.

The memory of one set of classes on Roy's *The Road to Altamont* illustrates the texture of our seminar classes. Larry Steele from Mount Saint Vincent took us through the passages that describe the car rides Christine shared with her mother. That prompted each of us to talk of family car drives, to explore regional variations, and to marvel at Roy's evocation of Manitoba vistas and how it contributed to our sense of Canada's expansiveness. Roy moved us from discussions of national symbols to meditations on place, home, and family. Kathleen Higney recalled *The Odyssey* after she read us this paragraph from *The Road to Altamont*:

> Sometimes a strange question rose from within me, as if from the bottom of a well. What are you doing here? Then I would cast my eyes around me. I would try to attach myself to something, familiar to me yesterday, in this world that was fleeing from me. But the troubling sense persisted that I was here only by chance

and that I had to discover the place in the world, as yet unknown to me, where I might feel rather more at home. The thought, seemingly so trivial and yet disturbing, accompanied me everywhere. This is over. This is no longer your place. Now you are a stranger here.

Little discussion followed Kathleen's comparison. There was so much shared experience in the room that no one needed to ask anything: we all knew what she meant. Such agreement is rare. Usually comments from the class are greeted with reservations and counter arguments.

Last year we took religious texts as our theme. Daniel Brandes and Eli Diamond led five classes in a reading of the book of Genesis; Gary Thorne led two sessions on the gospel of Saint John; Chris Austin took us through a Hindu sutra; Jamal Badawi explicated passages from the Koran and Tim Addison did the same with various Buddhist writings. Dave Puxley, who has made contributions to the Seminar in each of the past four years, introduced us to some of the devotional poetry of Rumi, with echoes of Leonard Cohen whom he had read with us the previous year. Patricia Robertson joined the class for a reading of John Donne, and Anna House discussed many examples of Medieval and Renaissance religious painting. In both the fall and spring, Paul Bowlby of Saint Mary's University joined the class, first to help us introduce the theme, then to help us read central passages of the *Bhagavad-Gita*, and finally to show us monumental Buddhist sculpture and architecture from various points on the Silk Road.

III

THE PREVIOUS PARAGRAPHS provide some impression of the kinds of subject matter that have been engaged with over the past eight years but I have also hinted at something deeper. To get closer to that sense I will describe something of what happened over two classes in the spring of 2013.

As part of our Canadian offerings I had asked my friend Irene Oore to lead two classes. She happily agreed, though with some apprehension about what she might contribute to the general theme. She chose

St. Lawrence Blues by Marie-Claire Blais as a text. The choice did not alleviate her anxiety. On the surface it is a difficult text and on the wrong day it might prove incomprehensible. But she admired Blais and wanted to talk about the revelation of a unique Quebecois sensibility. She succeeded. The students eagerly followed her exposition of the novel's boisterous activities, its exuberant depictions of passion and poverty, ribaldry and despair, devotion, salvation, and love. Irene, to help ground her observations, circulated Mary Meigs' illustrations for the novel and as we looked at them our excitement with what she was saying increased. She closed that section of the class by introducing us to a notion of the carnivalesque. Not long before the class was to end she came to a stop, exhausted by the energy she had expended. The room went still until Steven Wile, with great emotion, said "Bravo!" and everyone joined in a raucous celebratory cheer; Irene's apprehension had vanished. She smiled and thanked the class.

She returned the following week to lead a discussion of Blais' place in Canadian and French literature and at the students' request expanded on the nature of the Blais/Meigs collaboration. As the class ended with another display of affection, Irene turned to me and whispered, "This was so different, what a great pleasure!"

When Grace Morris and I were tidying up I asked who had brought the extraordinary chocolate chip cookies to the class. Grace glanced across the room, where an animated group of students were still peppering their professor with questions; she nodded and said, smiling, "Irene."

IV

THERE ARE GREAT rewards for participation in the Halifax Humanities Seminar. Our sense of particular texts deepens, we make new discoveries, we see things differently through other eyes. But there is something that goes deeper, something related to the act of reading, to those moments when we set down our book and thank Dickens or Stevens or Alice Munro. We feel gratitude for having our existence verified. On many occasions

Halifax Humanities students have taken Angus or me aside to say, "Thanks for believing in me." I can say nothing in return though an acute observer would hear a substantive sigh as my heart smiles in reciprocity.

Bibliography

Frost, Robert. "Out, Out—" In *Frost: Collected Poems, Prose, and Plays*. Ed. Richard Poirier and Mark Richardson. New York: The Library of America, 1995.

Roy, Gabrielle. *The Road Poast Altamont*. Trans. Joyce Marshall. Toronto: New Canadian Library, 2010.

Zwicky, Jan. "Five Songs for Relinquishing the Earth." In *Songs for Relinquishing the Earth*. London, ON: Brick Books, 1998.

Self and Other

Valedictory Address 2009

Jennifer Conroy

I HAVE READ that the Humanities are the stories and ideas that help us make sense of our lives and our world. The Humanities introduce us to people we have never met, places we have never been, and ideas that may have never crossed our minds. Seeing how others have lived and thought about life helps us decide what is important in our own lives and influences how we can make them better. We find what is true to our heritage and our history.

The Humanities teach us to balance passion with reason. We become informed; the Humanities give a voice to our feelings. Experiences are recognized and interests are explored. Life has a language and the venue in which you can hear it is through art, theatre, music, dance, literature, philosophy, poems. The Humanities awaken us to learning, inspire change, and invite us to join the greatest of minds, past and present, in a journey to seek meaning.

The first book that we read this year was *The Epic of Gilgamesh* (an ancient Babylonian text from about 2000 BC). It is a celebration of the humanity that resides in us all. Gilgamesh, the king, discovers what it is to be human through finding a loyal friend, Enkidu (the man who at first is more animal than human). Like Enkidu, Halifax Humanities has walked along our side as our friend and has gently led us through the great works and ideas of history. Halifax Humanities has encouraged and supported us. It has kept us feeling safe and interested in the process. But a friend can only accompany us so far on a journey; the rest we must continue alone.

This is a bittersweet goodbye. Lucky for us, we have been given a map should we become lost. It is in every book we have read. If we come upon a barrier in our progress, we can use the tools that have been taught to us—critical thinking, communication, the acknowledgement of difference, perspective, experience.

To my fellow classmates, as you move on and the memories of this experience seem to elude you, close your eyes—and see the vision before you today. A room full of people who have supported you on your journey and believed in you and your ability.

I hope that when our paths cross one day in the future, I will hear *your song*, as Walt Whitman says—I want to hear it loud and clear.

To the teachers, professors, and our "mother" Mary Lu, how do we say thanks to you? How do you thank the very people who brought passion back to the impassionate, reason to illness, and allowed those of us who are mothers to regain our voices and desires?

You have allowed us the time to grow, to heal, to nurture ourselves. The only way I know to repay a debt like this and to say thank you is by moving on in our lives with balance, substance, wisdom, and promise.

Thank you for the gift you have bestowed upon us and thank you for a truly life-changing experience.

NAPTIME WITH ELIZABETH

MADELINE REID COMEAU

lying soft together
on the big, messy bed
baby-bottle ballet
blurring the edges
between sustenance and sleep
like a skater making seamless strokes
across a shimmering pond
or a dance pair
suspended in waltz-time
on a dimly-lit ballroom floor

deep blue eyes
fixed intently on mine
like little sentinels on duty
a warm, miniature fist
locked around my pinky finger
baby-breath timpani
punctuating her passage
into dreamworld
like the stealthy arrival
of soft, feathery snowflakes in winter

curled up beside you
in this comfy cocoon

I remain transfixed
pondering the infant wisdom
gifted to me
on a big, messy bed
at naptime

$\mathscr{L}$ADY $\mathscr{G}$ODIVA

BRENDA DELORENZO

Back in the old days, mothers
wore aprons and baked and cooked
like Betty Crocker.

The doctors gave valium to mothers
to calm the chaos of raising children.

Mother called her teenage
daughter Lady Godiva.

She sat on a chaise-lounge
browning in the sun.

She would baste her skinny
arms and legs with baby oil.
The girl would eat warm tomatoes
from the garden.
The glass salt shaker at her side.

Mother nagged her to get a summer job.
She didn't pay no mind to
her mother's words.
Father called her lazy bones.
She didn't pay no mind to her
father's words.
The vegetable garden begged to be weeded.

The girl would day dream
about Tom who was a good lookin' hunk.
Mother warned her that she would
wrinkle like dried prunes sitting in the
sun all day.

The girl didn't pay no mind
to her mother's words.

She sat on a chaise-lounge
browning in the sun.

She would baste her skinny
arms and legs with baby oil.
The girl would eat warm tomatoes
from the garden.
The glass salt shaker at her side.
The vegetable garden begged to be weeded.

$\mathscr{I}$ NTERVIEW WITH AN $\mathscr{I}$ NUKSUK[1]

LAURA LEGERE

Ladies and gentlemen our Host—Bea Oetdare[2]

BEA OETDARE: Today we welcome our special guest, fresh from his recent role as logo for the Vancouver Winter Olympics[3]: Ingor Inuksuk.

INGOR INUKSUK: Thank you, thank you. It is good to be here and everywhere else too ... (*sits*)

BEA: So what vaulted you to the forefront of the art world?

INGOR INUKSHUK: The CBC Heritage Minute,[4] the short film clip. It shows Inuit people assembling an Inuksuk explaining to an injured man in military uniform that "now the people will know we were there." That went a long ways towards increasing my presence on the world stage. And before that—my image on the territorial flag of Nunavut. And, of course, the exposure of being the logo/symbol for the Vancouver Winter Olympic Games I guess.

BEA: Are you art or "assemblage?" What sets you apart from any other pile of stones?

---

1   pronounce *in-ook-shook*.

2   pronounce *be out'der*.

3   http://en.wikipedia.org/wiki/Inuksuk. Retrieved September, 28, 2013.

4   Canadian Heritage Minute video about the inuksuk (http://histori.ca/minutes/minute.do?id=10210)

INGOR: I am an ancient mark of Inuit presence and prescience (pun intended) and I can be a navigational aid. I am versatile and functional and yet "conceptual." I can be anything with form. Theoretically I could be a musical instrument if you recorded the sound of the arctic wind whistling and wailing through the gaps in my stones. Cutting an album and spending some time in the studio is on my horizon right now. But perhaps I can best be described through the art theorists for the most part, some collectors, maybe a historian or two, or the perspectives of the people who build me, recognize me as a friend or something more, a companion or guide.

BEA: How do you self-identify? You look like a man, a human, are you gender specific?

INGOR: Yes and no, literally.

BEA: Tell me something about your roots and the people who first shaped you from nature—the Inuit, formerly known as Eskimos, translated *Eaters of Raw Meat*.[5]

INGOR: I was originally made of local stone from Alaska to Greenland. I came into being close to the Arctic Circle, seldom far from a shoreline. We think that my earliest creators were of Mongolian descent and they came to the North American continent in three major waves. The first arrived about 40,000 years ago, the most recent, ten thousand years ago. During this time we think the complex culture of the nomadic Inuit originated and developed.[6] Now people everywhere assemble me for different reasons and some of those are the same as 40,000 years ago and some completely different but sometimes people just need to reach out and connect with the earth and leave something behind, something symbolic, spiritual and eternal to let others know they were there.

BEA: Initially, in the earlier days though, you even had spiritual significance didn't you?

INGOR: Yes, I was often assembled with great ceremony or "potlatch"

---

5 Carol Finley, *Art of the Far North* (Toronto: Random House, 1998), 11.
6 Finley, 157.

by Inuit Shaman and I worked hard to pay my dues back then, and I served. I was a point for navigation, a marker for travel routes, fishing places, hunting camps, herding caribou for slaughter, hiding caches of food and, yes, points of veneration. Every time someone builds me I acquire a new shape and size so I'm always evolving, reinventing myself or specifically enabling someone to do it for me,[7] and yet I am as timeless as Stonehenge.

BEA: You did say you were not gender specific but you are intended to represent human form, am I right?

INGOR: So, to come back to your earlier question about "my manhood," historically, the most common type of inuksuk was a single stone positioned in a vertical form outside. That is very manly. There is some debate as to whether the appearance of human- or cross-shaped cairns developed in the Inuit culture before the arrival of European missionaries and explorers. But the modern version does look human.[8]

BEA: So why, when and how did the drive to transform your image into iconic sculpture, fine art, tourist art or logo begin?

INGOR: One minute on the shore of Baffin Bay, the next in the gift shop in the Art Gallery of Nova Scotia. But generally it was part financial, part encouragement, part incentive, because in the 1950s[9] the Inuit had surrendered their nomadic way of life of travelling and hunting and fishing and settled into permanent Government provided and established communities. Incentives were put in place to encourage craft and artist co-operatives and commercial fishing ventures. James Archibald Houston (June 12, 1921–April 17, 2005) was a Canadian artist, writer and designer who featured significantly in developing the recognition and appreciation of Inuit art and who introduced printmaking to their culture. He immediately recognized the aesthetic appeal of the small sculptures he

---

7   Charlotte Gray, *The Museum Called Canada: Twenty Five Rooms of Wonder* (Toronto: Random House, 2007) 223.

8   http://en.wikipedia.org/wiki/Inuksuk. Retrieved September 28, 2013.

9   Ingo Hessel, *Inuit Art*. Editor, Sacko Usukawa. (New York: Collier-MacMillan Press, 1998), 157.

traded his own drawings for and he returned to the Canadian Handicrafts Guild in Montreal with roughly a dozen small carvings. With that they were able to procure a small grant in 1949 and the rest is history.[10]

BEA: But despite his obvious role in the development of Inuit printmaking and promoting northern art, he didn't change sculpture or carving?

INGOR: The significance of his bringing Inuit art to the Craft Guild cannot be overstated. He organized the first show of then "Eskimo Art." It was a complete success and he wrote promotional materials for sales in the south, was appointed a "Roving Craft's Officer" by the Canadian Handcrafts Guild, and resided in Cape Dorset.[11]

BEA: Certainly he prompted many of the Inuit to produce art for the south, yet they still imbued their art with traditional values, didn't they?

INGOR: Yes, he contributed to a new pride in being Inuit. There is much value in preserving traditions and history for their children. However, most Inuit art and sculpture (of which I am) categorically ends up elsewhere and is never seen again by our children or historians or anyone, for that matter.

BEA: Does art change when it becomes a performance piece or a collectable for others, especially for a commercial market? And yet another variation you have developed: small sculptures carved of northern stone and often beautifully polished that end up in gift shops and then travel all over the world. Have you become "Fine Art" or the opposite at that point?

INGOR: That is a kind of value judgment, placing quality over ethnicity. Inuit art cannot compare with that produced by traditional western values because the Inuit have been brought up within a largely egalitarian, non-judgmental, simple and yet complex, native lifestyle. Perhaps displaying their culture through their art has afforded the Inuit a way to hang

10   http://en.wikipedia.org/wiki/James_Archibald_Houston

11   Nancy-Lou Patterson, *Canadian Native Art* (Toronto: Collier-MacMillan Canada, 1973), 165.

onto the past in the face of rapid cultural change.[12]

BEA: Let's talk about adaptations to the Inuit way of life as a result of these significant changes.

INGOR: Well, traditional skills like hunting, fishing, and building shelter were no longer necessary and, because there weren't many opportunities for employment, in some villages almost half the population has become artisans, carving, sewing, drawing, painting or print making. Within a decade of James Houston's visits to Arctic Quebec, the Inuit carving industry on Baffin Island and the coast of Hudson Bay was booming. Initially it was to supply projects for government administrators, contracted art dealers, missionaries and even school teachers, and has since expanded.[13]

BEA: Wow—entire communities of artists and craftspeople. That sounds Utopian and is hopelessly romantic.

INGOR: Not really. The only person who benefits from the sale of an Inuksuk statue or sculpture is the artist who has created it, and the Guild fees, commission and taxes paid on the sale. Some of the individual artists, such as David Ruben Piqtoukun, have become world renowned and relatively successful.

BEA: With new laws emerging all the time governing the use of images, how do you—or can you—protect yours and decide who benefits from the use of it?

INGOR: Some images are intellectual property and trademarked but it is difficult to possess or dictate use of an image that can change with every single "assemblage" of stones or even with light and shadows. I am an *Inuksuk*; *I express* the Inuit belief that many things, like the land, belong to everyone and no one in particular.

BEA: And what about your modern usage? Does serving as a mainstream Canadian national symbol have its drawbacks?

---

12   George Swinton. "Foreword," Hessel, vii.

13   Patterson, 169.

INGOR: Well, it seems that I have either gained or lost significance as a religious object or shrine, depending on how you look at it. If everyone creates their own version of an Inuksuk by the side of the road or in their back yard rock garden, how do we justify the commercial success and maintain the commercial success/value that I presently enjoy; I certainly have tried to be mass appealing, simple yet complex.

BEA: Well, thank you Ingor Inuksuk and we will being seeing you real soon. (*To Audience*) Look for Ingor in his upcoming series of children's books and his very own feature cartoon, and fashion line too I'm told, lots of chunky knits and jewellery. (*Fade to commercial*)

SELF-RESPECT

DAVID MACEACHERN

Capturing prosperity has no need of disguise,
   one suffers from exclusion when kept aside.
Once open to the world at large,
   a sense of fearless exposure takes hold.
With hills to climb a reason unfolds,
   by conquering circumstance you shall reach on.
Variance in routine be source of relief,
   allowing fervor for virtue enlightens your day.
Full awareness and confidence walking the line,
   putting rise into advancement beyond darkened times.

"We learn better in a free spirit of curiosity than under fear and compulsion."

   —Saint Augustine

Freedom of Expression and the Crusade for Human Rights:
Joseph Howe and Carrie Best:
Two Nova Scotia pioneers

KIM KIERANS

SEPARATED BY A century, Joseph Howe (1804-1873) and Carrie Best (1903-2001) both challenged the Nova Scotia establishments of their time and fought for freedom of expression and civil liberties.

Howe: Freedom of the press

JOSEPH HOWE TOOK over the weekly newspaper, *The Novascotian*, in 1827 at the young age of 24. The weekly soon became the leading provincial newspaper among the reading classes.

Howe, a poor student, was largely self-educated. Historian Murray Beck writes in the *Dictionary of Canadian Biography* that Howe viewed the newspaper as an instrument of his own education and the education of his readers. Howe wrote:

> My books are very few, but then the world is before me—a library open to all—from which poverty of purse cannot exclude me—and in which the meanest and most paltry volume is sure to furnish some thing to amuse, if not to instruct and improve.

Howe introduced subscribers to poetry and to local authors such as Thomas Chandler Halliburton and his *Clockmaker* sketches. Writing as the "Rambler," he took readers on his annual travels along the country roads to sell subscriptions and gather stories in settlements across Nova Scotia.

He also took a keen interest in politics and was the first journalist to sit through debates and report in great detail on the activities of the Legislative Assembly. Howe's family had come to Halifax as Loyalists after the American Revolution. His father was part of the establishment but Howe came to witness too much corruption among the ruling classes. On January 1, 1835, he published a letter to the editor in *The Novascotian*, which reads in part:

> Mr. Howe, Sir. — Living as we do in a free and intelligent Country ... I will venture to affirm, without the possibility of being contradicted by proof, that during the lapse of the last 30 years, the Magistracy and Police have, by one stratagem or other, taken from the pockets of the people, in over exactions, fines, &c. &c. a sum that would exceed in the gross amount £30,000 ... [and] from the pockets of the poor and distressed at least £1000 is drawn annually, and pocketed by men whose services the Country might well spare. These things, Mr. Howe, cannot much longer be endured, even by the loyal and peaceable inhabitants of Nova Scotia ... THE PEOPLE.

Within months Howe faced a charge of criminal libel for publishing the letter. He chose to defend himself and, in the province's most celebrated trial, spoke with great passion for more than six hours. He argued for "an open and unshackled press" and concluded with this appeal:

> My public life is before you; and I know you will believe me when I say, that when I sit down in solitude to the labours of my profession the only questions I ask myself are, What is right? What is just? What is for the public good?

When the trial resumed the next morning, the jury took ten minutes to reach the verdict of not guilty. Howe proclaimed, "the press of Nova-Scotia is Free."

The fight for Howe's free unshackled press continues to this day.

Governments don't like media poking into the business of the public and they create laws to suppress information.

In 1938 the Supreme Court of Canada struck down a provincial law in Alberta that aimed to control and restrict the press. The court ruled that:

> Democracy cannot be maintained without its foundation: free public opinion and free discussion throughout the nation of all matters affecting the State within the limits set by the criminal code and the common law.

The SCOC also proposed for the first time the existence of an implied bill of rights to protect such civil liberties as a free press in recognition of certain basic principles underlying the Canada's fundamental law.

Best: Civil rights

CARRIE BEST, A poet, author, and journalist from Pictou County, understood the power of the media in her fight for the civil liberties of African Nova Scotians and other disadvantaged groups. In 1942 Best and her son Cal were arrested for sitting downstairs in the whites-only seats at The Roseland Theatre in New Glasgow. They were charged with disturbing the peace, convicted, and fined.

From that point on, Best became a vocal human rights activist. In 1946 she opened *The Clarion* in New Glasgow, the first black owned and published newspaper in Nova Scotia. It started as an 8" x 10" single sheet community bulletin and quickly expanded to become a small broadsheet newspaper and a powerful voice for racial understanding and social justice.

One of *The Clarion*'s first big stories was a case of *déjà vu* for Best. In 1946, Viola Desmond, a beautician and business woman from Halifax, was arrested, charged, and fined for sitting in the whites-only seats at New Glasgow's Roseland Theatre. Best continued to cover the story until Desmond won on a second appeal, helping to strike down segregation laws in Nova Scotia.

The Clarion was published from 1946 to 1956, and Best revived it briefly as *The Negro Citizen* in 1977.

Between 1968 and 1975 Best continued to use her writing to expose human rights abuses in a weekly column titled "Human Rights" in *The Advocate*, a weekly newspaper in Pictou. She tackled such weighty subjects as substandard conditions on First Nations' reserves and discrimination against black property owners on New Glasgow's Vale Road.

In a 1991 interview with CBC host Jim Nunn, Best, then 87, said she relied upon "intelligence, patience, a lot of prayer, a lot of forgiveness" in her fight against racism.

Rights and freedoms

WHEN CARRIE BEST spoke out against segregation in Pictou County in the 1940s, hers was one of the emerging voices in an international human rights movement that grew out of two great wars in the first half of the century. Article 19 of the 1948 Universal Declaration of Human Rights upheld the inalienable and inviolable right to freedom of opinion and expression, "to hold opinions without interference and to seek, receive and impart information and ideas through any media and regardless of frontiers."

This international endorsement of freedom of expression as a fundamental human right was reflected in various court decisions in Canada in the following years and was sacred to newspaper publishers like Carrie Best and George V. Ferguson, the editor of the Montreal *Daily Star*. In 1955 he wrote in *Press and Party in Canada* that "The general will of a political society cannot be fully expressed without this freedom. Freedom of information thus becomes an essential part of any system of democracy."

Not only the courts but also the government came to acknowledge the importance of freedom of expression in a democracy. In 1960 Prime Minister John Diefenbaker attempted to give it legal standing through passage of the Canadian Bill of Rights. Section One of the act recognized and declared that "in Canada there have existed and shall continue to exist without discrimination by reason of race, national origin, colour, religion or sex, the following human rights and fundamental freedoms, namely ... (d) freedom of speech ... (f) freedom of the press."

Today, the Canadian Bill of Rights remains on the statute books but is considered ineffective because it can be changed by a simple act of Parliament and is open to court challenges. Far more secure is the Canadian Charter of Rights and Freedoms, which was embedded as part of Canada's constitution in 1982.

Section Two of the Charter of Rights and Freedoms affirms that everyone has the following fundamental freedoms:

(a) freedom of conscience and religion;

(b) freedom of thought, belief, opinion and expression, including freedom of the press and other media of communication;

(c) freedom of peaceful assembly;

(d) freedom of association.

In 1835 Joseph Howe took the first steps toward a free press. In 1946 Carrie Best relied on those freedoms and used the media to advocate for racial equality and civil rights. Today, mainstream media face unprecedented threats to their very survival as advertising revenues and readers disappear, in both cases, to the Internet. Major North American newspapers have folded or are in serious financial trouble. Here in Nova Scotia the Halifax *Daily News* closed in February 2008 and the Halifax *Chronicle Herald* recently announced more major layoffs.

So this is a good time to remember the vital role of responsible journalism in our communities, our society, and our democratic system. Newspapers as we know them may not survive. The Internet is creating new ways of storytelling. But journalism—the act of independent reporting and verification of the facts, the act of questioning, challenging and criticizing government policy and official versions of events, the act of giving voice to the voiceless—the journalism of Joseph Howe and Carrie Best must survive. Citizens' ability to make informed choices depends on it.

Bibliography

Beck, J. Murray. "Howe, Joseph," *Dictionary of Canadian Biography*, vol. 10. University of Toronto Press; Québec: Université Laval, 2003. http://www.biographi.ca/en/bio/howe_joseph_10E.html. Accessed November 11, 2014.

Ferguson, George V. *Freedom of the Press: Seventh Series of Lectures Under the Chancellor Dunning Trust at Queen's University.* Toronto: Ryerson Press, 1955.

Government of Canada. *Canadian Bill of Rights S.C. 1960*, c. 44. http://laws-lois.justice.gc.ca/eng/acts/c-12.3/page-1.html Accessed November 11, 2014.

Government of Canada. *The Canadian Charter of Rights and Freedoms.* http://laws-lois.justice.gc.ca/eng/const/page-15.html Accessed November 11, 2014.

Grant, Cheryl. *Carrie M. Best: A Digital Archive*. Parliament of Canada. http://www.parl.ns.ca/carriebest Accessed November 11, 2014.

Nunn, Jim. "Civil Rights Activist Carrie Best." First Edition, Canadian Broadcasting Corporation, July 26, 1991. http://www.cbc.ca/archives/categories/society/celebrations/celebrating-black-history/civil-rights-activist-carrie-best.html Accessed November 11, 2014.

Province of Nova Scotia. "Joseph Howe: Defender of Freedom of the Press. Champion of Responsible Government in Nova Scotia." http://ns-legislature.ca/index.php/ about/joe-howe

Province of Nova Scotia. "The Newspaper Article that Brought about Freedom of the Press." http://nslegislature.ca/index.php/about/joe-howe/howepaper. Accessed November 11, 2014.

Province of Nova Scotia. "The Indictment for Libel and Mr. Howe's Defense." http://nslegislature.ca/index.php/about/joe-howe/howedefense. Accessed November 11, 2014.

Supreme Court of Canada. *Reference Re Alberta Statutes—The Bank Taxation Act; The Credit of Alberta Regulation Act; and the Accurate News and Information Act, [1938] SCR 100, 1938 CanLII 1 (SCC).* http://canlii.ca/t/

1nmz8. Accessed November 11, 2014.

United Nations. "The Universal Declaration of Human Rights." http://
www.un.org/en/documents/udhr/index.shtml#a19. Accessed November
11, 2014.

ROLAND IN PARADISE:
Teaching The Song of Roland *in Halifax Humanities*

NEIL G. ROBERTSON

Roland replies: "And may God grant to us,
It is our duty to be here for our king:
For his lord a vassal must suffer hardships
And endure great heat and great cold;
And he must lose both hair and hide.
Now let each man take care to strike great blows,
So that no one can sing a shameful song about us.
The pagans are wrong and the Christians are right.
No dishonourable tale will ever be told about me."

—*The Song of Roland*, laisse 79[1]

IT WOULD BE hard to find a text more unsuitable for Halifax Humanities than *The Song of Roland* and yet, as I want to argue in this chapter, nothing better takes us into what is essential to our work. This medieval poem from around 1100 CE has so many features that make its inclusion in the curriculum of Halifax Humanities deeply problematic: it is relentlessly, not merely Eurocentric, but indeed, Christian-centered in all that it says; it has language that is not only sexist and elitist but indeed racist; it seems to glorify war and violence in the name of personal honour and a sense of cultural and religious superiority. Of course, all of these aspects can and do

---

1   *The Song of Roland* (London: Penguin, 1990). Trans. Glyn Burgess,

become teachable moments in trying to problematize the sense that the high cultural aspirations that can seem to be at work in Halifax Humanities are not without serious, perhaps irresolvable, problems. Still, one doesn't choose to read a work, at least not in a programme under such severe constrains of time as Halifax Humanities, simply because it is so deeply problematic.

So it would seem that perhaps behind, or in spite of, these problems, *The Song of Roland* presents a certain richness of vision or insight that warrants its inclusion. But then one is faced with the remarkably simple, not to say simplistic, stance articulated in such passages as that quoted above: "The pagans are wrong and the Christians are right." This is in fact the unchanging perspective of the poem, where the "pagans," the Saracens, are portrayed in historically utterly inaccurate ways about an event that happened very differently from the way it is described in the poem. As a work of intercultural encounter, *The Song of Roland* is a massive failure.

But of course, while all of these contemporary concerns are entirely valid and need to be addressed, they can crucially mislead us, preventing us from entering into both what is truly medieval in the poem and what can speak to the participants in Halifax Humanities as we seek together to come to forms of self-understanding that aren't available in what is simply contemporary. The poem does have a kind of simplicity and naivety coupled with an almost massive incomprehension of the historical "other" that the poem appears to represent. But this "other" is in truth, and poetically, not a historical other—the historical Muslims of medieval Spain—but in fact a psychic, symbolic "other" that brings to light the moving principle of Medieval Latin Christendom. For the purposes of Halifax Humanities, this moving principle is not only worth considering in its own terms but it is also crucially disclosive of how the medieval functions not as dividing ancient from modern, but uniting and connecting the two.

So what is this moving principle? The simple and obvious way of describing it is the will, the will that appears in its constitutive function in the vow, in its motivational function as honour. This is really what the poem is about: what is the true will and how does it relate to its "other" that is deceit and treachery. The poem puts forward this question of the will in a disturbing and yet also moving form through the relation of Roland to his great friend and fellow vassal, Oliver:

> Roland is brave and Oliver is wise;
> Both are marvellous vassals.

Here we see the complementary virtues of Roland and Oliver, these companions who are connected not only by shared vassalage but by having been brought up together in the household of Charlemagne and who share the prospect of being joined in familial bonds by the marriage of Roland to Oliver's sister, Aude. Yet this relationship will be brought to the breaking point by the circumstances that face them in the deceit of not only the "pagans," but more pointedly of Ganelon, Roland's uncle. When the rearguard of Charlemagne's army—commanded by Roland—finds itself vastly outnumbered by a Saracen army as it leaves Spain, a debate ensues between Roland and Oliver about whether Roland should blow his horn to bring back Charlemagne's army to engage with this unforeseen eventuality. Roland refuses to blow his horn on the basis of the demands of his honour. What then ensues is precisely what Oliver foresaw: the slaughter of the French rearguard. This debate about the horn then recurs but more poignantly in the deepened extremity of the complete massacre of the French forces has become undeniable. In these new circumstances, Roland tells Oliver that he must blow his horn, so driving Oliver to the breaking point. After Roland refused to blow the horn when it might do some good, for Oliver the blowing of the horn now is both useless and declaration of the folly and recklessness that has led to the destruction of the rearguard. In his despair at Roland's folly he tells him: "If ever I see my noble sister Aude,/ You will not lie in her arms" (laisse 130). Indeed Oliver tells Roland:

> "Roland we can only rue your prowess;
> Charlemagne will have no aid from us.
> There will be none like him until the Day of Judgement;
> You will die here and France will be shamed by it.
> Today our loyal comradeship is at its end;
> Before evening there will be a sorrowful farewell." (laisse 131)

Roland's and Oliver's friendship is apparently shattered as Roland blows the horn to summon Charlemagne to avenge his soon-to-be-dead vassal. Yet even as Roland comes to destroy himself in the very act of blowing the horn, there appears in the poem a beautiful illustration of what is moving in it. Oliver, blinded by blood streaming from a head wound, mistakenly strikes a nearly fatal blow against Roland. This might well have brought about the end of Roland in the end of their friendship in vassalage as the standpoints of Roland and Oliver come into dreadful collision. But rather than its destruction, the truth of that friendship is recalled and resurrected in and through a touching display of courtesy:

> At this blow Roland looked at him
> And asked him in gentle, tender tones:
> "Lord Companion, do you intend to do this?
> This is Roland who loves you so dearly;
> You had not challenged me in any way."
> Oliver said, "Now I can hear your voice
> But I cannot see you; may God watch over you.
> Did I strike you? Pardon me for this."
> Roland replies: "I have not been hurt;
> I pardon you here and before God."
> With these words they bowed to each other;
> See how they part with such great love! (laisse 150)

This exchange takes us into the delicate heart of this medieval poem. There is a way in which the basic story of the *Song of Roland* can appear to be a kind of clash between a wisdom that takes the reality of the world seriously (Oliver's wisdom) and a kind of religious recklessness or fanaticism that would destroy all finite goods in the name of a supposed eternal other-worldly realm (Roland's "bravery"). In class we often consider whether Roland is displaying the kind of pride or fanaticism of the suicide bomber that would happily destroy this world for the sake of a supposed higher, purer world. Much in the text, in Roland's apparent blindness to the realities facing him, in his claims of honour and apparent belief that God will bring victory in the face of overwhelming opposition, seems to point to a kind of fanatical disregard for the realities of the world.

But such an account must be disrupted by just the kind of profound courtesy that Roland displays toward Oliver—even *in extremis*—and indeed to all his companions in vassalage as well as his care for Aude and for all the particularities that surround him and are infused by Roland with a deep and specific duty and love. How, then, are we to reconcile Roland's "recklessness" toward the finite and his deep regard for it? How, in the midst of failure, can Roland prove to be the most complete vassal, to the extent that the poem shows Roland, in his moment of death, returning his right glove of vassalage to the heavenly host—symbolic of his completed service?

> He proffered his right glove to God;
> Saint Gabriel took it from his hand.
> Roland laid his head down over his arm;
> With his hands joined he went to his end.
> God sent down his angel Cherubin
> And with him Saint Michael of the Peril
> With them both came Saint Gabriel.
> They bear the count's soul to Paradise. (laisse 176)

Here we are given the perspective of "Roland in Paradise." From Oliver's perspective such a recognition of Roland's actions as the fulfillment of fealty can make no sense. Oliver seems to assume in his "wisdom" a kind of Aristotelian prudence that would measure and order courage in relation to its context. For Aristotle, courage, as is true of the other virtues, is a mean between extremes. To one extreme is cowardice where we flee in relation to what we should stand fast before; on the other is recklessness, where we stand fast before what we should flee. When Oliver accuses Roland of recklessness, he is making just such a judgement. Roland, in his pride and folly, is refusing to see the context of his vassalage and so he is failing his lord, Charlemagne. Roland, in a way, agrees with Oliver here that his context will not determine his will: "God forbid ... That any man alive should say that pagans made me blow the horn ... "(laisse 85). Roland will not let the context determine his will: this is for Roland the truth of a vow. It is placing the principle of reality in a place that stands outside the context of the world: but how is this not then recklessness?

Here I want to suggest that we need to dwell on this standpoint of Roland in Paradise, indeed Roland in *Paradiso*. In Dante's *Paradiso*, Roland is found among the souls Dante encounters in the circle of Mars. And really Dante's text as a whole gives the true logic by which to understand what is at work in the earlier poem. For Dante, the logic of *Paradiso* is captured by Thomas Aquinas' expression, "Grace does not destroy nature, but perfects it" (*S.T.* 1.1.8). The logic of the central spheres of the ascent in the *Paradiso* is precisely that: it is a transfiguring of the ancient cardinal virtues of wisdom, courage, justice, and temperance into their supernatural forms of faith, hope and charity (love of neighbour in Jupiter and love of God in Saturn). The logic at work here is a "transhumanization" (*Paradiso*, Canto I) of the natural into the supernatural where the finite is not seen to be the full context but only present as derived from and contained within an infinite end. Here is the logic by which Roland can be understood not to be in the grip of a tragic *hubris* by which both he and his companions are destroyed, but rather as having within him an absolute *amor*, a truly infinite will, which loves and knows the finite, not as external context or constraint, but as properly derived from and residing in that will. Roland is the true vassal precisely because he knows that no pagan can make him "blow the horn." For Roland this in no way implies the destruction of the world, but that its truth is seen with spiritual eyes that alone can both ground and preserve the finite and particular. Even as Roland must disagree with Oliver's judgement—calling it "folly"—he still loves Oliver "with such great love." So the finite, nature, is not destroyed in this "transhumanization" but perfected. Courage is not destroyed, but transfigured into hope.

All of this may be true of *The Song of Roland,* but how does it speak to Halifax Humanities? I want to say two things here. The first is an historical point: that what we are witnessing in *The Song of Roland* and indeed other texts from the medieval section of the course is precisely the transition from the ancient to the modern standpoints. While the transhumanization at work in *The Song of Roland* is a religious one, and necessarily so, this transhumanization will underlie the possibility of secular modernity that looks not to virtue in a context but to a dignity and freedom that is not defined by any context or naturally given condition. Our modern concepts of freedom and dignity have in them an understanding of will and person that exist nowhere in ancient world. In so far as we understand ourselves as beings of freedom and dignity we reside within a "transhumanization."

I want to suggest that this transhumanization is for Halifax Humanities at the very core of its being. In both what formed and maintains Halifax Humanities is a judgement that a kind of ancient prudence is insufficient. The experts told us time and again that it was misconceived; that it served no practical end. The very existence of the programme is saying that we need not be defined or determined by our context. In my judgement, this is true not only for our little programme in its very being but for our students, for our faculty, for all who have aided and supported it. Together we are all saying—if I can use, in light of the poem, the term "pagan" to be a metaphor for the context that would seek to define and confine us—

> God forbid that any man alive should say that "pagans"
> made us blow the horn.

No, when we blow the horn, we shall do so freely and joyfully.

"I Loved Her That She Did Pity Them"
or, How I Learned to Love Othello

ROBERTA BARKER

IN 1998, MY first year as a PhD student at the Shakespeare Institute in Stratford-upon-Avon, the English actor Hugh Quarshie gave the annual Shakespeare Birthday Lecture at the Shakespeare Birthplace Trust. The level of Bardolatry in Stratford-upon-Avon in general, and at the Shakespeare Birthday Lecture in particular, cannot be overestimated. It is Shakespeare's town, and the Lecture is one of the pinnacles of the Shakespearean year. So the very fact that Quarshie chose to speak on the topic of his *doubts* about playing the hallowed role of Othello was surprising enough. In the event, he went further than anyone expected. He admitted that, as one of Britain's leading black actors, he had been asked to play Othello on numerous occasions. But, he declared bluntly, the play was the product of a racist early modern English society; in it, Shakespeare had adapted an already racist source text, a story by Cinthio, and made it more racist still; and *Othello's* subsequent long stage history had done little more than compound negative images of black masculinity. This being the case, he argued,

> If a black actor plays Othello does he not risk making racial stereotypes seem legitimate and even true? When a black actor plays a role written for a white actor in black make-up and for a predominantly white audience, does he not encourage the white way, or rather the wrong way, of looking at black men, namely that black men, or "Moors," are over-emotional, excitable, and

269

unstable ...? Of all the parts in the canon, perhaps Othello is
the one which should most definitely not be played by a black
actor.[1]

More than fifteen years later, I can still remember the ripple of utter horror
in the room when Quarshie answered a blunt question at the end—"Are
you saying that Shakespeare was a *racist*?"—with a simple, "Yes." "I can only
be sorry," intoned the questioner, "that your experiences have embittered
you so much as to convince you of something so wrong." Quarshie merely
smiled.

If Quarshie's position shocked the Bard-loving audience at the Shakespeare Birthplace Trust, by 1998 it was hardly controversial in academia.
The entanglement of *Othello*, with its ungovernably jealous and eventually
murderous Moorish tragic hero, in a long history of representations of men
of colour as irrational, violent, and even bestial, had been discussed in a wide
range of publications over the 1980s and 1990s. The year before Quarshie
gave his lecture in Stratford, Howard University Press published the important collection *Othello: New Essays by Black Writers*, which centered on
debate around the very points the actor raised.[2] Moreover, race wasn't the
only issue in *Othello* that exercised critics in this period. In his influential
1992 essay "When is a Character Not a Character?" Alan Sinfield cites the
play's representation of Desdemona as typifying early modern patriarchal
visions of femininity. Shakespeare is widely admired for his "invention of
the human:" his apparently miraculous ability to portray characters whose
aura of psychological complexity and emotional interiority epitomizes the
conceptions of the individual self emergent in the early modern period.[3]
But Desdemona, for Sinfield, is not a "character" at all; rather, she is "a
disjointed sequence of positions that women are conventionally supposed

---

1   Hugh Quarshie, "Second Thoughts About Othello," *International Shakespeare
Association Occasional Paper No. 7* (Chipping Campden: Clouds Hill Printers, 1999), 5.

2   Mythili Kaul, ed., *Othello: New Essays by Black Writers* (Washington, D.C.:
Howard University Press, 1997).

3   See Harold Bloom, *Shakespeare: The Invention of the Human* (New York: Riverhead Books, 1998).

to occupy."[4] *Othello*, such critiques suggested, was not only racist, but sexist, too.

I came of age in the midst of this massive and crucial questioning of Shakespeare's supposed status as the infallible author for all ages. Maybe it's no wonder, then, that I have always been a little afraid of *Othello*. When Mary Lu Redden asked me if I would teach it in Halifax Humanities 101, I nearly balked. *That* play, to that group of people? *That* play, to students who have experienced firsthand the brutal effects of institutionalized oppression and inequity? Won't it simply make everybody hate Shakespeare? My experience, quite unexpectedly, was the opposite. Halifax Humanities 101 is the classroom that made me love *Othello* again—less by convincing me that the critiques of Quarshie, Sinfield, et al. were wrong, than by convincing me that they were not, after all, the last word. *Othello*, I have come to believe, both represents and participates in very complex processes of identification and othering. Even as it depicts—and, to an extent, replicates—the brutal effects of hatred and stereotyping, it also portrays—and, to an extent, practises—the more hopeful possibilities opened up by compassion and identification across difference.

To consider how that might be, I want to look briefly at the first and the last scenes in the play in which we see its much-debated hero and heroine, Othello and Desdemona, together. Before we meet them, we hear their union described by Othello's disgruntled ensign, Iago, and Desdemona's spurned suitor, Rodrigo. "Your daughter and the Moor are now making the beast with two backs," Iago tells Desdemona's appalled father, Brabantio, asking him further if he wishes to see his daughter "cover'd with a Barbary horse."[5] Rodrigo offers a similar vision of the union, declaring that Desdemona has eloped from her father's house into "the gross clasps of a lascivious Moor" (1.1.126). The union of the Moorish general and his aristocratic

---

4   Alan Sinfield, "When is a Character Not a Character: Desdemona, Olivia, Lady Macbeth, and Subjectivity," in *Faultlines: Cultural Materialism and the Politics of Dissident Reading* (Oxford: OUP, 1992), 52–79, 53.

5   William Shakespeare, *Othello*, in *The Riverside Shakespeare*, ed. G. Blakemore Evans (Boston: Houghton Mifflin, 1974), 1.1.115–117, 111–112. All further references to the play will be to this edition and will appear in parentheses in the body of the essay.

Venetian bride is constructed as lewd, revolting, a kind of abomination: an act not only of miscegenation, but of outright bestiality.

Still, the couple we meet in the council chamber of the Venetian Doge looks and sounds quite different from the picture so hideously offered by Iago and Rodrigo. In answer to the accusations of Desdemona's father, Othello offers a very simple account of a love story founded in an exchange of personal narratives. He, the Moor who has risen to considerable status in Venetian society thanks to his military prowess, recounts how he used to visit Brabantio's house and tell of the "most disastrous chances" of his life, including his experience of "being taken by the insolent foe,/And sold to slavery" (1.3.137-138). He tells how Desdemona would "seriously incline" to listen to his tales (1.3.146), weeping and sighing at the thought of his sufferings:

> She swore, in faith 'twas strange, 'twas passing strange;
> 'Twas pitiful, 'twas wondrous pitiful.
> She wish'd she had not heard it, yet she wish'd
> That heaven had made her such a man. She thank'd me,
> And bade me, if I had a friend that lov'd her,
> I should but teach him how to tell my story,
> And that would woo her. Upon this I spake:
> She lov'd me for the dangers I had pass'd,
> And I lov'd her that she did pity them.
> This only is the witchcraft I have us'd. (1.3.160-169)

According to Othello's report, Desdemona—the sheltered young European noblewoman—begins by finding his experience radically other than her own: it is strange, passing strange. But she moves straight from wondering at it to pitying it. Pity, of course, can be taken as another form of othering. But this isn't where Desdemona stops, for she moves from pitying Othello to feeling a kind of identification with him across the lines not only of race but of gender: "she wish'd/That heaven had made her such a man." It was this movement of compassion and empathy, according to Othello, that sealed their union—and not, as Othello stresses, some racially determined form of "witchcraft."

To be sure, when Othello declares, "She lov'd me for the dangers I had pass'd,/And I lov'd her that she did pity them," we can hear him as asserting a binary difference between masculinity (which actively embraces dangers) and femininity (which passively listens and feels the tender emotion of pity). Strikingly, however, this easy binary is immediately challenged by Othello's own determination to let Desdemona speak for herself. "Here comes the lady," he says as she enters, "let her witness it" (1.3.170). As for Desdemona's words, she herself admits that they are not what one might immediately expect of a modest Venetian maiden:

> That I did love the Moor to live with him,
> My downright violence, and storm of fortunes,
> May trumpet to the world. My heart's subdu'd
> Even to the very quality of my lord.
> I saw Othello's visage in his mind,
> And to his honors and his valiant parts,
> Did I my soul and fortunes consecrate.
> So that, dear lords, if I be left behind,
> A moth of peace, and he go to the war,
> The rites for why I loved him are bereft me[.] (1.3.248-257)

In front of a roomful of much older men, Desdemona comes right out and declares that she wishes to live with—and, by implication, to have sex with—the man with whom she has just eloped. Moreover, she affirms that she has become *like* him, "subdu'd/Even to the very quality"—that is, both to the appearance and to the profession—of her lord. She not only loves him for his bravery, his "honors and his valiant parts," but she wishes to participate in it. Indeed, she has already done so, for like a soldier she has "trumpet[ed]" her love to the world through her "downright violence" to established social norms. Thus, she insists that she will not remain in the safely feminine and aristocratic position of the delicate "moth of peace," but will follow her husband as he returns once more to "the rites for why I loved him." The relationship between husband and wife, Moorish man and European woman, soldier and maiden, here appears as one of absolute identification and of (almost) complete defiance of the vicious prejudices that rule their world.

I say "almost" because, alas, the seeds of the destruction of this beautiful dream of union appear even as it is articulated. When Desdemona declares that she "saw Othello's visage in his mind," she implies that she saw *past* the visible racial difference that she might have perceived as ugly, straight into the beauties of his soul. Touching though this may be, it suggests that Othello's colour is more a deficit to be overcome than an attraction in her eyes. Othello hears this; and he hears, too, Brabantio's parting imprecation against Desdemona's unseemly feminine duplicity: "Look to her, Moor, if thou hast eyes to see;/She has deceiv'd her father, and may thee" (1.3.292-293). "My life upon her faith!" exclaims Othello (1.3.294), but the notes of racial and gender prejudice hang heavy in the air. It is upon these dissonant notes that Iago will play in order to bring about the destruction of both Othello and his bride.

Iago has been read in many ways by many critics: as an agent of absolute evil, as the image of the Machiavellian Italian so dreaded by the English of Shakespeare's age, as a Vice figure out of a medieval morality play, as an embittered and traumatized lower-class veteran of upper-class wars. He is all of these things, and more, as an actor chooses to play him. But in the context of my analysis of identification and othering in the play, he is perhaps above all a man who combines an exquisite understanding of another (in this case, of Othello) with an absolute lack of empathy for him. Slowly, cunningly, he appeals to Othello's insecurities, not claiming outright that Desdemona is deceiving him, but merely implying that this *may* be the case and letting Othello's deep-seated doubts do the rest. He understands perfectly that Othello is, *must* be, unsure of himself in the atmosphere of prejudice that surrounds him. With no pity whatsoever, he goes straight for the jugular by reminding Othello of both Desdemona's words and Brabantio's in the Venetian council room: "She did deceive her father, marrying you,/And when she seem'd to shake and fear your looks,/She lov'd them most" (3.3.206-208).

As soon as Othello is left alone, we see that Iago's evaluation of him has been impeccable. He muses on the differences between himself and his bride, rapidly concluding that they have turned Desdemona against him:

> Haply, for I am black,
> And have not those soft parts of conversation
> That chamberers have, or for I am declin'd
> Into the vale of years (yet that's not much),
> She's gone. I am abus'd, and my relief
> Must be to loathe her. (3.3.263-268)

Iago must be right, after all; Desdemona must be false, for Othello is not like her. He is black—and, moreover, brutish and old, not elegant and charming like the young noblemen around her. As for her, she is a whore, and he, "abus'd" by her, can only hate her. Difference and alienation win out over empathy and identification, with disastrous consequences. Othello murders Desdemona and then, when he realizes that Iago has deceived him and that she was faithful after all, kills himself. With almost his last breath, he compares himself to "a malignant and a turban'd Turk" that he once stabbed for traducing the Venetian state (5.2.353). Thus, Edward Berry argues that "[t]he most disastrous consequence of racial alienation for Othello is not the hostility or the estrangement of the Venetians, but his own acceptance of the framework by which they define him."[6]

And what of Desdemona? Well, when she revives for a last moment after Othello strangles her, she seems absolutely to confirm Sinfield's assertion that she is not a three-dimensional character, as modern liberal humanism has understood that term, but rather a patriarchal stereotype of femininity. When her maid Emilia asks her, "O, who hath done this deed?" Desdemona responds, "Nobody; I myself. Farewell!/Commend me to my kind lord. O, farewell!" (5.2.124-125). On this note, she dies. Her last words can be read as the very epitome of the woman's acceptance and internalization of her own victimization, just as Othello's self-comparison with the much-hated "Turk" suggests his acceptance and internalization of racist slurs against him.

But this is not the only, and perhaps not even the best, way of reading the tragic relationship between Othello and Desdemona. If she accepts her murder with her last breath, Desdemona does so in language that returns

---

6   Edward Berry, "Othello's Alienation," in *Studies in English Literature, 1500-1900* 30.2 (Spring 1990): 315-333, 331.

to her earlier absolute identification with her husband. When she calls her murderer "I myself," she can be read as asserting her oneness with Othello as well as acceding to her death at his hands. Othello too, in his very last words, tries to re-establish a shared experience between them. "I kiss'd thee ere I kill'd thee," he affirms; "No way but this,/Killing myself, to die upon a kiss" (5.2.358–359). His tragic *hamartia*, his error in doubting both himself and his wife, has ensured that they can be at one only in death. Nevertheless, at the last both seek that oneness. Their desire for identification survives, albeit in an exceedingly disturbing form.

Which, then, wins out in *Othello*: the powerful paradigms of otherness and prejudice, or the dream of defying those paradigms through empathy and compassion? The text itself cannot answer these questions for us. It can only lay out a field of possibilities for us to interpret. Very often, as Hugh Quarshie rightly asserted in that Shakespeare Birthday Lecture, history has responded by reading and performing the play in a manner that keeps stereotypes, oppression, and hatred firmly in place. But when I put these same questions on the table in Halifax Humanities 101, I was reminded that quite a different response is possible.

"I have been there," is probably the response I have heard most often when discussing the fates of Othello and Desdemona with the students of HH101. When we speak about Othello's terrible internalization of his society's view of him, many students identify with his experience and speak of their own struggles to look at themselves from outside the negative images dominant society would impose upon them. I well remember one student standing next to me at the sinks in the women's washroom and saying that she connected with Desdemona. "She doesn't want to marry those boring guys her father wants her to marry. She doesn't want to be a doll or a puppet. She wants to make her own choice and be her own person, and do something more interesting and exciting. We can all understand that." I was forcibly reminded, during this conversation, of the wonderful reminiscence of Henry Jackson, who saw a boy actor play Desdemona in Oxford in 1610. He described the experience as follows: "Desdemona, killed by her husband, although she always acted the matter very well, in her death moved us still more greatly, for as she lay in her bed, her face alone implored the pity of the audience."[7] Jackson was watching a teenaged male English apprentice playing an Italian lady. But the performance, and his "pity," made him so forget these massive differences that he referred to the actor/Desdemona simply as "she." Desdemona may be a mere patriarchal construct, as Sinfield suggests. But in both 1610 and 2013, she seemed real enough to audiences that they could empathize with her despite the powerful boundaries of difference.

Jackson and the students of Halifax Humanities 101 are linked across time and space by the same emotion that linked Desdemona to Othello: compassion. Is this, then, a solution to the problems with *Othello* so cogently underlined by Quarshie? Not in the least. Given its history, the play seems an equivocal standard-bearer at best for notions of empathy and identification. Racism and sexism form a key part of the play's text and of its cultural history. But so too do a profound resistance to them, and to all those forms of othering that would limit the possibilities for human growth and community. The resistance doesn't neutralize the problem, alas; but it can at least serve, as it did between Desdemona and Othello, to create dialogue across difference. And that, I now believe, makes *Othello* a play that remains worthy, if not of uncritical adulation, then certainly of the ongoing process of exchange that the students of Halifax Humanities 101 so powerfully model.

---

7 Quoted in Gamini Salgado, *Eyewitnesses of Shakespeare: First Hand Accounts of Performances, 1590-1890* (London: Chatto and Windus, 1975), 30.

Bibliography

Berry, Edward. "Othello's Alienation." *Studies in English Literature, 1500-1900* 30.2 (Spring 1990): 315-333.

Bloom, Harold. *Shakespeare: The Invention of the Human.* New York: Riverhead Books, 1998.

Kaul, Mythili, ed. Othello*: New Essays by Black Writers.* Washington, D.C.: Howard University Press, 1997.

Quarshie, Hugh. "Second Thoughts About Othello." *International Shakespeare Association Occasional Paper No. 7.* Chipping Campden: Clouds Hill Printers, 1999.

Salgado, Gamini. *Eyewitnesses of Shakespeare: First Hand Accounts of Performances, 1590-1890.* London: Chatto and Windus, 1975.

Shakespeare, William. *Othello.* In *The Riverside Shakespeare.* Ed. G. Blakemore Evans. Boston: Houghton Mifflin, 1974.

PUBLIC SPACE, DEMOCRACY, AND SILAS MARNER

STEPHEN CLOUTIER

EVERY CLASS HAS its own rhythm, and a lecturer must be able to gauge the tone of each class and develop strategies to help the students to engage with the texts. While a lecturer must be sensitive to the fact that students are often reluctant to speak in class, discussion truly is the best way to facilitate understanding within the classroom. There will, of course, always be an element of lecture in any class as the lecturer needs to provide the philosophical and political contexts and the literary movements that influence a text, but, for true understanding, the classroom needs to be a place where students are free to explore and shape their own ideas and experiences. I was conscious of this when I brought George Eliot's novel *Silas Marner* (1861) to Humanities 101 as the novel explores ideas of democracy and community that students can relate to their own lives. Further, it is also a novel that is malleable enough that other theories can be brought to bear on the text in order to investigate Eliot's themes. The idea of the "Public Sphere" developed by the German sociologist and philosopher Jürgen Habermas (born 1929) in his book *The Structural Transformation of the Public Sphere*, for example, can help readers to reveal the connections between the novel and the world around them. Using Habermas as a guide, the classroom can (and should) become an extension of the public sphere where the students are free to examine their own ideas and experiences in a democratic reading context that will help to shape their individual responses to the literatures they read.

When the novel opens, the title character is living in the deeply religious community of Lantern Yard. Marner is accused of stealing money from the church, a crime of which he is innocent (he was framed by his friend William Dane). As the community members believe that God would never let an innocent man be convicted of a crime, they leave the determination of Marner's guilt up to God's will and draw lots. Marner draws the wrong lot and is found guilty. Appalled that God would allow him to be convicted, he renounces his faith and leaves. He settles in the community of Raveloe, where he becomes a recluse, developing the reputation of being a "witch" among the other inhabitants of Raveloe. Replacing his spiritual beliefs with commercialism, Marner becomes obsessed by owning gold. Never spending it, he hoards it, reveling in the ownership of it.

Under the influence of the gold, Marner allows himself to become dehumanized. The narrative voice remarks that, "Marner's face and figure shrank and bent themselves into a constant mechanical relation to the objects of his life, so that he produced the same sort of impression as a handle or a crooked tube, which has no meaning standing apart"[1] and that his "prominent eyes that used to look trusting and dreamy, now looked as if they had been made to see only one kind of thing that was very small, like tiny grain, for which they hunted everywhere."[2] Marner seems more machine than human. Eliot shows her readers the dehumanizing effects of industrialization on workers. This dehumanization takes an obvious physical toll; he is described as "withered and yellow" and seems to have aged, so much so that "though he was not yet forty, the children always called him 'Old Master Marner.'"[3] Marner's alienation from the community symbolizes a danger inherent in the new industrialized society. Eliot's concern is to show that a sense of community needs to be an anchor in the rapidly transforming English society. Without community, we all risk becoming

---

1   George Eliot, *Silas Marner* (London: Penguin, 1996), 20.
2   Eliot, *Silas Marner*, 20.
3   Eliot, *Silas Marner*, 20.

like Marner: misanthropic, alienated, and alone.

This is the lesson Marner needs to (and will) learn in the novel. When Marner's gold is stolen by Dunstan Cass, the dissolute younger son of the local Squire, Marner goes to the local tavern, the Rainbow, an action that will precipitate the breaking down of his isolation and his reintegration into society. The Rainbow, then, holds an important place in the community. It is the gathering place for the community and, as I will argue, becomes a place where people are allowed to speak their minds in a democratic space they find in no other aspects of their lives. The idea of the "Public Sphere" put forth by Jürgen Habermas in *Structural Transformation* helps to illustrate the role of the Rainbow in the novel. In the book, originally published in German in 1962 and translated into English in 1989, Habermas defines the Public sphere as that domain of social life in which public opinion formed:

> The bourgeois public sphere may be conceived above all as the sphere of the private people come together as a public; they soon claimed the public sphere regulated from above against the public authorities themselves, to engage them in a debate over the general rules governing relations in the basically privatized but publically relevant sphere of commodity exchange and social labor.[4]

Habermas traces the idea back to the 18th century, when private people gathered as peers in coffeehouses. This free gathering was an important point in the development of democratic ideals as they mediated between society and the state. Places like coffeehouses provided forums for private citizens with no formal power to meet and engage in public rational argument. Through these forums, citizens were able to effect social change. The London Stock Exchange, for example, emerged out of Jonathan's Coffeehouse where stock brokers would meet. As feudal society broke down and the new capitalist society emerged, power began to shift from an absolute ruler to a bourgeois public. Thomas McCarthy, in his introduction to *The*

---

4 Jürgen Habermas. *The Structural Transformation of the Public Sphere: An Inquiry into a Category of Bourgeois Society*, trans. Thomas Burger (Cambridge, Mass.: MIT Press, 1991).

Structural Transformation, explains that:

> In its clash with the arcane and bureaucratic practices of the
> absolutist state, the emergent bourgeoisie gradually replaced a
> public sphere in which the ruler's power was merely represent-
> ed *before* the people with a sphere in which state authority was
> publically monitored through informed and critical discourse *by*
> the people.[5]

The Public Sphere is formed any place where people get together to
talk as citizens in order to create public opinion. The Public Sphere must
be a place where people gather voluntarily without any other agenda (economic or political) to discuss subjects of general interest and it must be a
place where there is no coercion and there is a guarantee of free assembly
and expression. As someone who grew up in Germany during the rule of
the Nazis (he was four years old when the Nazis came to power and 16
years old when Nazi Germany collapsed), Habermas clearly understood
the dangers of totalitarianism, especially as he characterizes his own father,
Ernst, as a Nazi sympathizer.

Eliot sets the novel historically in the period when feudal society is
breaking down and the new capitalist society is emerging. Marner lives in
a more superstitious past "when the spinning-wheels hummed busily in
the farmhouses—and even the great ladies, clothed in silk and thread-lace,
had their toy spinning wheels of polished oak,"[6] a time in which Marner's
trade was, perhaps literally, a cottage industry rather than part of an industrialized capitalist society; Marner's increasing focus on gold reflects society's
shift from the feudal to the market economy. Placed historically, then, the
Rainbow shows the Public Sphere as it is developing and becoming more
of a force within society. There are still vestiges of the feudal society. The
local landowners, the Cass family, are not nobility, but they are still at the
top of the social structure like Lords of the Manor. The family patriarch

---

5 Thomas McCarthy, "Introduction" to *The Structural Transformation of the Public
Sphere: An Inquiry into a Category of Bourgeois Society* by Jürgen Habermas (trans.
Thomas Burger. Cambridge, Mass.: MIT Press, 1991), xi.

6 Eliot, *Silas Marner*, 5.

Squire Cass "was only one among several landed parishioners, but he alone was honoured with the title of Squire."[7] The Squire may be in an honoured position in Raveloe, but the novel suggests that the days of the Squire are numbered (both this individual Squire specifically and the social position of Squire generally) telling the reader, "his sons had turned out rather ill."[8] The Squire's two sons reflect the decadence of privilege that will help to stimulate social change. The elder son, Godfrey Cass, is a weak-willed man who secretly marries the opium-addicted Molly Farren and then abandons her and their daughter Eppie. Dunstan "Dunsey" Cass, the younger son, is a gambler and thief who blackmails Godfrey with the knowledge of Godfrey's marriage to Molly. Social change is happening around them and neither Godfrey nor Dunsey has the will to halt its progress. Dunsey, in fact, dies in the novel though his body is not discovered until years later when a marsh is drained.

The tavern itself shows the lingering effects of the old system. Class distinctions are still visible: the wealthier patrons sit closest to the fireplace and drink spirits and water while the lower class drink beer.[9] What we see developing in the tavern, however, is a more democratic space. Everyone can speak should they wish to and, more importantly, others will listen to them. It becomes a place where disagreements are played out. Mr. Snell, the landlord, (described as "a man of a neutral disposition, accustomed to stand aloof from human differences as those of beings who were alike in need of liquor")[10] maintains a neutral position in the arguments and debates that swirl around him. Snell also ensures that no one is denied access to the tavern; Snell was "under the habitual sense that he was bound to keep his house open to all company, and confident in the protection of his unbroken neutrality."[11] The tavern becomes a place of refuge, a place where everyone is welcomed and accepted. Snell facilitates the conversations in the tavern in a way that allows community members to air their

---

7   Eliot, *Silas Marner*, 23.
8   Eliot, *Silas Marner*, 24.
9   Eliot, *Silas Marner*, 46.
10 Eliot, *Silas Marner*, 46.
11 Eliot, *Silas Marner*, 55.

grievances. Chapter 6, in part, concerns an argument about a cow. Mr. Snell, ever the mediator, comments that the truth "lies atween you; you're both right and both wrong."[12] In refusing to take sides, Mr. Snell gives a legitimacy to both sides, reinforcing if not the views themselves at least their right to have opinions. The Rainbow becomes a space for a kind of participatory democracy. There is not complete equality, of course; class and social distinctions are maintained in the tavern, and no one is going to become radicalized by what goes on there. These are still deeply superstitious people (Chapter 6 ends with a debate on the existence of ghosts), but the developing Public Sphere allows conflicts (even minor ones) to be exposed in the congenial atmosphere created by the landlord. When an argument threatens to get too heated, Snell steps in to mediate, saying, "a joke's a joke. We're all good friends here."[13] Snell's desire to temper the arguments allows community members to vent their frustrations in a controlled atmosphere that prevents serious conflicts outside the tavern.

Another consequence of the breakdown of traditional power structures that results from the developing market economy is the shift away from a society that is strictly controlled by the Church to a more secular society. With religion no longer providing a collective sense of community, Eliot shows how a sense of community can be created in a secular world. Strict religious belief, as represented by Lantern Yard, is unyielding and unforgiving; Marner told the truth and was excommunicated. The secular world of the Rainbow is the opposite; it is an accepting world, and, through this acceptance, Marner begins his reintegration into society. It is to the Rainbow that Marner goes when he has discovered that his gold has been stolen. Dunsey Cass has stolen the gold, but Marner does not know this, initially believing that it was stolen by Jem Rodney, the poacher, whom Marner accuses when he finds Jem at the tavern. Snell vouches for Rodney and gets Marner to tell his story. In the open atmosphere of the Rainbow's Public Sphere, Marner begins to reconnect with the society around him:

---

12   Eliot, *Silas Marner*, 47.
13   Eliot, *Silas Marner*, 49.

> This strangely novel situation of opening his trouble to his Rav-
> eloe neighbours, of sitting in the warmth of a hearth not his
> own, and feeling the presence of faces and voices which were his
> nearest promise of help, had doubtless its influence on Marner,
> in spite of his passionate preoccupation with his loss. Our con-
> sciousness rarely registers the beginning of a growth within us
> any more than without us: there have been many circulations of
> the sap before we detect the smallest sign of the bud.[14]

The "bud" is, of course, a sense of community that Marner lost with his expulsion from Lantern Yard. A true sense of community comes not, as we might expect, from a deep religious faith but a secular sense of togetherness and compassion. Eliot seemingly turns away from evangelical Christianity as a source of comfort in the novel to a secular collectivity. Eliot underscores the inability of religion to adapt to the emerging new society with the end of the novel. Marner decides to revisit Lantern Yard only to find that it is gone and no one remembers the religious community. "The old place is all swep' away," Marner says.[15]

Not only do they extend their sympathy to him when his gold is sto-len but they also offer a network of support when he decides to adopt a baby who has crawled into his cottage. The child, Eppie, is the child of Godfrey Cass, the elder son of the local squire, and Molly Farren, Godfrey's secret wife, who has died as a result of her drug addiction. Eppie com-pletes Marner's reintegration into society when, later in life, she accepts Marner as her father. Childless by his second, socially acceptable wife, God-frey publicly offers to recognize Eppie as his daughter but she chooses to stay with Marner, the man who raised her and she accepts as her "Father." Rejecting Godfrey's proposal, Eppie states, "he's took care of me and loved me from the first, and I'll cleave to him as long as he lives, and nobody shall ever come between him and me."[16] The significance of Eppie's decision is twofold. First, it shows the shift from the feudal society in which blood is the most important factor in determining "family" and all the benefits that

---

14   Eliot, *Silas Marner*, 57.
15   Eliot, *Silas Marner*, 179.
16   Eliot, *Silas Marner*, 172.

come with it to a more egalitarian communal idea in which family is based on true affection between people. Second, it ends Marner's journey out of social isolation. He even rediscovers his religious faith. For Marner specifically and for the community of Raveloe in general, the Rainbow helps to break down their isolation and alienation, giving them the sense of community they need to help make their lives more bearable.

We can see that, using Habermas' idea of the Public Sphere, Eliot imagines a new secular community. Social conflict is inevitable. What Eliot posits in *Silas Marner* is a way in which conflicts can be made public and still maintain social cohesion. The classroom can be used as an extension of Eliot's communal conception. In Habermas' definition of the Public Sphere, the classroom can never truly be a "pure" public sphere as the student-lecturer context does not allow for true equality between the groups (the lecturer is always leading the class and shaping the discussion); however, even within the limitations imposed by this context, Habermas' ideas can be used to transform the classroom into a vibrant democratic space that can stimulate student engagement and understanding. While consumer mass media and competition threaten to alienate us from the ability to shape the world around, the classroom can become a powerful tool to reassert the necessity of democratic ideals that may be lost under the relentless pressure of the commodification of education.

$\mathcal{D}$ E S C A R T E S

WARREN HEITI

When a stranger asked to see his library, he pointed to a half-dissected calf:
"There are my books," he said.—Anthony Kenny

My mind is tied like a helium balloon
to the pommel of the pineal gland.
It dwells like a fountain keeper
deep in the grotto of the royal gardens,
checking the mechanism and dredging
dead leaves from the waterwheel.

A zebra-skin rug, a gallery
of antelope skulls. On the screen,
cars zip around the circuit;
exoskeletons, ghost-controlled.

       Inside the watch is a ruby
       pierced through the pupil
       by the spindle of a gear.

And this antelope, you know,
is merely another automaton,
one of indefinitely many earthen
machines, swirling, in vortices,
in the jam-packed plenum. There's just one
God-sized crack, under the sink,
stop-gapped with steel-wool.

Waltham manufactured the first watch
with fully interchangeable parts.
A physics in miniature, a cosmology
that fits in a pocket.

They cannot speak, and so,
contrary to the juvenile
Pythagorean superstition,
it is no crime to use them
as trophies. On my wall, they are
what they were: soulless, inert.
Stopped clocks.

My speech distinguishes me:
it encodes my soul.

Yes, even you, Elisabeth. I received
commands from your naked hand,
signals from your lips. These twitches
seemed to be evidence of thinking—
but who knows? Like the antelopes,
like the elephant-foot umbrella-stand,
perhaps you are just so much
extended stuff, an aggregate
of aggregates, half-real,
a TV tuned to the séance
channel of yourself,
prone to fever, pneumonia.
I am
the axiom
in the system that secures the world.

Even the atom is divisible.

The division of time is done
by a clutch of wheels held
by the arbour fitted
into a frictionless hole.
A leafless tree grows
in that golden microcosm,
it is the axis mundi,
distilling light into the liquor
of night, privatizing the I,
calculating the if/then algebra
of contracts and language
and time.

My heart, the dark furnace, churns
the finest particles, drives them
up the chimney to the lump of fat
in my skull, where my soul
perches nervously, pinball
operator of the pineal gland.

But inside the watch is the transplanted
hair-spring of the grasshopper's
heart, gorgeous, almost organic, flexing
concentrically with force proportional
to what we have offered.

$\mathcal{C}$ L E M E N T I A:
On the Uselessness of Reading Together

MARY LU REDDEN, EXECUTIVE DIRECTOR

WHEN I APPLIED to be the director of Halifax Humanities 101 in the summer of 2006, I had been out of the workforce for 11 years, at home with my children and doing only very occasional part-time work. In spite of a good academic background—graduate studies in Philosophy of Religion at McMaster University and over a decade of teaching both university and college courses—I was doubtful that I would be considered, a middle aged woman with an 11 year gap in employment!

To prepare for the interview, I read Earl Shorris' book, *Riches for the Poor,* which tells the story of the beginnings and growth of the Clemente Program in the Humanities which was the inspiration for Halifax Humanities 101. I *was* hired, and two of Earl's insights have guided me in my work ever since. That work is remarkably multi-faceted: recruiting students, securing classroom space, keeping professors and board members in touch and informed, raising money for the programme, helping students navigate myriad obstructions to their continuing studies and, most importantly, providing continuity in the intellectual discussion that lasts eight months and covers more than two millennia of great writings with dozens of professors from the University of King's College, Saint Mary's University, Dalhousie University, Mount Saint Vincent University, NSCAD University, Atlantic School of Theology, and Acadia University.

The first of my guiding insights from Earl is his vision of adult education as providing a space for "reflection instead of reaction" for people with significant life challenges.[1] The second insight is Earl's somewhat unpolished description of the pressures on people with low incomes: he called this life context "the surround of force."[2]

I recognized Earl's insights from the experience of my own difficult childhood. I knew both the need for a space of reflection and the surround of force. As a child, when the tensions in our family became too much, I escaped into a world of books.

As I read Earl's *Riches for the Poor*, I was deeply moved by the beauty of offering excellent education to adults who are shut out of so much: universities, concerts, art galleries, and much of the cultural life of our city.

I reflected on my mother's life, too. My mother was a very intelligent and well-read woman, an excellent pianist, and lover of Charles Dickens, Thomas Hardy, George Eliot and Jane Austen. She spent her adult life raising her unruly brood of five on a woefully inadequate income, and doing menial part-time work. How my mother would have benefited from a regular opportunity to sit and discuss great literature with others!

As we tidied up after the graduation ceremony at the end of my first year, David Heckerl of Saint Mary's University, one of our deeply dedicated teachers, said to me that what he loved most about the program was its "beautiful uselessness." I protested vehemently that our program, while beautiful, was in no way useless: "We are teaching important skills of critical thinking, classroom participation, time management."

Over time, I have come to see that what David said to me that day is in fact the heart of Halifax Humanities. When I read Earl's book, my first thought had been the beauty of it all. Now I spend a lot of time thinking about the nature of that beauty and how it liberates people even though it offers them no direct financial gain or job skills.

I have come to think of the Halifax Humanities as our intellectual Central Park.

Let me explain. As the director of Halifax Humanities, I have visited

---

1 Earl Shorris, *Riches for the Poor: the Clemente Course in the Humanities* (W.W. Norton & Co., 2000), p. 98.

2 Earl Shorris, *Riches for the Poor*, Chapter V "The Surround of Force."

many similar programmes in Canada and have twice attended the annual meeting of American Clemente directors. Since I must travel through New York City to get to the directors' gathering at Bard College, it only makes sense to stay in NYC for a while. How I've come to love the city!

In both of my visits to NYC I stayed very close to the west side of Central Park. Free to wander the public paths and gardens in beautiful spring weather, I love to drink in the beauty and justice of the Park. The beauty of Central Park is obvious. Perhaps its justice less so. In the midst of one of the most scandalously expensive cities in the world, underprivileged families from Harlem have as much right to play in the playgrounds as the Park Avenue children with their attentive nannies. Central Park is a public good, open to all and restricted to none because of income, race, ethnicity, or education level.

In Halifax Humanities, professors from seven universities come together with students who live with economic deprivation and what we share is our desire to explore. We explore the world of books where many of us hid, lonely, as children seeking to escape the "surround of force" into a space of reflection. In Halifax Humanities, we explore the intellectual space of great texts. The professors may have spent more time in this space than the students have, but the students' insights and questions open new vistas onto this familiar landscape. The great texts we study—Homer's *Odyssey*, Dante's *Divine Comedy*, Shakespeare's *Merchant of Venice*, Ibsen's *A Doll's House,* among so many others—can be neutral territory where people of disparate backgrounds, income levels, education, and life experience come together for a guided but free flowing exploration.

This is the beauty of Halifax Humanities: shared exploration with no particular agenda apart from the joy of reflection, discussion, and discovery. From many points of view this is quite "useless." This is what I have come to see: the critical thinking skills, the inspiration to pursue further education, and the restored sense of dignity that our students often experience are lovely by-products of that joy of exploration, but they are not its aim.

Students often tell me that the course and its community are important to them precisely because Halifax Humanities is not agenda-driven. Life on a low income, especially if one has mental or physical health worries, is often focused on treatment and therapy. These are, of course, very important but they can seem to turn a person into a patient, someone defined by a condition, weakness, or flaw. Specialized helpers focus on the condition and a person can feel as if she or he disappears into the role of the patient, recognized by others only as a condition—a problem to be treated, improved, and controlled.

In Halifax Humanities, according to many students, there is a freedom to leave your "condition" at the door and enter a free space of intellectual exploration. Here, what matters most is your intelligence and curiosity—your strengths—not your weaknesses.

I cannot count the times I have been told by middle-aged women, worn from years of raising children on their own with inadequate incomes, that this is the first time they have done anything "just for myself." Similarly, I've been told again and again by students living with serious mental health conditions that it is a relief to be in our classes where they are students, not patients. As one student said: "It's not therapy; but it sure is therapeutic."

Our programme, while part of a caring and supportive network, is quite different from many of our sister programs across Canada and the United States. That each specific community has developed a Clemente inspired program to suit its situation is one of the best parts of Earl Shorris' legacy. Like the American Clemente Program in the United States, we have stayed with the idea of a curriculum based on the so-called "Great Books" of the Western tradition. However, unlike those programs, we offer those books in a curriculum that might be described as an integrated conversation among disciplines and across history rather than in Earl Shorris' proposed schema of five discrete thematic sections of Literature, Art History, Philosophy, American History and Critical Thinking. In some of the American Clemente program these strict divisions in curriculum are handled in a flexible manner depending on which faculty members are available to teach.

Our focus on "core texts," whereby we read only primary texts and not critical analyses, is also in sharp contrast with our Canadian sister programs. Other curricula are often more social science based and at times focus expressly on social issues such as gentrification, gender politics, aboriginal affairs, and race relations.

The American Clemente programme offers its students the opportunity to earn a credit from Bard College. However, this credit is granted based on a very site-specific set of guidelines. While some American programmes require tests and assignments, not all do. Granting credit to students is a route that none of the Canadian programs has taken. While each of the Canadian programs has found ways to assist those students who wish to move on to credit studies at either community college or university, none has taken transition to credit studies as a primary focus. For some reason, all of the Canadian programmes take the shared intellectual experience of reading and discussion as primary. And interestingly, at their yearly Bard College gathering, the American Clemente directors often reflect intensely upon the value of their programmes to students who do not or cannot complete the requirements to earn a credit.

Regardless of whether a program is for credit, or the curricular focus is classical literature and philosophy or current social issues, the experience of the students in such courses is remarkably similar. Students speak eloquently of the experience of being seen not as "poor," "disabled," "a patient" to be treated or a "case" to be managed, but as a person with intelligence and reflections worth sharing. As a recent graduate of an American Clemente program wrote:

> The world improves when each one of us becomes better. The Odyssey Project achieves one of the kindest acts: it encourages us to look within ourselves, to seek a better world and the most important, it gives us hope to find it.[3]

It was pure coincidence that Earl Shorris held the first gathering of his free adult education program at the Roberto Clemente Family Resource Centre in Manhattan. But how lovely that coincidence proved to be. The name "Clemente" comes from the Latin *clementia*, which means "humanity, mercy, gentleness, kindness." I have come to see that this serendipitous

---

3   *The Odyssey Project's Journal,*   October 2012. http://clementecourse.org/news/52/15/October-2012-The-Odyssey-Project-s-Journal

juxtaposition of our unique programmes in adult education and the Latin for "humanity, mercy, gentleness, kindness" is entirely appropriate.

Halifax Humanities is characterized by sharing, generosity, and love: the love of the scholars for the texts they are eager to share with students; the generosity of the students' willingness to be guided into unfamiliar intellectual territory; and, most importantly, the sharing at the heart of each class when teachers and classmates meet with enthusiasm and civility in the intellectual Central Park of great texts and together build a space of reflection, sheltered for a precious short time from "the surround of force."

SURPRISES

VALEDICTORY ADDRESS 2008

KATHLEEN HIGNEY

THE HALIFAX HUMANITIES 101 experience may be expressed with ten verbs. Verbs are words that are used to show activity or state of being. Halifax Humanities 101 is a programme of learner-friendly study that invites participation on many levels. The words I have chosen to describe my year of learning are: *having, reading, discussing, eating, talking, writing, thinking, imagining, remembering* and *knowing*.

Having a destination, which promised to be interesting, on Tuesday and Thursday afternoons was extremely important to me. It also felt good to know that I would be seeing familiar faces and that I would be expected and welcomed at each class.

Reading books for the programme that I probably would not have read otherwise was good for my mind, will and emotions. And because we were given the books to keep, I could write comments in the margins. Not having to worry about library fines if I kept an item too long was a bonus too!

Discussing the books in class gave me the incentive to finish reading the ones I found difficult. It was challenging and rewarding to be able to express my ideas to people who had read the same works and to hear their opinions, though they were sometimes very different from mine.

Eating snacks with the other students and with the teachers was an enjoyable and important part of the classes. Getting to know someone is easier over a cup of tea or coffee.

Talking with classmates on the phone or at coffee shops after class allowed us to discuss the readings further and gave us a chance to socialize more.

Writing about the books and ideas we were studying allowed us to become more aware of what we thought and believed and enabled us to express ourselves in a more organized and permanent manner.

Thinking about different ways of looking at things as expressed by the authors of and characters in the books we read was exciting. It is helpful to understand that people may hold opposing views about the same issues. We can learn from each other if we remain teachable and humble.

Imagining that having a voice and being treated with respect like we were in Halifax Humanites is how our everyday lives might look in a better world.

Remembering the experience of being valued and empowered the next time we are treated badly or unfairly is another gift to Halifax Humanities students because we have our self-esteem strengthened during the classes.

Knowing that as individuals and members of community groups we can help to bring about changes that we and our loved ones need to lead happier and fuller lives is something we as graduates of Halifax Humanities 101 will carry with us forever.

Thank you!

THE GIFT

MADELINE REID COMEAU

I KNEW MY visit to Aunt Carrie that Christmas would most likely be my last. I felt some trepidation at the prospect of seeing her in St. Patrick's Nursing Home, St. John's, where she shared a small hospital-like room with another resident. A fiercely independent woman all her life, the medical specialists had convinced her that she should abandon the comfort and status of her apartment at Elizabeth Towers before her condition worsened. This was a "lady" (the term she preferred) who had chauffeured her friends to church, served up meals on fine china, beat everyone at cards, and mixed a mean drink (whether you wanted one or not). At ninety years of age, she could still talk your ear off about local politics and was always up on the latest gossip, especially with regard to the priests and nuns.

I pondered for some time over what kind of gift to bring. I wanted it to be different, special. I walked through Shoppers Drug Mart—nothing, then moved on to Lawton's—more of the same. As I was heading out empty-handed, I spied a display of teddy bears, the kind that could take up a chair in your living room. I was drawn to the medium brown one with the sporty tartan bow around his neck. I was not deterred by the fact that my aunt's space was limited to the standard bed, chair, and bedside stand. This was a gift that resonated with me; if she didn't like it, well, there was no point in going there. We (the bear and I) shared a seat on Air Canada, then a taxi to the nursing home. As I pranced down the corridor with teddy globbed onto the front of me, I could feel a smile emanating from somewhere deep inside me.

Aunt Carrie was indeed delighted to see me. At the sight of the bear, she blurted out: *In heaven's name Madeline, what have you got there?* She probably thought I had bought it for a niece or nephew. When faced with the reality that it was a gift for her, she put up some resistance: *Why did you do that, waste your money like that?* followed by *Sure, I've got nowhere to put it.* Seeing this gift-giving thing was not going as planned, I hastened to change the topic of conversation. I laid teddy aside, planning to unobtrusively take him away with me and spent the next hour chatting with my dear aunt, remembering all the wonderful summer holidays in Marystown, my mother's family home. As I was about to leave, she had a change of heart regarding teddy, telling me: *Since you brought it all the way here, you may as well leave it. I'll find someplace to put it.*

When I went into her room the next day, teddy was propped up in the chair where I had left him. I noticed that Aunt Carrie had a wicked sort of smile on her face; she was itching to tell me something—maybe another juicy bit of gossip. She proceeded to inform me that after I had left the previous evening, teddy and she had spent the night together. With her signature kind of chuckle, she added: *At my age, my dear, it was the next best thing dear to having a man in my bed.* We both cracked up laughing as we headed, hand in hand, to the dining room to share a strong brew of orange pekoe tea in delicate bone china cups with slices of dark, moist Christmas fruitcake, the homemade variety of course.

I often reminisce about that Christmas visit and the intense pleasure that I experienced when the gifted teddy bear found its way into my aunt's heart. I realize now, many years later, that her embracing of my gifted teddy with such humour was a beautiful gesture, her way of gifting her love back to me.

NEEDING ENTERTAINMENT

KATHLEEN HIGNEY

I tell the truth except you say
It is so hard to bear
And so I lie and weave my words
With cunning and with care

Spin me one more tale you ask
The evening seems so long
So traveling back to bygone days
I search for word and song

There in grace and splendor
Ancients live a better life
Resting from their labours
Accomplishment minus strife

I timidly approach them
And on my bended knees
Seek wisdom to cheer my friend
Who entertainment needs

A quick look at the others
A sound without a word
One stands up to answer me
And this is what I heard

We notice your commitment
And caring for your friend
And because you are not selfish
Wisdom we will lend

Suddenly back in my living room
I open my mouth wide
And sweet words flow like honey
Somehow they turn the tide

My old friend brightens and with a smile
Starts walking towards home
And I grateful and in awe
Am seemingly alone

Alone I think of great ones
Whose faces we see no more
But their strength remains within us
Until we reach the other shore

SORRY MR. CONNORS!

CATHERINE JOUDREY

IN 1974 MOM bought encyclopedias from a doortodoor salesman. We had five full sets: two general, one on science, another on world cultures, and a set of military medical guides (I have no idea why we had those). We also had lots of books about Germany from when my parents were posted there, and a ton of cookbooks. At my grandfather's in Woodside, there were *National Geographics* all over the house, and I'd read one after the other, especially my three As: Astronomy, Archaeology, and Anthropology. Grandad had books everywhere, and a big reading pile out in the porch where there was a pleasant rocking chair.

I read obsessively. I read everything I could get my hands on, and was a member of the library's summer reading club—easily surpassing the hundred book goal each summer. When Donnie moved in, he put nightlights through the house. He was afraid of the dark. I found them great to read with. I read whole series in the space of days—*Star Trek*, *Star Wars*, the *Belgariad*, and *Wheel of Time*. I'd drop one when it was done, and pick up the next, like they were chips in a bag. I got into comic book collecting, gathering up past issues at flea markets, and had an account on file for my orders at the local comic book shop, The Cardboard Jungle. I spent much of my babysitting money on books and comics.

Around 1989 I discovered WW2 and the Holocaust shelves of our local library. I read every book. It was heavy reading for a kid. We read Anne Frank at school, and I wonder if that triggered it. I was consumed with the need to know what war was, and how people experienced it. I was involved in cadets and met many veterans—I wanted to know their stories.

My interest went on for years and branched out into WW1, other military campaigns, and the biographies of world leaders.

I read in inappropriate places—doing my paper route I collided with parked cars because I was reading a book.

My reading lead to other problems too.

Once, I was sitting in Mr. Connors' Biology class in grade nine, reading and obviously not paying attention (though I remember clearly we were on the section about osmosis, and he was doing something cool with a tube and a carrot). He was a nice teacher, and usually calm, but my reading enraged him. He slammed his metre stick on my desk so hard the book flew from my hands to the floor. Picking up the book, he began reading the back summary in a singsong voice to the class ... his voice got soft, and he stopped reading as he realised the topic: Forced sexual slavery in WW2 and women's lives in the aftermath. He put the book on his desk.

Later, he apologised for hitting my desk, but asked me to please stop reading in his class.

JUSTIFIED CONCLUSION

DAVID MACEACHERN

Spoken in the wonder of its answer,
a theory seeks approval as its wish.
How words can open minds with reason,
so thoughts are exchanged in true concern.
Carried on through respect of one another,
the conversation holds direction to new themes.
Being wise in agreement depends upon trust,
while what is at stake has precedence.
When success comes without loss for righteousness,
then justice shows that prevention has won.

COULD YOU PLEASE DEFINE THAT WORD?

STEVEN BURNS

SHAKESPEARE USED ABOUT 50,000 different words in his plays and poems. There are many thousands more in English and new ones are added every day. Yet the average English-speaker gets by most of the time with a vocabulary of fewer than 5,000 words. So it is no wonder that we often run into words that we are not familiar with.

There are four main things that you can do when you don't understand a word. (1) You can give up trying to understand the speaker. (2) You can listen carefully and hope that the context will make clearer what the word must mean. (3) You can check it in a dictionary. (4) You can ask the speaker, "You used a word I don't recognize; could you please define it for me?"

There are professors who seem to use at least one word per sentence that no one else will understand. I suspect that they are trying not to be understood. But when a teacher wants to be understood, the strategy (4) is a very good one.

Sometimes, though, you just cannot ask for a definition. The following story is about a student at Dalhousie who was not allowed to ask for the meaning of a word.

The PLATITUDE has Outlived its Usefulness

WHEN I WAS a young Assistant Professor of Philosophy, I was recruited to be a judge at a debating tournament organized by the Dalhousie Debating Society. I was very new at the game and was not invited again so I imagine that I did not do a very good job of it. I did, however, last long enough to witness an amazing transformation.

One of the disciplines in a debating tournament is the "Impromptu." The contestants take turns; each picks a topic from a hat, has two minutes to ponder the matter, and then must rise and address the audience on the given topic for five minutes. A young man, who looked nervous even before the event began, stood up to take his turn. He fished a slip of paper from the hat and visibly blanched as he looked at it. After an awkward pause, he read the topic aloud: "The platitude has outlived its usefulness." He spent his two minutes in apparent discomfort; a bell called him to his feet and he began to ramble. It became clear after a short while that he did not know the meaning of the word "platitude." He paused, stumbled, sweated, and stuttered. It was embarrassing for him, and the audience was also very uncomfortable. But suddenly he regained some calm, colour came back to his face, and he said:

"But you must be thinking that I do not know the meaning of the word 'platitude,'" he intoned in a suddenly steady voice. "But of course I do. The platitude is a small, furry mammal that lives above the Arctic Circle. It is renowned for its gift for reproduction and they breed like rabbits. In fact their population grows so rapidly that they are noted for their mass suicides when large numbers of platitudes stampede over the edge of a cliff to die on the rocks or in the ocean below. The remaining platitudes immediately return to their busy reproductive activities and the population grows again. They are cute little animals. But you might wonder whether they are of any use.

"You probably also know about the caribou which also live in the north of Canada. They migrate over vast distances and for centuries they provided an important source of food for the native Inuit all across the territory. But not long ago their numbers began to dwindle and this threatened the Inuit with a serious shortage of traditional food. Scientists were sent to study the problem and they determined that it stemmed from the growing shyness of the caribou. They did not make friends easily and suffered from a low sex drive and thus were becoming increasingly incompetent at the reproductive act. It is this unfortunate fact which explained their dwindling population.

"Fortunately, however, it has recently been observed that the caribou have found themselves among the platitudes. Whenever they look down at their feet, they see platitudes mounting one another with enthusiasm and evident delight. Guided by the example of the platitudes, the caribou have re-learned how to reproduce. So the platitude turns out to have been very useful, after all.

"But the scientists now assure us that the caribou have learned the lesson well, and that the herds are again growing, and the northern food supply is again secure.

"So we must conclude, Ladies and Gentlemen, that the platitude has indeed outlived its usefulness."

And a relieved young debater sat down, to enthusiastic applause.

AUGUSTINE'S CONVERSION

NICHOLAS HATT

UPON READING AUGUSTINE'S *Confessions* for the first time, students in both Halifax Humanities and the Foundation Year Programme at King's College are usually struck by the harsh words Augustine has for infants: "[N]one is pure from sin before you, not even an infant of one day upon the earth," he says, quoting the Book of Job.[1] Such a claim is difficult to reconcile with our presumed innocence of babies. It is as though Augustine has taken away from us some final, remaining refuge of purity and goodness.

For Augustine, however, the situation merits close consideration. Infants, he says, are born into a veritable paradise supplied with mother's milk in abundance. Their mother or nurse desires to give what her body supplies and her baby desires to eat just as much as is given.[2] And yet, Augustine observes, babies often scream and cry for milk when hungry, striking out at their parents and elders, even if what they want might be harmful to them; they often appear jealous of other babies who share in their own nurses' milk, even when they themselves have had enough. Is this paradise? "If I were to do that now ... I would be laughed at and very properly rebuked,"[3] he writes. By his reckoning, the only innocence that lies in an infant is the weakness of its limbs, not its mind! Paradise, it seems, is hardly innocent at all, replete with contradiction.

---

1   *Confessions*, I.vii.11. The translation used is that of Henry Chadwick.
2   *Confessions*, I.vi.7.
3   *Confessions*, I.vii.11.

As Augustine grows up into boyhood, the contradictions only intensify. His elders send him off to school, placing on him a "moral duty" to obey his teachers and do well in school. Why? He tells us plainly: "that I should succeed in this world, and should excel in the arts of using my tongue to gain access to human honors and to acquire deceitful riches."[4] Like many young boys, he preferred to play games rather than complete his school work. His schoolmasters, in turn, beat him and his friends for neglecting their studies but they themselves were hypocrites: their schoolmasters were just as much engaged in games and recreation, although they call their own games "business!"[5] The older we get, the more the contradictions abound, on both an individual and social level.

Years later, these contradictions reach a breaking-point for Augustine. On the verge of his conversion to Christianity, he tells us that he was at conflict within himself, unable to give up his old habits and way of life:

> In my own case, as I deliberated about serving my Lord God which I had long been disposed to do, the self which willed to serve was identical with the self which was unwilling. It was I. I was neither wholly willing nor wholly unwilling. So I was in conflict with myself and was dissociated from myself. The dissociation came about against my will.[6]

It is the same moment Paul describes in his Letter to the Romans when he tells us about his own inner struggle—a parallel Augustine himself makes, too:

> I do not understand my own actions. For I do not do what I want, but I do the very thing I hate … I can will what is right but I cannot do it. For I do not do the good I want, but the evil I do not want is what I do.[7]

For Augustine, the resolution must come from without: he hears a child's voice singing over the garden wall, urging him to pick up the Scrip-

---

4   *Confessions*, I.ix.14.
5   *Confessions*, I.ix.15.
6   *Confessions*, VIII.x.22.
7   Romans 7:15, 18b-19.

tures and read them. In the famous story, he opens the book to Romans 13, and finds it fully instructive, demanding that he give up his old habits: "I neither wished nor needed to read further," he writes, "… it was as if a light of relief from all anxiety flooded into my heart."[8]

We, too, live in these contradictions every day, both as individuals and as a society. Who amongst us has not experienced some injustice because of them? Hopefully Halifax Humanities has been a refuge from them, a place where we have been able to step aside and consider a way out of them. We approach and engage with innocence the texts we are reading with no other goal than trying to understand what they teach us about ourselves and the world in which we live. We do not read them in order to get a job or acquire a skill so we can become better participants in the hypocritical and contradictory society to which each of us—teacher and student alike—has perhaps fallen victim at least at some point in our lives. We desire something more.

---

8 *Confessions*, VIII.xii.29.

BOX MAKER

JESSE BLACKWOOD

ONCE THERE WAS a silly old man who loved boxes. He loved boxes for what they held inside, how they carried things and stored them, for how they helped people with all the different things they held, and just for being boxes. He loved the boxes themselves.

Ever since he was a little boy he loved boxes and he dedicated his whole life to building them and making them better. He believed that each box should be built according to its need; that whatever purpose it might fill, if it was built to fulfill that purpose it might fulfill it better.

He built boxes of paper and of wood, of glass and of clay, of iron and even of water—square boxes of ice, to keep things cold, of course.

He lived in a little city where everything was not too old and not too new. It was not too far from the ocean but not too close either. The mountains were just close enough to be seen but far enough that they could not easily be got to. And the wild forests where things came and went and did as they pleased were quite entirely out of the way so that those wild things almost never came. And although the city was not altogether remarkable, an unremarkable city has many of the same needs as a remarkable one and the box maker spent his life building boxes to help with these.

He built boxes to hold all that the city needed. He built some to hold sugar and flour, others to hold oil and matches. Some were meant to be opened right away. Others were built to be stored away and only opened on special occasions. He built little metal boxes with intricate locks and combinations to guard fine jewels. For each different thing that needed to be held, he built a box. In tiny paper boxes he placed the seeds of flowers and

317

trees; and in great large boxes he placed great large things, tools, machines, materials, and all manner of things that might be useful to the city.

He even built beautiful wooden boxes for the citizens who had died. He built these with special care given to each. He believed that these boxes should be beautiful rather than melancholy and he worked long lonely hours so that the outside of the box might portray some of the beauty of life. However, he was always exhausted by this sort of box making and was saddened that the beauty of the citizens' lives should be so fragile and fleeting.

Year after year the box maker built boxes. And in the eyes of the people of the city he was a very important man. His boxes were everywhere and aided every day in growing the city's life. Often the mayor would come to the box maker and ask for his help. He had come to the box maker with a crisis of water, a crisis of schools, a crisis of criminals, and even a dragon crisis. Each time the mayor came the box maker built a box to solve the crisis. He built boxes to store water when it had run out, he built boxes to bring in books when the teachers had none, and he built enticing boxes for criminals that could be broken into but not broken out of. He even built a box to house a dragon who could not find his way home.

More and more the city grew and prospered because of the boxes and because of the attention the box maker paid to both how he built them and to what they might hold. However, the boxes he made were mostly simple and practical; each one was built to serve a purpose but rarely did the box remain after its purpose had been taken outside of it. Only did his coffin boxes continue to portray the beauty that they held after their purpose had been served. But even these were only beautiful on the outside and they troubled the box maker as he grew older.

Nevertheless, in the eyes of the city and in the eyes of his accountants he was a very successful man and only when he had been making boxes his whole life and was become an old man, only then did he discover that there was something missing from his life. He had never thought what to do after he stopped making boxes. He had no children nor grandchildren and this made him sad. He saw that even he could not make boxes forever. And he believed there must be something more to boxes than to throw them away after they were emptied of what they held.

Still, he did not neglect the work of his box making. Neither did he give up hope. And that is, of course, why he found the solution that he did.

The first part of his solution, you will say, was quite simple and I daresay that for the box maker it was not this part that made him sad. That is, because the old man could not make boxes forever, he had to find someone who could make the boxes in his stead. And of course he did just that. He selected a young man from the best of his craftsmen and he trained him in all that he knew.

Then one day, when the young craftsman was in place, the old man withdrew a small sum from his accounts and bequeathed his factories forever to the city and to the care of the young man.

The city was saddened by his departure and the citizens could not understand why such a man should want anything else, yet they did not eagerly petition him to stay lest he should resume the wealth of the factories he had bequeathed.

Of course what really saddened the box maker had to do with the boxes themselves. Each box was built to fulfill a need and once it had done that it might be used for something else or it was discarded. When the box was emptied it nearly always ceased to be a box.

It was to solving this problem that the old box maker resolved to dedicate his remaining days. He decided to leave the city and moved to a small town that was built at a crossroads between the forest and the ocean. The town was a little more than a day's journey from the city and was only a short distance from the ocean which it overlooked from the height of a hill that was nestled and protected by tall trees and by the forest. Not far below, winding from the heart of the forest and around the foot of the hill was a brook where, near the mouth of it, the salty ocean mixed with the fresh water of the mountains and where the laughter of children was often heard. It was for this laughter chiefly, as well as the beauty of the landscape, that the old man chose to live among the townspeople.

Now we have again reached the point at which we started, with a silly old man who loved boxes.

The old man settled in a little house overlooking the ocean and brook then he walked down the hill and let his feet dangle in the water and he considered the problem of boxes.

"Boxes," he thought to himself, "are built to come and to go. They are needed one day and then not needed the next." He recalled how much trouble the great big dragon box had been after the dragon had gone back home. No one could decide what to do with the box after it was not needed and it frightened them because it reminded them of the dragon.

"A box is only as valuable as what it holds," the box maker thought. You could not make boxes that were meant to be empty, nor could you make boxes that were meant to hold their contents inside and never let them out. What was the point of that?

"There is also the problem of the outside of the boxes," the old box maker sighed. Why was it that only the inside of the box ever seemed to matter? Suddenly a great cloud passed overhead and caught in the reflection of the water below the box maker's feet. Then the old man had an idea of what he would do.

The first thing he did was to take what remained of his money and buy an old warehouse that had been used to store toys and trinkets for all the surrounding countryside and toyshops. It was a big job fixing it up, cleaning out all the dust, organizing the toys and trinkets that had been left behind, and installing a great many new windows. But the old box maker whistled while he worked and soon the warehouse was beautiful, inside and out. The townspeople wondered whether he might be building a new box factory but there were so many windows looking out in every direction that there was no room for any box making machines and besides all the odd shaped windows provided too many distractions.

But the old man had no desire to start a new factory. Instead, the old box maker took one small room which had once been used as the office of an accountant but which now stood empty and near the path that all the town's children took between the river and the schoolhouse. The old box maker took that room and turned it into a little toyshop.

It was not a normal sort of toyshop where one thing was exchanged according to the value of another. That was exactly what the box maker wanted to avoid.

And that is why he didn't sell toys at all. He developed a little system of exchange where one thing was given for another. The children came into the shop and told the old box maker secrets and stories from their adventures in the wild woods and filled the old warehouse with the sound of their laughter. In return the box maker gave the toys and trinkets away. Of course the children liked this better because they hardly ever had any money. And the box maker too, because the stories never lost their value.

Yet however pleasant it is to give things away the toyshop did not solve the problem, at least not entirely.

But the toyshop was only a small part of the warehouse and the rest of it was used by the old man to solve the problem of the boxes.

Some said that the box maker was able to do it because he had gotten a little magic off one of the dragon's scales. Others thought that he had himself been born in the wild forests where wild things lived. More likely, he loved the work of making boxes and that is how he managed.

For each story and secret and all the little bits of laughter, the old box maker went into his warehouse and built a new box. He built boxes to hold secrets and to share them, to remember stories and to tell them, to house the music of laughter and to let it out. And because of the nature of such things and how the boxes were built, the old man succeeded in solving the problem. Such things as they held within had also to be held without.

"How simple!" the old man cried with delight. And of course he was right.

In one way even these new boxes were very normal boxes and that is because they were boxes. In another way they were a very special sort of box and of course that had to do with the nature of what they were built to hold. First of all they did not have the regular six sided squarish shape that belongs to most boxes. Instead they were octagonal, pentagonal, hexagonal, circular, cylindrical, and sometimes no particular shape at all. They were also built so that the inside and the outside got altogether mixed up. What was put into the boxes might equally have been said to be the thing that held the boxes together from without. It is difficult to describe. They could be as easily opened and closed as normal boxes. But that was because what was in had gotten into the part that was out. And because all the boxes held the secrets and the joys not only on the inside only but also shared them on the outside.

In all his box making these box secrets and box stories reminded the old man most and least of his making of coffin boxes. For these new boxes were often beautifully carved and intricately painted—often poorly the old man thought—so much did the beauty of the secrets and stories excel the mastery of his craft.

Yet in two important ways these new boxes were in no wise like the coffin boxes. The first and the simplest was the great joy the old man took in making them. The second is that the coffin boxes were built with life portrayed on the outside and death housed on the inside. Their beauty was of a representational quality. However, the boxes of stories and of the children's laughter were quite the opposite. The inside and the outside grew and blossomed together. Neither did the boxes deteriorate and fall to dust or grow dull from too much light. Rather the inside secret grew more splendid as the outside beauty blossomed and grew more radiant.

For many years the old man built these beautiful boxes. And over these years he emptied the warehouse of all its trinkets and toys and filled it with new beautiful boxes of laughter and stories until at last these boxes began to overflow into his toyshop. The children marveled at the sight of them and were filled with wonder at what the old man showed them from within and without. Then one day, when the old man was quite quite old and full of years and full of life and at last when his beautiful warehouse could contain no more boxes, the old box maker died.

The townspeople had never quite understood the old man though they were glad for the free toys—free as they saw it—that he gave the children. They had heard that he had been the famous box maker of the city, the master craftsman who had caught the dragon and saved the city. But the townspeople did not know more than that. Nevertheless they notified the mayor who decided to make the journey to see for himself if it really was the old box maker. The young apprentice, now in middle age and a master box maker himself, also decided to make the journey for he knew the old man better than anyone else.

Over the years the mayor had grown old and was nearly blind and deaf from his work in the city and was quite fat from too many election campaigns. For this reason, as the two men traveled together, they spoke very little. The mayor complained of the distance while the young box maker examined the beauty of the journey and the trail that lay ahead. When at last the two men arrived it was the mayor who entered the toyshop first and who confirmed as best as he could that the old man was the great box maker. The next moment, however, the old mayor became befuddled by the stacks and stacks of empty boxes. One after another he opened them and became more angry as each time as he found the next one empty again. He could neither hear nor see any of what was all about.

Next the young box maker entered. He recognized the great master and he began to cry. Then bending down he perceived that the old box maker was smiling, even in death. It was then that the young man heard the music of the boxes that filled the room. Indeed, all around was a great uproar of joyous laughter and the stories and secrets of the wild wild wood. And that is the story of a silly old man who loved boxes.

$\mathcal{T}$ERRIBLE THINGS TO GREAT LITERATURE:
Reflections on the Literary Moot

BEN FRENKEN AND MIKE MURPHY

THE ANNUAL LITERARY moot, presented by the Weldon Literary Moot Society at Dalhousie's law school and now in its fifth year, "does terrible, terrible things to great literature" (as Mary Lu Redden said preparing the crowd for the imminent butchery of Mary Shelley's *Frankenstein*). A severe injustice to the literary canon of the Western World, the Literary Moot could not have worked out any better.

The Literary Moot started as a distraction for a group of us in our second year at the Schulich School of Law, Dalhousie University. While preparing for our compulsory moot court assignments in the fall of 2010, we decided it would be a lot more fun to contest the legal merits of an Aeneas leaving Dido or a Creon's responsibility for Antigone's death.

We had come to know Halifax Humanities 101, primarily through volunteering in the Odyssey Live! fundraiser the previous year. I had also worked as the charity's writing coordinator the year prior to starting law school. We were pretty sure that Mary Lu, Brian Flemming, and the rest of HH101 would be open to trying one of the characters the students meet over their eight-month course.

The formula was simple: take one classical text; choose one dominant theme; devise one legal issue; pair two third-year law students with two practising lawyers; find four witnesses to subject themselves to bringing the story to life; and, ask a real judge to preside.

Legal improv theatre. That's easy. In order to make this an event to fundraise successfully for HH101, though, the event needed a lot of support. We quickly learned how much Halifax loves HH101. The law school gave us space and helped us pay to host 200 attendees. Local businesses sent us various gifts for our silent auction. Law firms in Halifax and Toronto provided sponsorship funds that would go directly to HH101. *The Coast* and CBC provided free advertising and interviews.

At that first Literary Moot, Justice Peter Bryson (as he then was) agreed to preside over the mockery. Laurie Jones and Tony Amoud, practising downtown lawyers, paired with third-year law students, Andrew McCoomb and Andrea Buncic (who are now both litigators in Toronto). Laura Penny (who has been a part of every moot since), Costas Halavrezos and a couple of University of King's College students joined up to play the witnesses. Best of all, participants at HH101 agreed to act as our jury.

That first Literary Moot saw Odysseus, the hero, tried for the wrongful death of the suitors. Facts were few and far between. If there was any professional civility, it came in the form of flirtation with the bench. Homer's characters were subjected to unthinkable (and hilarious) suggestions and accusations. It was fun.

But the humour and irreverence of the event masks real engagement with some of the best questions with which the classics leave their students. The Literary Moot, for an evening, brings a classic to life. Literarily it's anachronistic and legally it's a jurisdictional non-starter. Subjecting Homer and his poem to contemporary society and its laws worked, and the event continues to work because we are still anchored in those texts and our issues are not so far removed from theirs.

Anyone who has had the good fortune to attend an HH101 class knows the classics become present every Tuesday and Thursday. HH101 participants grapple with thoughts, problems, criticism, and analyses that have defined Western culture and they do so as if the great thinkers and writers are there in the public library of the North End.

The Literary Moot hopefully shares that quality to some degree with

HH101. Since we devised an acceptable means of ignoring our compulsory school work, it has always made sense that the Literary Moot in Halifax could only be a fundraiser for HH101.

It is for that reason that students at the Schulich School of Law set up a student association, the Weldon Literary Moot Society, whose sole purpose is to ensure that the Literary Moot is staged annually to support HH101. The WLMS will be putting on the 5th iteration of the event later this academic year.

VOCATION:
Halifax Humanities 101—a Reflection

COLIN DODDS

WHEN GARY THORNE introduced me to the idea of adapting the Clemente Programme that had been pioneered in the USA by Earl Shorris, it was an easy sell. It was from that beginning that the Halifax Humanities 101 developed. Under Gary's leadership, institutional commitments were sought and made, the curriculum developed with the assistance of volunteer instructors, donors were signed up, and the North End Library partnered as the locale for classes. What a powerful partnership.

As my vocation is education, accessibility and lifelong learning have been guiding principles for me. Hence when I was working and living in the UK, I wanted to give back and share the education I had been privileged to enjoy. I achieved this in many ways including teaching in extension programs in the mining communities I was part of. When the Open University was founded in the early 1970s, I became a counsellor and tutor for the Foundation Social Sciences course and taught the economics courses, the latter taking me into a high security correctional facility.

Feeling that I needed to know more about the Arts and Humanities, I enrolled as a student so was immersed in sharing the music, literature, philosophy and critical thinking—conversations that are the foundations of Halifax Humanities. I learned so much and not just from the curriculum but from others in the program, and the Halifax Humanities programme has rekindled my interest in going back to re-read the texts.

The key assets for the success of the Halifax Humanities programme have been that it is barrier-free and community based. All participants needed were a love of learning and a willingness to share with others. They can put aside the many challenges they might face outside of the classroom and immerse themselves in the classics and have the texts to read at home.

With my own discipline being Economics—the dismal science—I have not had the opportunity of participating directly in the programme—my loss. Rather I have watched it develop into a wonderful educational partnership of dedicated teachers and learners engaged in passionate conversations of classical literature and art that can be placed in the context of today's world. I know from the instructors that they themselves experience new insights and avenues to explore back at their own universities.

I have witnessed the pride in family members of the graduating students and the pride of the students themselves, some of whom have gone on to further studies on scholarships provided.

So, as Halifax Humanities enters its second decade, it has established a legacy of enriching the minds of students who otherwise would have missed out on the experience. The instructors, supporters, and donors have participated in the opportunity of witnessing the joy of learning from those who in the past have been marginalized in our community.

$\mathcal{W}$HAT $\mathcal{I}$ $\mathcal{L}$EARNED

WILLIAM BARKER

1

I STARTED PARTICIPATING in Halifax Humanities shortly after it started and have remained involved with the programme for almost every year since. Even though I teach regular university classes and have been working in and near the traditional institutional classroom for just about fifty years, I will say there is something especially engaging in Halifax Humanities. That's because you never know what is going to happen.

Now and then I have been asked to present one of the great books of the programme and I have been there for Grimms' fairy tales, Joyce's *Ulysses*, Coleridge's *Rime of the Ancient Mariner*, and Tolstoy's *Death of Ivan Ilyich*, possibly others. In these classes, you never know where the discussion is going to travel and a conversation about Grimm can lead to a discussion about child abuse or a favourite kind of cake or a distantly remembered version of some old tale. This is true unfettered response and it is liberating for the teacher, who is often humbled by the clear authority of the students when we are moved to talk about the world we live in.

My main involvement has, however, been with the student writing. Shortly after the programme began, I commented to someone (Angus? Mary Lu?) that some organized writing would be very helpful for the students. So I began to teach the equivalent of a first-year writing course. It did not go well. Many students could not finish the assignments because they were too removed from our "magisterial language" (that's what our university way of speaking is called by Pierre Bourdieu, a French sociologist). My every attempt to get a one-size fits all, perfectly written assignment from each student (what we try to do in the university), failed hopelessly. So I just followed the students; we began to try other things and we ended up with something entirely different. I might propose a topic but the writers brought whatever they could: letters to the editor, memoirs, short stories, poems, articles, critical essays. Sometimes the genres were jumbled together in a single piece of writing. I typed up the handwritten scripts and copied it all. In class we would read the script along with the oral presentation, usually by the author, and then comment on anything that grabbed us—a description of a hair colour, a missing comma, personal memories of bars in Halifax, a wayward child. Anything seemed to go. The conversation was often hilarious, sometimes very moving. And the strangest thing happened— the writing got better and better.

One year there were sixteen students in the class and one by one they dropped out; another year there were only three (I called them the Poet, the Critic, and the Storyteller, and it was a very rich year for us). More recently there have been eight or so of us, a very tight group. Usually I bring a piece of my own writing. I admit that I am as shy as any student to show my writing. We have a few sharp-eyed commentators and I have even received emails objecting that what I wrote did not ring true. (As if I didn't often already know, as I read it aloud!). My own writing may be a poem, a reflection, or a memory. Sometimes the students are very excited about a piece of writing—on how many days have I wished that piece had been my own! I look on some of the work I have seen with awe.

The results have been gratifying. Some students have already been published and some are now getting published. A couple have taken university courses, including creative writing. Some of the hair-raising life tales that I have heard are a reminder that everyone has stories. The hard part is setting them down. The class story, if it were all told, would contain the adventures and insight of an epic worthy of Homer.

I admit to a feeling of guilt. I can only run this group for about half a year at a time. I know if I tried to go year round it would fail (or I would). This is a provisional event, a meeting at a crossroads. As soon as we plan to meet forever, the journey must end.

2

HERE IS A poem I wrote for the class. After I finished reading it, the students called me a "crowmunist." I think it expresses something of what I feel in relation to Halifax Humanities.

I WANT TO BE A CROW

I watched you out my window,
Sitting on a gutter pipe
A quick glance to left, then right
You jab your bill under your wing
Then, a quick shrug, looking round once more,
And off you go, who knows where.

What an excellent life to be a crow.
No baggage, just a twiggy nest
somewhere with a few old bones
maybe with a shiny earring
found beside a discarded sandwich
on a deserted early morning curb.

Who ever tricked a crow?
I sometimes tiptoe up behind you.
You never raise your head, you just carry on
And as I take one step more,
You lazily lift off, untroubled
By my best attempts to get a closer look.

No need to show off amongst your fellow crows.
Every crow is the same model,

Jet black feathers, deep black bill,
No old crow gets fatter than the others,
And none of you wears a medal
or sports designer clothes.

When I see you gather at the sunset,
a massive crowding in the sky,
each one of you is just a dot amongst the others,
and not one of you seems to lead the pack,
to outrun the others,
to be carried on an airy throne.

5 May 2014

Nothing like an uninformed observation of nature. Crows do compete
when they do their flying stunts, though to my knowledge a crow has not
yet received an Olympic medal or an Order of Canada for exceptional
performance.

3

WHEN I STARTED to write this account, I began to list the things that I
have learned from my years in Halifax Humanities. Here are a few of them:

—You are right to be afraid to show your creative work. But
in a truly supportive group, almost anything can and should be
shown, and discussed.

—Marks are often the enemy.

—Random conversation can lead to interesting ideas and
interesting ideas often need random conversation to be discovered.

—Structured content is useful but too much structure makes
you lazy.

—Each person comes to a class with an interesting life story from which an understanding may evolve.

—Life challenges are too easily forgotten in the traditional classroom. They are never forgotten in the HH classroom!

—Never assume anything about a student. And now that the barrier is down, the student also learns never to assume anything about the teacher.

—First comes the false humility of a way of talking; that is followed by the discovery of the deeper humility, even embarrassment, by teacher or student, in the face of learning with others.

—The students are better at some things than the teacher.

—The traditional classroom teaches passivity, self-aggression in relation to marks, sometimes theatrical performance in relation to others. The HH classroom teaches the art of conversation, the requirement to listen, even to things that are ridiculous and entirely off topic, because one never knows when the insight will arrive. Because there are no marks, the outer limit of understanding is never reached.

—The ancients saw learning emerge out of the student's nature, the teacher's program of learning, and practice. Practice is still needed in Halifax Humanities. That is why I like to teach a class in writing. Students learn to bring something to every class.

—The Storyteller, the Poet, and the Critic all have something to say to one another.

—The classroom has to be a safe place so that licensed rough and tumble of ideas and comment can occur. The teacher is there to preserve that safety. His or her presence is often all that is needed.

—Sometimes silence is good. Just being together in a room is comforting and encourages thought.

—We all can talk too much. Rather than leap to stop the talkers, in our classroom we let them have their say. We learn when to stop ourselves.

—It is possible to be a generous critic—to be kind, yet critical. It's a fine line, and in our classes we learned over time to know that this line should not be crossed.

OUR OWN MASTERPIECES

TRACY MONIZ

STORIES ARE ETERNAL. They cross generations, cultures, and continents. Stories linger long after the last word is written and long after the last word is read. Stories heal and stories humour. Stories teach, shape and inspire.

In Halifax Humanities 101, students read and reflect on the literary "masterpieces" of Western culture and, along the way, they develop as learners, as thinkers and, for some, as writers too.

I lead a writers' circle for Halifax Humanities students. Over twelve weeks, students write and share stories—works of creative non-fiction and poetry that stem from their experiences, observations, and curiosities. Students write in response to prompts and every two weeks we gather as a writing community. We read and discuss contemporary works of fiction, non-fiction, and poetry, with some selections chosen from among student suggestions. We discuss elements of writing such as detail, scene setting, and character development. Interested students read their work to peers and, as a group, we celebrate the strengths and offer suggestions to further refine the pieces. This builds a sense of community and students look to one another for feedback, support, and inspiration. Whether students have written for years or recently picked up the pen, the writers' circle offers a consistent and structured space where students can explore and uncover their writer's "voice."

The writers' circle brings together a diverse group of adult learners and this diversity permeates the stories they tell. The students share a devotion to honest storytelling. They embrace their enjoyment of literature and respect for words and follow their impulse to translate lived experience into

337

shared stories. Collectively, their stories paint a portrait of everyday, human life—the challenges, the triumphs, the losses, the joys. Their stories reach into and across communities and cultures, capturing voices and perspectives often underrepresented.

It takes courage to write. It takes even more courage to share what we write with others. The students drawn to Halifax Humanities and, more specifically, to our writers' circle show courage every day. I thank them for their bravery, generosity, and trust. I thank them for the gift of their words.

My time with Halifax Humanities is precisely that—a gift. When I first learned about the programme, I immediately connected with its vision. By engaging in the study of the traditional humanities, students can nurture insights and skills for thoughtful reflection and the ability to think critically and reflectively may, in turn, change a life. I wanted to learn from this community of thinkers and learners as much as I wanted to teach within it.

And learn I have.

From the students' example, I have learned about commitment and perseverance. From the students' stories—their own "masterpieces"—I have learned about hope. I feel honoured to be part of the Halifax Humanities community.

Best wishes for the next ten years.

THE ᴍIRACLE ON ɢOTTINGEN ꜱTREET

BRIAN FLEMMING

EIGHT YEARS AGO, Professor Angus Johnston and Professor Neil Robertson invited me to lunch at the Mezza Restaurant on Quinpool Road. They would not tell me why they wanted to meet so urgently but they assured me the subject matter was important. At that lunch I first learned of the achievements of the New Yorker, Earl Shorris, author of *Riches for the Poor* and founder of the Clemente Course in the Humanities on the lower east side of Manhattan. Angus and Neil told me how our local visionary, Rev. Gary Thorne, rector at St. George's, had founded a pilot project in Halifax—the St. George's Friends of Clemente Society—to bring Shorris' ideas to Halifax. But there were some organizational issues facing the Society. Would I agree to take the Chair of the Society and help sort out its financial and organizational problems?

I was skeptical at first. How was it possible that people who had been left behind financially, educationally, and socially by our society could study the Western Canon of great works from *Gilgamesh* and Plato to T.S. Eliot and James Joyce over an eight month period and be made happier and better citizens? I asked to be able to go to the North End Library to witness what was happening there each week. It did not take many visits to the Miracle on Gottingen Street for me to become convinced that this was a cause worthy of strong support.

I have been lucky enough to get to know most of the students over the past eight years and to have attended many of the regular lectures.

Several important truths have emerged from these encounters. The first is that the programme—which has not been watered down in any way from that taught at the University of King's College in the Foundation Year—has bestowed a life of the mind on people who never dreamed of having one. The most common claim graduating students have made to me over the years is: "Halifax Humanities changed my life forever." When you are poor or disadvantaged in some way—particularly if you are a woman—you are invisible. Breaking the education barrier had removed that invisibility for those in the program. Many who were living lives of quiet desperation have been able, thanks to the programme, to climb to the sunlit uplands of visibility and to be respected for the first time.

So many of the students have told me that, for the first time in their lives, someone actually listened to their opinions and valued those opinions. Incredibly, most have. Thanks to the extraordinary cadre of teachers from all local universities, Halifax Humanities students have been able to connect the present with the past and to luxuriate in the wisdom of their ancestors. It is passing strange that this connection comes at a time when the Humanities are slowly being abandoned by universities around the world in the name of crass credentialism and a false sense of vocationalism. If ever there was an argument for improving access to higher education at low, or no, cost, Halifax Humanities provides that argument. It is also passing strange that maintaining and encouraging a strong connection with the past should be more alive on Gottingen Street than in many of the ivy-covered buildings around town that claim to be universities.

To be fair, the senior administrators of Halifax's universities have always strongly supported the work of Halifax Humanities 101. I just wish that this support for the Humanities had been as evident in what these same administrators were encouraging, day to day, in their own institutions. There, grabbing grants and tilting heavily towards the kind of research that the Humanities cannot do have impaired the teaching of literature, philosophy, beauty and belonging that only the Humanities can provide.

But the wheel will turn. It always does. And when it does, the "pilot light" of learning that is kept burning on Gottingen Street might finally move further south.

Floreat Halifax Humanities! May your fierce flame of learning keep lighting the darkness for another decade or two.

IN CONCLUSION

SERIOUS FUN: THE JOYS OF HALIFAX HUMANITIES
Laura Penny

A SCRAP WE CAN'T AVOID:
THE ESSAY I DIDN'T WRITE FOR HALIFAX HUMANITIES
(AND THE ONE I DID)
Alexander MacLeod

ELEMENTS
Jon David Welland

Serious Fun: The Joys of Halifax Humanities

LAURA PENNY

"Man's maturity: to have regained the seriousness that he had as a child at play."

—Nietzsche, *Beyond Good and Evil*

SERIOUS FUN MAY sound like an oxymoron but I think it's the best way to describe the implausible good time that is Halifax Humanities. I've had the genuine pleasure of participating in the programme since 2006 and I'm still not quite sure how we do it. But I am sure that it is a hell of a lot of fun. That is why I do it. That is, I think, one of the reasons why so many people—students, grads, professors, volunteers, community allies—keep coming to Halifax Humanities and tend to stick around.

It is an admittedly unlikely recipe for fun. Take a roomful of people who have suffered the indignities and tedium of living on a low income, among other deeply serious challenges. Add some of the most influential, complex authors in western history and the serious nerds who study them. Put them all in a lively library on a scrappy street. Somehow, the result is fun, real fun, serious fun.

Our culture tends to define fun as a product or service one purchases, be that in the form of trips, toys, fancy meals, or booze. Brief interludes of sunshine, distraction, gluttony, or insensibility are allegedly one's reward for working, for creating some value or another for the Great Mammon of the economy. Consequently, one of the gruelling and dispiriting aspects of life

345

on a low income is the sense that fun is not a legitimate budget line item. The sheer difficulty of acquiring the basic necessities of life—shelter, food, transport—while on assistance or living on poverty-level wages means that the impoverished are often barred from much of what passes for a good time in North America in 2015.

Moreover, our cruel and punitive prejudices against the poor are so powerful and pervasive that the poor themselves sometimes internalize them. Even if the impoverished could afford fun, they might be disinclined to think they deserve leisure or pleasure. Most of the advice or counsel North American culture offers the poor boils down to "don't be poor." Simply exhorting people to pull themselves up by the bootstraps—when they're fiscally barefoot—denies the structural and systemic problems that keep reliably producing poverty.

This attitude allows us to attribute poverty to personal choices, even though there are plenty of affluent people who make totally abysmal choices and remain quite comfortable, while other folks do absolutely everything right and still wind up beyond broke. To bum a line from Herman Melville, "Of all the preposterous assumptions of humanity over humanity, nothing exceeds most of the criticisms made on the habits of the poor by the well-housed, well-warmed, and well-fed" (Herman Melville, *Billy Budd and Other Stories*, [Ed. Frederick Busch, New York: Penguin Classics, 1986], 46).

Halifax Humanities is emphatically *not* in the bootstrap business. We do not do job training. We do not labour under the pretence that reading the classics is a path to wealth or "empowerment," which is usually just self-helpese for wealth. Instead, we provide very modest offerings: a stack of free books and a few hours of thoughtful conversation every week, some bus tickets, and snacks.

In return for these small boons we ask a great deal of our students. This good time is a lot of hard work. We demand they do hours and hours of difficult reading. Then they must reckon with the parade of volunteer nerds who enthuse, all-too-briefly, about that reading. They must do something that is not as easy as it may sound: learn to sit in a room and talk to—and eventually, *with*—people who differ wildly.

Year after year, our students do this and so much more. They create friendships. They become part of a growing community of alums, volunteers, and community allies. They discover, or recover, interests and strengths eclipsed by bad circumstances and brute necessity. They sometimes stump and frequently delight their professors. And they do most of this laughing.

Certainly other, wiser contributors to this volume have made eloquent cases for the civic, moral, and/or spiritual value of the humanities. Fun probably seems like a comparatively slender or superficial justification for studying the liberal arts. But I think part of the vivifying power of Halifax Humanities is learning that learning, however hard it may be, is fun. This hard-won fun is liberating in two ways. Our students free themselves from their past and present troubles by devoting their time, care, and attention to their own intellectual development. Our students free the treasures of the western tradition from an increasingly inaccessible, overpriced, and instrumental university system.

This is simply to say that Halifax Humanities also provides a valuable service to the professors who volunteer for it. When I served as a section coordinator for Halifax Humanities, I invited dozens of my colleagues into our classroom. Despite their many differences, in doctrine and disposition, every single one of them said the same thing about their experience: "Wow! I really enjoyed that," or "that was so fun." Halifax Humanities 101 offers professors a chance to engage with texts that matter to them, without all the hobgoblins of institutional life, such as grade-grubbing students, tedious meetings, and administrative folderol. Our students ask audacious questions and surprise even seasoned nerds who have devoted decades of their lives to these books.

Our students are the animating force of our programme, and they deserve most of the credit for the joys we all share. This will doubtless embarrass the holy heck out of her, but Mary Lu Redden's heartfelt hospitality is also responsible for the warm and welcoming atmosphere our students and profs enjoy. Whether she's furnishing us with tasty—and nutritious!—snacks, gently helping students in distress, or pointing out consistent threads from section to section, Mary Lu's sharp mind and capaciously kind soul set the tone for all of us.

This tone—playful *and* thoughtful—is also clearly evident in our benefit events, which really put the fun in fundraiser. In our marathon readings of *The Odyssey* and the literary moot trials the good people of Weldon Law School have generously organized on our behalf, we wed the serious and the deeply silly. Our 24 Hour *Odyssey* is likely the only place where one can watch a team of readers from a local law firm bring Odysseus to life with hilarious costumes, prop bones from KFC, and inexplicable Scottish accents, and then marvel at the readers from Dal Classics singing the hero's song in perfect Greek and Latin.

The other thing that is really special about our fundraisers is the way they unite broad swaths of the local community. Our marathon readings and literary moots draw well-heeled South End professionals, decidedly less comfy university students, curious cultural dabblers, and generations of our own students. Unlike, say, a five-hundred-bucks-a-plate gala for the homeless, where the homeless themselves are utterly unwelcome, our charitable events level the differences between donors and donees. These events connect the rich and the poor, as well as dead authors and their living readers. And they create this spirit of camaraderie by being fun.

Fun—serious fun—frees us to approach the profound issues we confront in Halifax Humanities sideways, obliquely, with a smile. To bum some lines from Emily Dickinson, fun allows us to "Tell all the truth but tell it slant—/Success in Circuit lies" (*The Complete Poems of Emily Dickinson*, [Ed. Thomas H. Johnson, New York: Back Bay Books, 1976], 506). Or, as Nietzsche suggests, we experience true maturity only when we regain the openness, quality of attention, and sense of possibility that we enjoyed as children at play. Halifax Humanities combines the raucousness of recess and scholarly rigour to restore precisely this playfulness. It is my fond hope that we will continue playing together for decades to come.

A SCRAP WE CAN'T AVOID:
the Essay I Didn't Write about Halifax Humanities 101 (and the one I did)

ALEXANDER MACLEOD

I WAS GOING to make a sandwich. That was my original plan. I was going to divide my little essay on Halifax Humanities 101 into three parts, following the celebrated structure of "the criticism sandwich." You are familiar with the template, I'm sure. In the fourth century BC, Aristotle laid out his guidelines in *On Rhetoric* and we've been following them ever since. The trick of persuasion, he says, is to appear "fair-minded" while strategically appealing to your listeners to feel a real emotional connection, "pathos," for the subject we are discussing. In the modern criticism sandwich, you slip something serious and important, maybe even something slightly negative but constructive, between two more pleasant, easily digested asides and away you go.

For my essay, I planned to start off light and easy with a little anecdote that would make my readers feel at ease. I thought I would lead with a story about the time when I did my best to raise money for Halifax Humanities 101 and to advance the greater cause of the Arts in our society by stripping down to just my bathing suit and a yellow Sou'wester in front of the biggest classroom at King's. This was all done in service of a great dramatic vision, our English Department's production of "Buck Naked on a Plank," the contemporary, slightly comedic, clearly Atlantic Canadian re-telling of

349

Book Five of Homer's *Odyssey*. We had everything we needed: a packed house, randomly tossed glasses of water working as special storm effects, puppets, beautiful but petty gods wearing faux feather boas, and me, our version of the drowned Odysseus, belting out his lines in a soggy, slightly drunken mix of Newfoundland and Cape Breton accents. If you were there, you remember this, the awkward positions we put ourselves in for the greater good of Halifax Humanities 101. If you weren't there, fear not. I'm sure there is photographic and even video evidence out there waiting patiently in a hard drive, ready to reappear publicly whenever I make my first run for serious political office.

That would have been a good start, I think. Once my readers understood that I was (and I am), at root, a deeply silly person, once we were all comfortable with this fact, then I could move into the substantial meat of the matter in the middle section of my essay. That's where I'd talk about the serious mission of the program, the Big Picture significance of HH 101, its progressive ideals, its fight for what I see as the completely right model for community education. I planned to say a lot about all the good work that gets done in the North Branch of the Library on Gottingen Street, the cookies and the coffee that are always waiting, the acceptance of everyone, the welcoming of children for all the lectures. And I wanted to include some reflection on the way that lofty ambitions often have to work themselves out in under less-than-ideal conditions and about how much raw effort that takes, how much long term commitment, and all the steadily invested time it requires to trigger a small but fundamental change. I'd draw attention to the fact that the most important structural work of the program is never glamorous or highfalutin. My middle section would be all about grinding it out, pushing for better outcomes, how much I appreciate that.

After the serious argument, I'd come back to the heart-warming stuff for the conclusion. This is where I'd put the graduations and the impressive valedictory addresses, the many victories great and small that Halifax Humanities 101 has enjoyed for the last decade. I'd set it up so the whole thing built to a nice congratulatory crescendo. If everything came together correctly—two pieces of bread and some salami in the middle, maybe some zingy mustard thrown in for kick—everybody would come out feeling good. My seven pages would make a quick but satisfying little snack. It would tick all the boxes and hit on all the substantial, but also the very positive, thoughts and emotions I associate with this program. I would make it clear that I think Halifax Humanities 101 is probably the most valuable Arts and Humanities program currently at work in our city and our province. It could have been great.

Unfortunately, it didn't turn out that way. Instead of pulling together a feel-good, consistently hopeful story, I have been wrestling with this piece for weeks, starting and re-starting it many different times, but never making much progress. It has been bugging me for a long while, bringing up some serious, nagging, unavoidable questions that simply will not go away. Why won't this essay settle down and behave? If it is supposed to be such an easy assignment, such an optimistic celebration, then why the persistent sense of uncertainty, the gaping potholes in what I, like Paul Simon, hoped would be a "smooth ride?" Is there something in the subject itself, something that resists the sandwich, something that strains against the most easily digested feel-good thematic? If so what is it?

Faculty, students, and staff associated with Halifax Humanities 101 do not have to look very far to see the problem. Anybody who values the Arts or, more specifically, anybody who thinks Arts education is valuable, knows that we are living through dark times right now and that our most basic assumptions about the obvious benefits of the Humanities are being tested like never before. Despite our best efforts, fewer people than ever are interested in taking Arts courses and places like Saint Mary's, Mount Saint Vincent, Dalhousie, and King's, just like their sister institutions, Harvard, Princeton, Oxford and Yale, are all struggling to make compelling arguments for the social value of what they teach and study. The *New York Times* reports that Humanities research and teaching now receive less than one half of one percent—yes that is the figure, less than one half of one percent—of the funding that goes to Science and Engineering and that governments around the industrialized world are suggesting that Arts students should now pay higher, rather than lower, tuition because they are clearly making "nonstrategic" decisions with their educational choices.

This issue, clearly, is the monster at the end of this book, the spectre haunting my much more optimistic and hopeful reflections on Halifax Humanities 101. The threat is real and substantial and it will not and, in the end, cannot and should not be ignored. Facts are facts: in the ten years this program has been doing its good work, the relationship between public money and the Arts, between wealth and Humanities education, has become steadily more problematic, more politically toxic. The dramatically declining enrollments and all the empty, though easily available, seats in our classrooms show us that the general population has turned away from Arts education in an unprecedented way and the collective futures of already established Humanities programs inside and outside of universities are far from guaranteed. In every corridor, "attrition" is the killer buzz word of the age. Everywhere we look, the same arguments are repeated: the state should not be required to subsidize the luxurious intellectual choices of the elite, nor the apparently wrong-headed decisions of poor people who should know better the true value of a dollar. Come on, the critics say, nobody in the "real world" can afford to care about the things that "Arts People" care about. It is all a scam, a trick that fans of atonal music and sound poetry have been pulling off for years, a fraud that has finally played itself out. If top flight humanities education is valued only by rich people who already have their economic destinies guaranteed, then those people should just pull out of the public system—as they have in health care and so many other areas—and simply pay top dollar for what they really want, the kind of premium Arts education offered up in exclusive private schools.

This is powerful rhetoric of a different kind: persuasive, maybe, but certainly not rooted in pathos. It does not call for greater connections within our communities. Instead it appeals to other powerful emotions, strong motivators like anger and insecurity and fear, and it uses these to establish deep social divisions. Economic logic and an economic vocabulary are always prominent in these arguments and, so far anyway, people in the Humanities have not done a very good job responding to the charges levelled against our work. When loaded but conflicted terms such as "cost," "value," "price," and "payment" get brought into the debate, we suddenly become inarticulate or, worse, we dismissively reject the critique and say things like "The entire system itself is flawed." When my colleagues get worked up about the current state of affairs, our senior administrators tell us to think about the student loan program. Do we think it would be wise for a very smart but very poor seventeen-year-old student from New Glasgow to take out a crippling $75,000 loan to pursue her degree in Canadian Literature? Is this the kind of academic advising the people who deliver the courses would support? I don't think so. The situation often feels very bleak and sometimes I admit that my faith waivers.

Although the stakes are high in this charged debate and though it often doesn't go down very well in polite conversation, I think that, rather than derailing Halifax Humanities 101, these current struggles zero in exactly on why HH 101 has been so important to me and exactly why it makes such an essential contribution to the cultural life of this city. I meant it when I said that Halifax Humanities 101 is, to my mind, the best model we currently have for Arts education. Instead of shying away from the political relationship between money and culture, between education, knowledge, and value, Halifax Humanities 101 is squarely focused on exactly those negotiations. The struggle for access to quality learning and the battle against exclusivity and elitism in education are in fact the core reasons why the program exists in the first place and they provide its central motivation. One only needs to look through the coloured windows and the cantilevered walls of the new Central Library and to think about the more than 12,000 jubilant people from all walks of life who stormed through its doors on opening day to see that the community actually shares these values and wants to nurture them. When the critics say "Only wealthy people care about literature," HH 101 invites them to come and sit down for a Tuesday lecture. When they say, "Questions from the fields of philosophy or history or music or drama or classics have no bearing on our day-to-day lives," the program replies: "Why don't you ask these students right here what they think?"

There is indeed a battle for the relevancy of the Arts going on right now, but I do not think its front line is inside the university classroom or around the big table in a dean's office where courses are launched and cancelled on a regular basis. If perspectives were re-ordered, we would see that it is not the visiting professors who are providing the essential service at the North Branch. Instead, it is the students, the public participants, who are doing the most valuable work because it is their interest, their everyday presence, and their commitment to learning—even when there aren't necessarily any grades or any tradable credits to be earned—that shows us there is something important, something vital, something essential, that can be explored and understood exclusively through the kind of education, the kind of investigation, only the Humanities can provide and sustain.

I realize now, maybe too late, that that is the essay I actually wanted to write about Halifax Humanities 101. I am happy for the program, of course, and I do want to celebrate its achievements, but I don't think this is the moment for self-congratulatory puff pieces designed to draw attention to all the great volunteer work that has been carried out by a great team of academics. Instead, I think we need to look back and see the true social contours of this project. Yes, HH 101 has been fighting the good fight for ten years but, in our rush to celebrate its achievements, we shouldn't forget that it has actually been participating in a real ongoing fight, a battle against powerful opposing forces, with serious consequences at stake. Think about it: Halifax Humanities 101 has been running full tilt for a decade with no end in sight because the fragile connections it is trying to forge are under constant threat and there are fundamental systemic problems out there— killer forces of cultural, economic, racial, and gendered division—that are continually tearing our communities apart in merciless, violent ways, faster than we can ever rebuild them. HH 101 stands against these forces and it has been constructing and sometimes reconstructing our city one Tuesday and Thursday at a time, from one lecture to the next, for more than ten years. That is the real work that needs to be foregrounded, the scrap that shouldn't be ignored. You can't have victories without obstacles, can't overcome resistance until that resistance is met head on, can't recognize what Raymond Carver calls "A Small Good Thing" without a deep and intimate awareness of the tide of Big Bad Things that are out there, always threatening to swamp our best efforts.

If you are the kind of person who appreciates essays with nice ring-like rhetorical structures and if you feel a satisfying sense of closure when arguments cycle back to where they began, then I invite you to think again about the real Odysseus, lashed to a piece of wood, "Buck Naked on a Plank," and tossed into the middle of a stormy sea. Here is a powerful symbol from a narrative that was composed thousands of years ago. I first read this story when I was a student in a Humanities class and I remember there were valuable lessons in there, insights from long ago that were still applicable to my daily life. Odysseus and the storyteller who made him up and the millions who passed his tale along and the teacher who led us through the scene and the students who gobbled it up: we all recognized a common world and a familiar situation and we all shared an understanding for the way things go. Odysseus knows all about fragility in the face of massive forces. He knows about risk and vulnerability and about how hard it is to take a stand against long odds, how difficult it can be to just hold on through another night. And yet, he persists, he stubbornly carries on. God knows, the storm scene happens in the very early stages of the game, in Book Five. Poor Odysseus still has a long way to go on his epic journey and many more obstacles to overcome. Like Halifax Humanities 101, *ta da*, he has been through a lot already, but his story is still only beginning and we get the shared sense that he will survive for many years to come.

ℰLEMENTS

JON DAVID WELLAND

EARTH

IT IS SOLID, unyielding matter. Thoughts can be fixed in permanent form through action performed on the material plane; routine and ritual become material through constant repetition until they are etched indelibly on the human soul. It is the pattern that forms life out of inanimate matter, and it is the matter that it becomes after death. It is pattern, the force that gives thoughts their permanence. It is the order that staved off chaos and it is the crux of meaning and significance.

FIRE

FIRE REPRESENTS PURE unbridled energy: it is the key to both creation and destruction; one always involves the other. It is anger, rage and violence, but it is also passion and all intense feelings, whether positive or negative, creative or destructive. Without its energy there is inertia and stagnation. It represents change in the most drastic and fundamental nature. It is activity, motion, the primal force that gives life purpose and the power behind all patterns of thought.

AIR

IT IS EPHEMERAL, shifting from moment to moment. It is the realm of concepts and ideas. They waft by, like the stars in the sky. All you need to do is reach out and snatch them from the ether before they are wafted away. It can be shaped by the will into thought constructs, mental experiments. Alone, without the pattern and the stability of earth, these patterns will vanish and be replaced by countless variables, countless notes to haunting songs now forgotten.

WATER

A STILL, REFLECTIVE pool, a crystal clear pond that reveals secrets, hidden truths, but also lies and deception. Beneath the surface lies the depths of the human soul. Its waters can restore life, can heal and invigorate, but only in the midst of a strange disturbing dream, a deep sleep where there is no pain, but also no passion and drive. It is where you may be entranced by your own reflection, at which you stare as the years drift by without meaning, as you slowly age, then pass away, carried by the water flowing past your feet.

Congratulations

MATTHEW MCCARTHY

JENNIFER WATTS

MAUREEN MACDONALD

MEGAN LESLIE

MATTHEW McCARTHY

BRANCH MANAGER,

HALIFAX NORTH MEMORIAL PUBLIC LIBRARY

I MANAGE HALIFAX North library, which I am proud is a home to Halifax Humanities. The programme is ten years old and I am so delighted to wish it a happy birthday, it has such a lot to be proud of.

5 things I like about Halifax Humanities.

1. I love the surprises that Halifax Humanities has to offer. Who would think to match the under-served and the excluded with classic literature?

2. The idea that literature is incredible, relevant, transformative, that it is worth it.

3. When you enter their classroom, as I do from time to time, to just say hello and welcome, you get a rich sense of connection. The students aren't inattentive, they aren't distracted. The students are there, busy taking a wonderful leap into the unknown. They have their eyes on their changing horizon.

4. The students make a brave decision, a commitment, and it's empowering to them. You can see it in their faces as the year progresses.

5. The words that are left behind on the flip chart each week surprise and amaze me, as I wheel the tables around to set up for the next programs. Wow, what were they looking at this time? I'm going to look that up! They make me so glad to be in such a space.

JENNIFER WATTS

COUNCILLOR DISTRICT 8, PENINSULA NORTH,

HALIFAX REGIONAL MUNICIPALITY

ON BEHALF OF residents of North End Halifax, I am very happy to send congratulations to graduates, volunteer teachers, and board members of the amazing Halifax Humanities Society programme. It is fantastic that the programme is celebrating ten years of engagement in our community. Your experience of learning together is a wonderful model and reflects the importance of education at all ages and stages of our lives. Thank you to Halifax Humanities 101 for enriching the lives of students and teachers for over 10 years and for making our community a more inclusive place.

Maureen MacDonald

MLA HALIFAX NEEDHAM,

LEADER, NOVA SCOTIA NEW DEMOCRATIC PARTY

CONGRATULATIONS HALIFAX HUMANITIES 101!

We unfortunately inhabit a world where all too many people have capacities that never find expression due to circumstances outside their control, i.e. poverty, sickness, racism, disability.

For ten years Halifax Humanities 101 has given almost 100 unique human beings the opportunity to grow as individuals and to expand their intellectual capacities through the study of the classics and other contemporary fields of study.

I am inspired, humbled, and extremely grateful to the volunteer Board of Halifax Humanities 101, the faculty and academics throughout our excellent university system who have given their time to this important endeavour, and, of course, to the students.

Congratulations on ten years of a truly remarkable program.

MEGAN LESLIE

MP, HALIFAX

Dear Friends,

AS MEMBER OF Parliament for Halifax, I am pleased to congratulate current and former students, volunteer professors, and board members on the 10th Anniversary of Halifax Humanities 101.

The Humanities teach us to think reflectively and Halifax Humanities 101 has been offering the riches of a Humanities education for free to people in our community who would otherwise not have the opportunity to study the Humanities. I have often heard former students talk about how much they have enjoyed the opportunity to read classic texts in philosophy, literature, history and art, and participate in lectures and discussions. Many former students have told me that Halifax Humanities 101 was a pivotal life-changing opportunity for them—they often credit their growth in confidence and self-esteem to Halifax Humanities 101.

Thank you especially to the volunteer professors for providing such academic excellence in such a warm and supportive environment that has enabled so many in our community to experience a truly wonderful learning experience.

Best wishes on your Tenth Anniversary and continued best wishes for continued success.

CONTRIBUTORS

ROSE ADAMS received her BA from Acadia University in 1979, her MA in Canadian Literature from Carleton University in 1981, her BFA in 1982 and MFA in 1986 from the Nova Scotia College of Art and Design University, and her Masters in Adult Education from Dalhousie University in 1994. She teaches at NSCADU and serves on the Halifax Humanities Board of Directors.

DR. ROBERTA BARKER is a member of the Joint Faculty of the University of King's College where she teaches in the Foundation Year and Early Modern Studies programmes, and of Dalhousie University where she teaches Theatre in the Fountain School of Performing Arts. She is a volunteer teacher with Halifax Humanities and has served the program as a curriculum section coordinator.

DR. WILLIAM BARKER, former president of the University of King's College, is a professor of English at Dalhousie University. He has served as a writing instructor in Halifax Humanities for 10 years and has also offered classes on Shakespeare, fairy tales, and Tolstoy.

DR. JOHN BAXTER is a Professor in the Department of English at Dalhousie University with a special interest in early modern poetry, Elizabethan and Jacobean drama, rhetoric, and religion and literature. He has taught classes on Shakespeare in Halifax Humanities since the second year of the programme and has served as a curriculum section coordinator.

ANNE BEEK is a graduate of Halifax Humanities 101 and a keen member of the Seminar class

JESSE BLACKWOOD is a writer living in Petite Rivière, Nova Scotia. A graduate in Early Modern Studies and Classics from the University of King's College, he has volunteered and worked in numerous capacities with Halifax Humanities and Saint George's YouthNet programs.

DR. STEVEN BURNS began teaching in the Dalhousie Department of Philosophy in 1969. In 1993 he was cross-appointed to the Contemporary Studies Programme at the University of King's College. He has taught in Humanities 101 since its inception. Now retired, his latest publication is a chapter on *Beautiful Losers*, in *Leonard Cohen and Philosophy* (Open Court, 2013).

DR. GEORGE ELLIOTT CLARKE was born near the Black Loyalist community of Windsor Plains, Nova Scotia, raised in Halifax and holds an Honours B.A. in English from the University of Waterloo, an M.A. in English from Dalhousie University and a Ph.D. in English from Queen's University. In 2001, Clarke won the Governor General's Award for Poetry for his collection *Execution Poems*, published by the Gaspereau Press. A recipient of eight honorary doctorates. Clarke was appointed a member of the Order of Nova Scotia (2006) and the Order of Canada at the rank of Officer (2008).

SHARI CLARKE is a musician and music teacher and was the class valedictorian for Halifax Humanities in 2013. She now serves on the Board of Directors.

DR. STEPHEN CLOUTIER is a part-time lecturer at St. Mary's University. After receiving his BA (Hons.) from St. Mary's and his MA from the University of Windsor (Ontario), he obtained his PhD from the University of Leicester (United Kingdom). His research areas include Twentieth Century British writing (the two world wars in particular) and left-wing political theory and literature. He has also taught in Ontario, Newfoundland, and England.

LISA COMEAU was the class valedictorian of Halifax Humanities 101 in 2012 and is an artist and writer living in Halifax.

MADELINE REID COMEAU is a writer of creative non-fiction and poetry. Her reviews for *Atlantic Books Today* (ABT) spanned a period of six years and included a cross-section of literary genres. A graduate of Halifax Humanities, she gets a lot of joy out photography and considers herself a life-long learner.

JOHN B. COX is a long-time disabilities rights activist, sitting on boards nationally, provincially, and locally. He is the author of *Getting Included: How Labelling Individuals has Impacted Inclusion* (Halifax, 2012). He is a graduate of Halifax Humanities 101 and an active member of the weekly seminar.

JENNIFER CONROY is a student at Saint Mary's University and was the class valedictorian for Halifax Humanities in 2009. She has also served on the Board of Directors of the Halifax Humanities Society.

BRENDA DELORENZO is a painter, a poet, and a very creative woman, and has been her whole life. Halifax Humanities 101 opened a whole world of literature and philosophy that she continues to explore through the Halifax Humanities weekly seminar.

LAMONT DOBBIN is a writer, photographer and anti-poverty activist. He was class valedictorian for Halifax Humanities 101 in 2011 and volunteers at a local food bank.

DR. SUSAN DODD is an Associate Professor in the Foundation Year Programme at the University of King's College and the author of *The Ocean Ranger: Remaking the Promise of Oil* (Black Point, N.S.: Fernwood, 2012). She has served on the Board, coordinated sections, fundraised, and taught with Halifax Humanities since its pilot year in 2005.

DR. COLIN DODDS is the president of Saint Mary's University and a long-time supporter of the work of Halifax Humanities.

HOWARD EPSTEIN is a retired lawyer and politician. Prior to attending law school he researched Lewis Carroll and the Alice books as a graduate student in English Literature.

BRIAN FLEMMING, CM, QC, DCL, is an international lawyer, writer and public policy advisor. He is a former senior adviser to Prime Minister Pierre Trudeau. The only Senior Fellow of the Van Horne Institute in Calgary, he is one of Canada's leading experts on transportation policy. He is a former Chair of the Board at University of King's College and of Halifax Humanities 101.

BEN FRENKEN is an associate in the litigation group at Norton Rose Fulbright Canada LLP (Toronto). He worked as writing coordinator for HH101 in 2008-2009 and volunteered at HH101 fundraising events while he lived in Halifax until 2012. His efforts are now directed towards a sister charity in Toronto.

DR. RONI GECHTMAN teaches history at Mount Saint Vincent University and has taught for Halifax Humanities. He grew up in Buenos Aires, Argentina, and has lived in Jerusalem, New York, Toronto and Vancouver. His PhD is from New York University.

CORRINE GRITTEN is a writer who lives in Dartmouth and studies English at Dalhousie University.

DAWN HALE is a retired health care worker and a graduate of Halifax Humanities.

DR. RON HAFLIDSON is a faculty member at St. John's College in Annapolis, Maryland. Previously he was Senior Fellow and Teaching Fellow in the Foundation Year Programme. He has a BA in Classics and Early Modern Studies from King's College, a MA in Religious Studies from McMaster University, and a PhD in Theology from the University of Edinburgh. His research is on St. Augustine of Hippo, whose *Confessions* he has taught in Halifax Humanities.

SYLVIA D. HAMILTON is a Nova Scotian filmmaker and writer whose films have won national and international awards. She is published in several journals and anthologies including *The Dalhousie Review*, *West Coast Line* and *The Great Black North*. Gaspereau Press published her poetry collection, *And I Alone Escaped to Tell You*, in 2014. She holds the Rogers Chair in Journalism at the University of King's College's in Halifax.

NICHOLAS HATT is the Dean of Students at the University of King's College. He studied Classics and Contemporary Studies at the University of King's College and Dalhousie University and is also a graduate of the Atlantic School of Theology. He has volunteered with Halifax Humanities since 2010.

WARREN HEITI lives in Halifax where he has taught at Dalhousie, King's, and Saint Mary's universities. He is the author of /*Hydrologos*/ (Pedlar Press, 2011).

KATHLEEN HIGNEY has been a Halifax Humanities 101 student since 2007 and served as a Board member for two years. She loves to write and appreciates the opportunity to share the cultural richness she has enjoyed being a student in the programme. When she is not reading or writing, she likes to spend time with her children and grandchildren, take photographs and knit.

DR. ANGUS JOHNSTON retired as an Associate Professor in the Foundation Year and the History of Science and Technology Programmes at the University of King's College. His interest is in the history of philosophy, ancient and modern. He is a founding Board member of the Halifax Humanities Society and Chair of its Curriculum Committee; for its first eight years he coordinated the Halifax Humanities Seminar and has taught and coordinated for Halifax Humanities 101 as well as Halifax Thinks.

CATHERINE JOUDREY is is a participant in HalifaxThinks. A Constituency Assistant to Graham Steele, MLA, for over 12 years, she recently served as Communications Officer for Saint Mary's Faculty of Arts.

KIM KIERANS is a high school dropout. In her mid 20s she was accepted into the University of King's College Foundation Year Programme as a mature student and went on to complete an honours degree in Classics while working 30 hours a week. In her late 40s she completed an MA in Atlantic Canada Studies at St. Mary's University. She is a Professor of Journalism at and Vice President of the University of King's College.

HELEN LANGILLE is a dedicated community volunteer. She was one of two class valedictorians at the first graduation ceremony for Halifax Humanities and has served on its Board.

LAURA LEGERE is an artist, writer, activist and seamstress. Currently a student attending Nova Scotia College of Art and Design University, Laura is a graduate of Halifax Humanities 101 who is determined to have her degree by the time she is 65. She is currently training for a triathlon.

MEGAN LESLIE is the Member of Parliament for Halifax. She is both the Deputy Leader and Environment Critic for the Official Opposition.

MAUREEN MACDONALD is the MLA for Halifax Needham and leader of the Nova Scotia New Democratic Party.

SCOTT MACDOUGALL was born in Moncton, New Brunswick. He currently lives happily in Halifax with his wife and second son and worries, often in library reading rooms, if he will ever sort out Stanley Cavell's thoughts on scepticism.

DAVID MACEACHERN is a graduate of Halifax Humanities 101 and is involved in the Seminar class. He came to Halifax from rural Nova Scotia and lives with a disability. He has a desire to help others who struggle and is hoping to become someday a published author.

DR. ALEXANDER MACLEOD is Associate Professor of English at St. Mary's University. His BA is from the University of Windsor, his MA from Notre Dame University, and his PhD from McGill University. His collection of short stories, *Light Lifting*, was published in 2010.

MATTHEW MCCARTHY is branch manager at Halifax North Memorial Public Library. He first got to know Halifax Humanities as a Youth Librarian at the same branch in 2008.

TRACY MONIZ is an Assistant Professor in the Department of Communication Studies at Mount Saint Vincent University and the editor of *Writing History: A Collection by New Writers* (Life Rattle Press, 2013). She has volunteered with Halifax Humanities since 2013, leading a writing group of interested students.

GRACE MORRIS has had a long career working in the retail sector. She was the class valedictorian of Halifax Humanities in 2010 and has served on the Board of Directors. She is a steadfast member of the Seminar Class.

DR. MICHAEL MURPHY received his JD from the Schulich School of Law at Dalhousie University. While in law school, Michael acted as Editor-in-Chief for the *Dalhousie Journal of Legal Studies* and was his class valedictorian. Along with three of his classmates, he founded the Weldon Literary Moot Society in 2010. In addition to his practice, Michael enjoys writing and was shortlisted for the Margaret and John Savage First Book Award at the Atlantic Book Awards for his first novel, *A Description of the Blazing World*, in May 2012.

DR. LAURA PENNY is a professor at the University of Kings College and the author of the bestselling *Your Call is Important to Us: The Truth About Bullshit*, a study of the phenomenon of bullshit and its role in modern society. In 2010 she published *More Money Than Brains: Why School Sucks, College is Crap, and Idiots Think They're Right*, a consideration of anti-intellectualism and a defence of the arts and humanities. She has been a dedicated teacher in Halifax Humanities since the program began.

DR. VERNON PROVENCAL is a Professor of Classics at Acadia University. He is the author of the forthcoming book on the Greek historian Herodotus, *Sophist Kings: Persians as Other in Herodotus* (Bloomsbury Academic Press, 2015).

MARY LU REDDEN is the Director of The Halifax Humanities Society. She has an Honours BA in Philosophy from Huron University College and an MA in Philosophy of Religion from McMaster University where she also pursued doctoral studies. She has worked as a university and community college instructor.

CHRIS RICE was a student of English and Early Modern Studies at the University of King's College before going on to study philosophy at the University of Sussex. He recently finished a second MA in English at Dalhousie University. His thesis looks at Herman Melville's *Moby-Dick* through the forms of tragedy and autobiographical narrative.

DR. NEIL G. ROBERTSON is an associate professor in the University of King's College Foundation Year, Early Modern Studies and Contemporary Studies programmes. Dr. Robertson has a BA from the University of King's College. He went on to take an M.A. in Classics at Dalhousie University, and in 1995 completed his PhD at Cambridge in Social and Political Science. He teaches frequently in Halifax Humanities and has served on the Board of Directors, of which he is currently vice-chair.

BONITA SHEPHERD was the first applicant to the pilot project of Halifax Humanities in 2005. She was class valedictorian in 2007, serves on the Board of Directors, and continues to pursue her love of study with the Seminar class and through auditing classes at Dalhousie University.

DR. COLIN STARNES went to Bishop's, Harvard, McGill and Dalhousie universities. He tutored in the first year of the University of King's College Foundation Year Programme, was its second Director, and taught for 30 years in Dalhousie's Department of Classics. President of King's from 1993-2003, he is now Chair of the Halifax Humanities Society. He teaches Dante in HH101.

JYMY TANNER was one of two class valedictorians in the first year of Halifax Humanities in 2006. She served for many years on the Board of Directors of the Halifax Humanities Society and was a dedicated member of the Seminar class. Jymy passed away in the spring of 2014.

DR. GARY THORNE serves as the chaplain at the University of King's College and the Anglican chaplain to Dalhousie University.

Prior to joining the King's community in 2006, Father Thorne served as rector of Saint George's Anglican Church for 16 years. During that time he founded Saint George's YouthNet, an inner city youth ministry, and Halifax Humanities 101, a program to deliver university level teaching to those living in material poverty.

DR. JANNETTE VUSICH has served as a teaching fellow, senior fellow, and associate director, academic, in the Foundation Year Programme at the University of King's College and as an assistant professor in the Early Modern Studies Programme at King's. She holds a BA from the University of Toronto and an MA and PhD in the History of Art from Johns Hopkins University.

JENNIFER WATTS is the City Councillor for District 8, Peninsula North, Halifax.

GILLIAN WEBSTER is a retired librarian and a writer and skydiver.

JON DAVID WELLAND is a working writer and artist living in Dartmouth, N.S. He has been a Halifax Humanities student for eight years and has become a dedicated life-long learner.

BARBARA WHITBY is a writer who lives in Truro. She is the author of *The Last Beothuk* (2007), *Strange and Supernatural* (2009), and numerous essays and poems. She emigrated from Britain in 1960, travels widely and explores locally.

ACKNOWLEDGMENTS
for our 10th Anniversary Book Project

We, the editorial committee—Shari Clarke, Lamont Dobbin, Susan Dodd, and Mary Lu Redden—thank everyone who contributed to this book in any way.

We are particularly grateful for contributions to the physical production and distribution of this book:

Thank you to our proof readers Cheryl Bell, Susan Dodd, Peter Glenister, and Victoria Goddard.

Doug Bamford kindly allowed us to use a photo of his wonderful sculpture "North is Freedom" for our cover. Brenda DeLorenzo allowed us to reproduce her amazing painting, "What's Behind Her Skull?" Thank you.

Thanks also to Jesse Hiltz and Victoria Goddard who collaborated on designing our book's cover, and to Lamont Dobbin and Victoria Goddard for the cover photographs.

Thank you to our "launch committee," who worked to let people know about this book: Cheryl Bell, Carolyn Gillis, Breton Murphy, and Mary Lu Redden.

Thanks also to Fernwood Publishing and Gaspereau Press for helpful advice about the pros and cons of self-publishing.

Victoria Goddard designed this book and guided us through the revolutionary process of self-publishing and print-on-demand technology; the book you now hold in your hands is Victoria's artwork.

We are delighted and honoured by the writings that the contributors shared with the Halifax Humanities community, and we could not be more grateful. We are grateful, too, to all those who were unable to submit writings but who inspired this anthology through their brilliant and beautiful reading, talking and sharing.

Thanks to Supporters of Halifax Humanities

Over the past ten years, many individuals, foundations, churches, and public institutions have provided financial support to Halifax Humanities. Countless more have given time, expertise, energy, and joy as students, professors, volunteers, caring professionals who tell clients about us, and friends.

There are so many contributors to the true heart of Halifax Humanities—reading, talking, and community life—that we cannot possibly do more here than to say: *Thank you!*

A FINAL NOTE

If you might be interested in participating in Halifax Humanities 101 or HalifaxThinks, or if you would like to donate, please contact our Director, Mary Lu Redden, through our website: www.halifaxhumanities101.ca.